INDEX TO SONG BOOKS

Da Capo Press Music Reprint Series

GENERAL EDITOR

FREDERICK FREEDMAN

VASSAR COLLEGE

INDEX
TO SONG BOOKS

**A Title Index to Over 11,000 Copies of Almost
6,800 Songs in 111 Song Books Published
between 1933 and 1962**

Compiled by
ROBERT LEIGH

DA CAPO PRESS • NEW YORK • 1973

Library of Congress Cataloging in Publication Data

Leigh, Robert, writer on music, comp.
  Index to song books.

  (Da Capo Press music reprint series)
  1. Songs — Indexes. I. Title.
ML128.S3L45   1973   016.784′8   72-8344
ISBN 0-306-70553-2

This Da Capo Press edition of
Index to Song Books is an unabridged
republication of the first edition
published in Stockton, California, in 1964
by Robert Leigh. It is reprinted by special
arrangement with Robert Leigh.

Published by Da Capo Press, Inc.
A Subsidiary of Plenum Publishing Corporation
227 West 17th Street, New York, New York 10011

INDEX TO SONG BOOKS

INTRODUCTION

Many hundreds of song books have appeared since Sears' SONG INDEX SUPPLEMENT was published in 1934. In selecting from these books for this index my aim has been to include those most likely to be found in library collections. Only books published in the United States are included. No pocket-size books are included. Only a comparative few of the flood of paperbound song books are included, these mainly for popular songs of this century which are not to be found in hard-cover books. Many books have been omitted because a check of the Union Catalog of the California State Library indicated that very few if any libraries possess copies. Finally, only books giving both words and music are included.

This index is intended solely to aid the librarian in the location of a copy of a desired song. Therefore, information about the names of the author and composer, the genre, and the nationality is generally omitted; such information is included only if it aids materially in identification. It has been my experience as a reference librarian that a patron knows the title, more or less accurately, of the desired song, or some of the words; however, it is very unlikely that he would remember the author or composer but not the title. For example, it seems highly improbable that a person would remember that the song's words were by Eastburn or that the music was by Winner, but be unable to remember the title: "Little brown jug." Accordingly, this index is primarily a title index, with many cross-references from alternate titles and memorable lines. There are no author or composer entries.

The use and spelling of colloquial forms of words vary from song book to song book as well as in the way library patrons remember them. For example, the song given in ROBBINS MAMMOTH COLLECTION OF WORLD FAMOUS SONGS as "I'se gwine back to Dixie" appears in SINGING TEEN-AGERS as "I'm going back to Dixie." In order to simplify, the dictionary form of a word is used, and cross-references made from colloquial spellings (e.g. I'se <u>see</u> I'm). When referring from this index to a song book, check colloquial spellings if the title is not listed under the same spelling given here.

Example of entry:
Vom himmel hoch: B5 H4(e.g.) <u>From heaven above</u>
    (<u>high</u>) C2(e.g.) S3(e.g.) T6 <u>Y</u>

Explanation: The song appears under the title "Vom himmel hoch", with English words only, in the book indicated by B5, and with both English and German words in the book indicated by H4. The same song appears under the title "From heaven above" or "From heaven high", with English words only, in the books indicated by T6 and Y, and with both English and German words in the books indicated by C2 and S3.

LIST OF SONG BOOKS INDEXED

A   Album of favorite songs of the gay 90's. M.M. Cole, Chicago, 1942.

A2   Attaway, William - Calypso song book. McGraw-Hill Book Company, New York, 1957.

A3   Austin, Arthur - The family book of favorite hymns. Funk & Wagnalls Company, New York, 1950.

B   Boni, Margaret - The fireside book of favorite American songs. Simon and Schuster, Inc., New York, 1952.

B2   Boni, Margaret - Songs of the gilded age. Golden Press, Inc., New York, 1960.

784.5
mem
BON
B3   Boni, Margaret - The fireside book of love songs. Simon and Schuster, Inc., New York, 1954.

784.4
BON
B4   Boni, Margaret - The fireside book of folk songs. Simon and Schuster, Inc., New York, 1947.

783
BON
B5   Boni, Margaret - Favorite Christmas carols. Simon and Schuster, Inc., New York, 1957.

B6   Best, Richard L. - Song fest (same as New Song Fest). Crown Publishers, Inc., New York, 1955.

784.4
BIK
B7   Bikel, Theodore - Folksongs and footnotes. Meridian Books, Inc., Cleveland. 1960.

B8   Brand, Oscar - Bawdy songs and backroom ballads. Grove Press, New York, 1960.

B9   Brand, Oscar - Singing holidays; the calendar in folk song. Alfred A. Knopf, Inc., New York, 1957.

C   Carmer, Carl - Songs of the rivers of America. Farrar & Rinehart, New York, 1942.

783.6
CAR
C2   Carols of Christmas from many lands. Augsburg Publishing House, Minneapolis, 1958.

C3   Castagnetta, Grace and H. W. Van Loon - Folk
      songs of many lands. Simon and Schuster, Inc.,
      New York, 1938.

C4   Cavalcade of song hits.   Leo Feist, Inc., New York,
      1947.

C5   Cavalcade of songs of the 30's.   Harms, Inc.,
      New York.

C6   Cazden, Norman - The Abelard folk song book.
      Abelard-Schuman, New York, 1958.

C7   Cazden, Norman - A book of nonsense songs.
      Crown Publishers, Inc., New York, 1961.

C8   Cole, William - Folk songs of England, Ireland,
      Scotland and Wales.   Doubleday & Company, New
      York, 1961.

C9   Cross, Milton - Favorite arias from the great
      operas.   Doubleday & Company, New York, 1958.

C10   Carmer, Carl - America sings.   Alfred A. Knopf,
      Inc., New York, 1942.

C11   Chin-Hsin Yao Chen and Shih-Hsiang Chen - The
      flower drum and other Chinese songs.   John Day
      Company, Inc., New York, 1943.

C12   Cancionero popular americano.   Pan American
      Union, Washington, D. C., 1950.

D   Downes, Olin and Elie Siegmeister - A treasury
      of American song, 2nd edition.   Alfred A. Knopf,
      Inc., New York, 1943.

D2   Deutsch, Leonhard - A treasury of Slovak folk songs.
      Crown Publishers, Inc., New York, 1950.

E   Everybody's favorite Neapolitan songs.   Amsco
      Music Sales Company, Boston, 1938.

E2   Everybody's favorite songs.   Amsco Music Sales
      Company, Boston, 1933.

E3 Everybody's favorite songs of the gay nineties.
Amsco Music Publishing Company, Boston, 1943.

E4 Ewen, David - Songs of America. Ziff-Davis
Publishing Company, New York, 1947.

E5 Engel, Lyle K. - America's greatest hit songs.
Grosset and Dunlap, Inc., New York, 1962.

F The family music book. G. Schirmer, Inc., New
York, 1957.

F2 Felton, Harold W. - Cowboy jamboree: western
songs and lore. Alfred A. Knopf, Inc., New York,
1951.

F3 Flanders, Helen Hartness and others - The new
Green Mountain songster. Yale University Press,
New Haven, 1939.

F4 Frey, Hugo - Music for millions, volume 5: a
collection of songs America loves best. J. J.
Robbins & Sons, New York, 1950.

F5 Frey, Hugo - Robbins mammoth collection of
American songs. Robbins Music Corporation,
New York, 1941.

F6 Frey, Hugo - Robbins mammoth collection of songs
of the gay nineties. Robbins Music Corporation,
New York, 1942.

F7 Frey, Hugo - Robbins mammoth collection of
world famous songs. Robbins Music Corporation,
New York, 1939.

F8 Fowke, Edith and Joe Glazer - Songs of work and
freedom. Labor Education Division, Roosevelt
University, 430 South Michigan Avenue, Chicago,
1960.

G Greenberg, Noah, W. H. Auden, and Chester
Kallman - An Elizabethan song book. Doubleday
& Company, New York, 1956.

G2   Greenberg, Noah - An English songbook. Doubleday
      & Company, New York, 1961.

G3   Goodwin, George - Song Dex treasury of humorous
      and nostalgic songs. Song Dex, Inc., New York,
      1956.

G4   Goodwin, George - Song Dex treasury of operas.
      Song Dex, Inc., New York, 1957.

H   Harlow, Frederick P. - Chanteying aboard
      American ships. Barre Gazette, Barre,
      Massachusetts, 1962.

H2   Harms hits through the years. Harms, Inc.,
      New York.

H3   More Harms hits through the years. Harms, Inc.,
      New York, 1955.

H4   Hausman, Ruth L. - Sing and dance with the
      Pennsylvania Dutch. Edward B. Marks Music
      Corporation, New York, 1953.

H5   Hillie, Waldemar - The people's song book. Boni
      and Gaer, New York, 1948.

I   Ives, Burl - The Burl Ives song book. Ballantine
      Books, Inc., New York, 1953.

I2   Ives, Burl - Irish songs. Duell, Sloan and
      Pearce, Inc., New York, 1958.

I3   Ives, Burl - Song in America. Duell, Sloan and
      Pearce, Inc., New York, 1962.

J   Jordan, Philip D. and Lillian Kessler - Songs of
      yesterday. Doubleday, Doran & Company, New
      York, 1941.

J2   The "Joy" book: 60 sensational standard songs.
      Joy Music, Inc., New York, 1960.

K   Karpeles, Maud - Folk songs of Europe. Dufour
      Editions, Chester Springs, Pennsylvania, 1957.

K2   Kemp, David - The skiers' song book. Pacific Books, Palo Alto, California, 1950.

L   Lomax, John A. - Best loved American folk songs. Grosset and Dunlap, Inc., New York, 1953. (same as Folk song U.S.A. Duell, Sloan and Pearce, Inc., New York, 1948.

L2   Landeck, Beatrice - Echoes of Africa in folk songs of the Americas. David McKay Company, Inc., New York, 1961.

L3   Leiper, Maria and Henry W. Simon - A treasury of hymns. Simon and Schuster, Inc., New York, 1953.

L4   Leisy, James - Let's all sing. Abingdon Press, Nashville, 1959.

L5   Loesser, Arthur - Humor in American song. Howell, Soskin, New York, 1942.

L6   Lomax, Alan - The folk songs of North America in the English language. Doubleday & Company, New York, 1960.

L7   Lomax, John A. and Alan Lomax - American ballads and folk songs. Macmillan Company, New York, 1934.

L8   Lomax, John A. and Alan Lomax - Our singing country. Macmillan Company, New York, 1941.

L9   Latin-American song book. Ginn & Company, Boston, 1942.

L10   Landeck, Beatrice - Songs my true love sings. Edward B. Marks Music Corporation, New York, 1946.

M   Miller, Mitch - Sing along with Mitch. Random House, New York, 1961.

N   Niles, John Jacob - The ballad book. Houghton Mifflin Company, Boston, 1961.

O   O'Sullivan, Donal - Songs of the Irish. Crown
        Publishers, Inc., New York, 1960.

P   Pawlowska, Harriet - Merrily we sing; 105 Polish
        folksongs. Wayne State University Press, Detroit,
        1961.

P2   Pitts, Lilla Belle and others - Singing teen-agers.
        Ginn & Company, Boston, 1954.

R   Reed, W. L. - The treasury of Christmas music.
        Emerson Books, Inc., New York, 1961.

R2   Richman, Gloria - Ivy League song book. Rolor
        Publishing Company, Greenville, Wilmington 7,
        Delaware, 1958.

R3   Robbins, Rossell Hope - Early English Christmas
        carols. Columbia University Press, New York,
        1961.

R4   Rubin, Rose N. and Michael Stillman - A Russian
        song book. Random House, New York, 1962.

R5   Rubin, Ruth - A treasury of Jewish folksong.
        Schocken Books, Inc., New York, 1950.

S   Seeger, Ruth C. - American folk songs for
        Christmas. Doubleday & Company, New York,
        1953.

S2   Scott, Tom - Sing of America. T. Y. Crowell
        Company, New York, 1947.

S3   Simon, Henry W. - A treasury of Christmas songs
        and carols. Houghton Mifflin Company, Boston,
        1955.

S4   Shaw, Martin and Henry Coleman - National
        anthems of the world. Pitman Publishing Company,
        New York, 1960.

S5   Silber, Irwin - Songs of the Civil War. Columbia
        University Press, New York, 1960.

S6   Silliman, Vincent and Irving Lowens - We sing of

life. Starr King Press (distributed by Beacon Press, Boston) 1955.

S7   Smith, Reed - American anthology of old-world ballads. J. Fischer & Bros., New York, 1937.

S8   Song hits of the fabulous fifties. Remick Music Corporation, New York.

S9   Song hits of the fabulous forties. Harms, Inc., New York.

S10   Song hits of the roaring twenties. Remick Music Corporation, New York.

S11   Seeger, Pete - American favorite ballads. Oak Publications, New York, 1961.

S12   Sandburg, Carl - New American songbag. Broadcast Music, Inc., New York, 1950.

S13   Silverman, Jerry - Folk blues. Macmillan Company, New York, 1958.

S14   Simon, Henry W. - A treasury of grand opera. Simon and Schuster, Inc., New York, 1946.

S15   Spaeth, Sigmund and Carl O. Thompson - 55 art songs. C.C. Birchard & Company, Boston, 1943.

S16   Swarthout, Gladys - Album of concert songs and arias. G. Schirmer, Inc., New York, 1946.

T   Taylor, Mary C. - Rounds and rounds. William Sloane Associates, New York, 1946.

T2   39 country and western songs. Hansen Publications, Inc., New York.

T3   31 songs to remember. Shapiro, Bernstein & Company, Inc., New York, 1953.

T4   31 more songs to remember. Shapiro, Bernstein & Company, Inc., New York, 1959.

T5   Thirty years thirty hits, No. 1. Miller Music

Corporation, New York, 1950.

T6   Thomas, Edith Lovell - The whole world singing. Friendship Press, New York, 1950.

T7   Those wonderful years of song, 1900-1910. M. Witmark & Sons, New York, 1961.

T8   Those wonderful years of song, 1910-1920. M. Witmark & Sons, New York, 1961.

V   Vigneras, Marcel - Chansons de France. D. C. Heath & Company, Boston, 1941.

W   The Weavers' song book. Harper & Bros., New York, 1960.

W2   White, Florence and Kazuo Akiyama - Children's songs from Japan. Edward B. Marks Music Corporation, New York, 1960.

W3   Wier, Albert E. - Songs for the leisure hour. Longmans, Green and Company, Inc., New York, 1941.

W4   Wheeler, Opal - Sing in praise. E. P. Dutton & Company, New York, 1946.

W5   Wier, Albert E. - Young America's music, Vol. 1. Charles Scribner's Sons, New York, 1939.

W6   Wier, Albert E. - Young America's music, Vol. 2. Charles Scribner's Sons, New York, 1939.

W7   Wier, Albert E. - Young America's music, Vol. 3. Charles Scribner's Sons, New York, 1939.

W8   Wier, Albert E. - Young America's music, Vol. 4. Charles Scribner's Sons, New York, 1939.

W9   Wheeler, Opal - Sing for America. E. P. Dutton & Company, New York, 1944.

Y   Young, Percy M. - Carols for the twelve days of Christmas. Roy Publishers, New York, 1954.

Z   Zanzig, Augustus D. - Singing America. C. C. Birchard & Company, Boston, 1941.

ABBREVIATIONS

a.	Albanian	gk. Greek	p. Polish
af.	Afrikaans	h. Hebrew	pd. Pennsylvania Dutch
am.	Amharic	hn. Hindi	pe. Persian
an.	Annamese	hu. Hungarian	pr. Portuguese
ar.	Arabic	hw. Hawaiian	r. Russian
b.	Basque	i. Italian	rm. Roumanian
be.	Bengali	ic. Icelandic	ro. Romansh
bu.	Bulgarian	in. Indonesian	s. Spanish
c.	Czech	ir. Irish	sc. Serbo-Croatian
cg.	Congolese	j. Jugoslav	sl. Slovak
ch.	Chinese	ja. Japanese	sn. Sinhalese
cm.	Cambodian	k. Korean	ss. Swiss
cr.	Creole	l. Latin	sw. Swedish
ct.	Catalan	ld. Ladino	t. Turkish
d.	Dutch	lt. Lithuanian	tg. Tagalog
dn.	Danish	lv. Latvian	ty. Tyrolean
e.	English	lx. Luxembourgian	u. Urdu
es.	Estonian	m. Macedonian	uk. Ukrainian
f.	French	ml. Malay	w. Welsh
fi.	Finnish	mt. Maltese	wa. Wallonian
fl.	Flemish	mx. Manx	y. Yiddish
g.	German	n. Norwegian	z. Zulu
ga.	Gaelic	np. Nepali	

If English words only are given, English is not indicated.
If English and another language are given, abbreviations
for both are listed.

a (article) see next word of title
A Atocha va una nina: L9(e. s.)
A, B, C tumble down D: W5
A Belen cantando see To Bethlehem, singing
A bhean ud thios ar bhruach an tsruthain: O(e. ir.)
A cada instante te miro: L9(e. s.)
A cantar a una nina: L9(e. s.)
A co to tam stuknelo: P(e. p.)
A fhuisgi, croi na n-anamann: O(e. ir.)
A Frangesa: E(e. i.)
A Geneyve: R5(e. y.)
A ghaoth andeas: O(e. ir.)
A kak po lugu: K(e. r.)
A 'l chiante 'l gial: K(e. i.)
A la claire fontaine: B7(e. f.) V(f.)
A la puerto del cielo see At the gate of heaven
A mhaithrin, a' leigfea 'un an aonaigh me: O(e. ir.)
A moi les plaisirs: G4(e. f.)
A na tom zvolenskom moste: D2(e. sl.)
A pombinha voou: L9(e. pr.)
A tam w Krakowie we mlynie: P(e. p.)
A tanto amor: G4(e. i.)
A-tisket a-tasket see Itiskit, itasket
A w niedziele porankiem: P(e. p.)
A wy juchy, wy mazury: P(e. p.)
Aba l'ogum: L2
Abalone: S12
El abandonado: L7(e. s.)
Abdul, the Bulbul Ameer: B6 E2 G3 L5 Ivan Petrofsky
    Skevar: L7
Abe Lincoln (Now old Abe Lincoln, a great big giant of a
    man was he) H5
Abe Lincoln went to Washington: S5
The Abe-iad: J
Abends will ich schlafen gehn: G4(e. g.)
Abide with me: A3 E2 F L3 W3 W4 W7
Aboard the "Henry Clay": H

The abolitionist hymn: D F8 I I3
About the May pole: G2
About the year of 1 B.C: B6
Abraham's daughter: B9 D S5
O Absalom, my son: I T
Abscheulicher, wo eilst du hin: G4(e.g.)
Abschiedslied: K(e.g.)
Absence makes the heart grow fonder: A E3 G3
ach see next word of title
Acordei de madrugada: L9(e.pr.)
Acres of clams: F8 H5 I I3 Old settler's song: B6 L
Across the western ocean: H
Across the wide Missouri see Shenandoah
Action song: W7
Adam: B6
Adam catched Eve: T
Adam in the garden pinning leaves: L8
Addio (by Tosti) E(e.i.) Good-bye: E2 G3 W3
L'addio a Napoli: E(e.i.) G3
Addio del passato: G4(e.i.) S14(e.i.)
L'addio del voluntario: G3 (i.)
Addio dolce svegliare alla mattina: G4(e.i.)
Adelita: C12(s.) G3(s.)
Adeste fideles: B4 B5 F7 L4 R2 O come all ye
    faithful: A3 C2 E2 F G3 L3(e.l.) P2 R S3(e.l.)
    S6 W3 W8 Y
Adeus, adeus: L2
Adieu donc ma mie: K(e.f.)
Adieu sweet Amarillis: G T Z
Adieu to Bon County: L7
Adieu to Maimuna: H
Adieu to the stone walls: L8
Adios con el corazon: K(e.s.)
Adios, florecita blanca: C12(s.)
Adios ke aloha: G3
Admiral Jack and General Tom: W6
Admiral's song (from Pinafore) G3
Advance Australia fair: S4 Australia: F
Aeire cinn bo ruin: K(e.ir.) O(e.ir.)

A-fishing (Gold Coast song) T6
After a dream: S15
After he'd been drafted see Hej, ked sa janicko na vojnu
    bral
After hours: S13
After the ball: B E4 F F4 F6 G3
Afterwards: F7
Again, as evening's shadow falls: L3
The Agincourt carol see Deo gracias anglia
Agnese la zitella: G4(e.i.)
Agnus Dei (by Bizet) W3
Agnus Dei (by Tallis) G2(e.l.)
El aguinaldo: C12(s.)
Ah see next word of title
Ah'm see I'm
Ai nostri monti: E(e.i.) G4(e.i.) Home to our
    mountains: W3 W8
Aija, anzit, aija: K(e.lv.)
Aime-moi, bergere: V(f.)
ain (article) see next word of title
Ainsi que la brise legere: S14(e.f.)
Ain't going to rain no more see It ain't going to rain no
    more
Ain't going to study war no more see Down by the
    riverside
Ain't it hard to be a right black nigger: L8
Ain't no more cane on the Brazis: L L7
Ain't that a rocking all night: S
Ain't that a shame: A E3 F4 G3
Ain't we got fun: S10
Ain't working song: L8
The Air Force: B9
Aithri Sheain de Hora: O(e.ir.)
Ak koyun: K(e.t.)
Akh ty, dushechka: R4(e.r.)
Akh ty, nochenka: R4(e.r.)
Al chante il gial see When the cock crows
Al fin son tua: G4(e.i.)
Al harim: B7(e.h.)

Al naharot bavel: R5(e. h.)
Al pasar la barca: L9(e. s.)
Al pasar por Sevilla: L9(e. s.)
Al rumor de las selvas hondurenas: C12(s.)
Al son de la mangulina: C12(s.)
Al suon del tamburo: G4(i.)
Alabado: D(e. s.)
The Alabama: J
Alabama bound: L7 S11 T3
Alabama jubilee: S8 T8
Alabama lullaby: C4 F5
Alalimon: L9(e. s.)
Alas departing is ground of woe: G2
Alas, what hope of speeding: G2
Alaska harvest moon: S12
Albanian National Anthem: S4(e. a.)
Alberta, let your hair hang low: S13
Aldapeko: K(e. b.)
Alexander: B2
Ali v'er: R5(e. h.)
Alice, where art thou: F7 G3
Alikazander: G3
All are architects: S6
All creatures of our God and king: S6 Z
All day on the prairie see The cowboy
All for the love of a girl: T2
All for the men: L6
All glory, laud and honor: A3 B4 L3 T6
All God's children got wings see Heaven, heaven
All hail the power of Jesus' name: A3 B4 L3 L4 W4
All in a stable see Kerstlied
All in to service: T
All looks be pale: G
All my heart this night rejoices: H4
All my love: S9
All night long: L6
All on account of Eliza: G3
All on the grass see Sur le gazon
All people that on earth do dwell: A3 L3

All praise to thee, my God, this night: L3
All quiet along the Potomac: C D I3 S5
All the pretty little horses: L L7
All things bright and beautiful: L3
All through the night (Ar hyd y nos) B B6 C3 C8(e.w.)
    F L4 R2 W3 Z Welsh lullaby: W5
All throughout the great wide world I wandered see
    Vsiuto ia vselennuiu proekhal
All we do is sign the payroll: F4 F5
All we here: T
All you that in this house: Y
Alla en el rancho grande: E5(e.s.) L7(e.s.) L9(e.s.)
Alla vita che t'arride: G4(e.i.)
Allan Water: C8
Alleghany moon: J2
Alleluia see also Hallelujah
Alleluia (by Mozart) S3
Alleluia (All creatures of our God and king) see   All
    creatures of our God and king
Alleluia, song of gladness: L3
Alleluya psallat: G2(e.l.)
Alligator, hedgehog see The bestiary
Die allmacht see Omnipotence
Allmacht'ge jungfrau: G4(e.g.)
Alma redemptoris mater: R3
Almost day see The chickens are a-crowing
Almost done: L
Almost persuaded: A3
Aloha oe: B2 C3 E3 F(e.hw.) F7 G3
Alone (Russian song) C3
Alone in the fields (Feldeinsamkeit) S15
Along the lowlands: H
Along the Peterskaya Road see Vdol po Piterskoi
Along the Santa Fe Trail: S9
Alouette: B4(e.f.) B6(f.) B9 F4(f.) G3(f.) L4(f.)
    R2(f.) V(f.) Z(f.)
Als die alte mutter see Songs my mother taught me
Als ich bei meinen schafen wacht see While by my sheep
    I watched at night

Di alte kashe: R5(e.y.)
Altwiener tanzlied: K(e.g.)
Always: G3
Always a bridesmaid: F6
Always one rain: A2
Always take mother's advice: E3 F6
Am I blue: S10
Am I born to die: L6
Am stillen herd: G4(e.g.)
Am weihnachtsbaum die lichter brennen see As candles
    glow
Amapola: E5(e.f.s.)
Amapola, la Creole-a: L2
Amarilli: B3(e.i.)
Amaryllis (Tu crois, o beau soleil) V(f.)
Amaryllis (from Prince Ananias) G3
Amazing grace: L L7
Amber tresses tied in blue: F5
America: A3 E2 F F4 F5 G3 L3 P2 S6 W3 W7 W9
    Z
America the beautiful: A3 C12 F F4 F5 G3 I3 L3 S6
    W9 Z
America triumphant: S6
American beauty rose: E5
The American flag: F5
An American frigate see Paul Jones
The American hymn: F5
Amhran na bhfiann: S4(e.ir.) A soldier's song: I2
Amhran na mbreag: O(e.ir.)
Amici: G3
Amis, l'amour tendre et reveur: G4(f.)
Amo, amas: L5
Amol iz geven a mayse: R5(e.y.)
Amor (Cuando al pie de tu ventana) G3(s.)
El amor que te tenia: L7(e.s.)
O amore (from L'amico Fritz) G4(e.i.)
The amorous goldfish: G3
L'amour de moi: B3(e.f.)
Amour, viens aider ma faiblesse: C9(e.f.)

Amours divins: G4(f.)
an (article) see next word of title
Analization: L5
An ancient Irish proverb: G3
Ancient of days: A3 L3
And her golden hair was hanging down her back: A B2
   E3 F5 F6
And when I die (don't bury me at all) G3
Andantino (starlight and sunshine) F7
Andorran National Anthem: S4(e. ct.)
Andreas Hofer: G3(g.)
The angel band: S
The angel Gabriel: S3 Y
Angel voices, ever singing: L3
The angelical hymn: Y
Angelina Baker: F4 F7 G3 W3
Angelique O: C12(f.) 'Gelique O: L2
Angels from the realms of glory: A3 B5 L3 R S3 W3
   W8 Y
Angels of great beauty came down to earth see
   Przylecieli tak sliczni anieli
Angels we have heard on high (Les anges dans nos
   campagnes) B4 C2 L3 R2 S3(e. f.) Gloria in
   excelsis deo: B5
The angelus (from The Serenade) G3
Angelus ad virginem: G2(e. l.)
Les anges dans nos campagnes see Angels we have heard
   on high
Anges purs: S14(e. f.)
Anicka, dusicka, kde si bola: D2(e. sl.)
Anicka, dusicka nekasli: D2(e. sl.)
Anicka malicka: D2 (e. sl.)
Anicka mlynarova: D2(e. sl.)
The animal fair: L5
Annchen von Tharau: G3(g.)
Annie Laurie: B3 B4 B6 E2 F F4 F7 G3 L4 P2 R2
   W3 W7 Z
Another little drink: D
Another man done gone: L L6 S12

Another round see Preab san ol
Antagata dokosa: W2(e. ja.)
Anthem of the ILGWU: F8
Anvil chorus see La zingarella
Any old place I can hang my hat is home sweet home to
    me: A
Any rags: A E3 F6
Anyam szive: B7(e. hu.)
Anything goes: H2
An apple for the teacher: J2
Apres un reve see After a dream
April in Paris: C5 H2
April is in my mistress' face: Z
April showers: H2
Ar fall promesau: K(e. f.)
Ar hyd y nos see All through the night
Are ye able: L4
Are you from Dixie: T8
Are you the O'Reilly: A B2
Are you there, Mo-ri-ar-i-ty: I2
Are you washed in the blood: A3
Aren't you the girl I met at Sherry's: F6
Argentine National Anthem: S4(e. s.)
Arioso see Vesti la giubba
Arise (Chinese song) see Chee lai
Arise and wake: R3
Arise thou, my soul: S6
The Arkansas traveller: B4 L5 L7
The Arlberg ski school: B6 K2
An armored knight is returning see Jedzie, jedzie
    rycerz zbrojny
Armorer's song: G3
The army of the free: S5
around see also round
Around a western water tank: L6
Around her neck (she wore a yellow ribbon) B8 She wore
    a yellow ribbon: M
Around the corner (and under a tree) P2

A-roving: B4 B6 C6 H H5 R2 The maid of Amsterdam:
 I I3 L4
Arre, buey: L9(e.s.)
Arroyo claro: L9(e.s.)
El arroyo que murmura: C12(s.)
Arroz con leche: L9(e.s.)
Art thou troubled: S16
Art thou weary; art thou languid: L3
Arthritis blues: S13
Artillery song: G3 Caisson song: F P2
Artsa alinu: R5(e.h.)
As candles glow (Am weihnachtsbaum die lichter brennen)
 C2(e.g.)
As I roved out one fine summer's evening: L6 As I went
 a-walking one fine summer's evening: L8
As I roved out one May morning see I'm seventeen come
 Sunday
As I set down to play tin-can: L8
As I walked out one May morning see I'm seventeen
 come Sunday
As I was going to Banbury: K
As I went a-walking one fine summer's evening see As I
 roved out one fine summer's evening
As I went out for a ramble: L8
As I went over Tawny Marsh: T
As Joseph was a-walking: B5 S3
As now the sun's declining rays: L3
As off to pasture I did go see Lisette
As the backs go tearing by: R2
As the sun doth daily rise: L3
As time goes by: C5 H2 S9
As with gladness men of old: L3 R
As you go through the hills see Ked pojdes cez horu
As your hair grows whiter: G3
The ash grove (Llwyn on) C8(e.w.)
Ashrey ha-ish: R5(e.h.)
Asi eres tu: L9(e.s.)
Ask if yon damask rose be sweet see Frag' ob die rose

Asleep in the deep: G3
The Asra: S15
At a Georgia camp meeting: B E3 E4 F4 F6 G3 W3
At dawning: P2
At our door see Chodi suhaj
At sundown: T5
At sunset (Finnish song) Z
At the ball: S15
At the Castle of Tardets see Atharratze jauregian
At the cross: A3
At the gate of heaven (A la puerto del cielo) Z(e.s.)
At the gates of paradise see Sus in poarta raiului
At the making of the hay: W8
At the water's edge one evening see Nad woda
    wieczornej porze
At work beside his father's bench: S6
Atharratze jauregian: K(e.b.)
Atmest du nicht: G4(e.g.) S14(e.g.)
Atomic blues see Talking atomic blues
The attache: J
Au chateau d'hirondelle: K(e.f.)
Au clair de la lune: B4(e.f.) B6(f.) F(f.) F4(f.) L4(f.)
    V(f.) W5
Au joli bois: V(f.)
Auch ich war ein jungling: G3(g.) G4(g.)
Auf flugeln des gesanges see On wings of song
Auf, ihr brieder: H4(e.pd.)
Auf wiedersehen, my dear: M
auld see also old
Auld lang syne: B4 B9 C3 E2 F F4 F7 G3 L4 M R2
    W3 W7
Aunt Clara: S12
Aunt Dinah's quilting party see The quilting party
Aunt Harriet Becha Stowe: J
Aunt Rhody: B6 I S11 W Go tell Aunt Nancy: L The old
    gray goose: L7
Aunt Sal's song: L6
Auntie next door see Tonari no obasan
Aupres de ma blonde: B(e.f.) B6(f.) R2(f.)

Un aura amorosa: G4(i.)
Aura Lee: B3 B6 F7 G3 L4 R2 W3
Aurore pradere: L2 L7(e.cr.)
Aus meinen grossen schmerzen: B3(e.g.)
Australia see Cape Cod girls
Australia (advance, Australia fair) see Advance
    Australia fair
Austrian National Anthem see Osterreichische
    bundeshymne
Automation: F8
Autumn (There are nuts on the trees) S6
Autumn in New York: H3
Autumn song: W6
Avadim hayinu: B7(e.h.)
Avalon: M S10
Avant de quitter: C9(e.f.) S14(e.f.)
Ave Maria (Hail, blessed flower of virginity) (English
    carol) R3
Ave Maria (by Gounod) E2 F7 W3 W7
Ave Maria (by Mascagni) F7 W3 W7
Ave Maria (by Mozart) S3
Ave Maria (by Schubert) E2 F F7 W3
Ave Maria (by Verdi) G4(e.i.)
Ave, plena gratia: R3
Ave rex angelorum: R3(e.l.)
Ave verum corpus: L3(l.)
The Avondale mine disaster: L6
Awake (from Die Meistersinger) Z
Awake, awake: C6
Awake, my soul, and with the sun: L3
Awake, my soul, stretch every nerve: L3
Awake, my soul, to joyful lays: S
A-walking and a-talking: C6
Awate dokoya: W2(e.ja.)
away see also way
Away down East: J
Away in a manger: A3 B5 C2 G3 L3 L4 R S3 Y
Away, Rio see Rio Grande
Away, Whigs, away: C8

Away with these self loving lads: G
ay see also next word of title
Ay, ay, ay: B3(e.s.) C12(s.) E2 G3
Ay la le lo (Spanish song) K
Ay te tsi nye te: B7(e.uk.)
Ayer vite en la fonte: K(e.s.)
Ayil, ayil: B7(e.h.)
Ay-lye, lyu-lye, lyu-lye: R5(e.y.)
Aysem: K(e.t.)
Az men fort kayn Sevastopol: R5(e.y.)⊱

B

Ba, be: G3
Baa! baa! black sheep: E2 F7 W5
A babe is born: B5 S3 Y
Babe of Bethlehem: S
The babes in the wood: W5
Baby born today: S
Baby Bunting: W5
Baby bye, here's a fly: W5
Baby, did you hear: C
Baby doll: S8
Baby in a guinea-blue gown: S12
Baby, please don't go: S13
Babylon: N
Babylon is fallen: S5
The bachelor's lament: J
The bachelor's lay: L8
Il bacio: E(e.i.)
Back home again in Indiana see Indiana
Back of the bread: T6
Bacon and greens: G3
Bacon on the rind: L5
The bad girl: L6 see also I been a bad, bad girl
Bad luck blues: S13
Bad man ballad: L7
Badger hill: C7

Badouma paddlers: L2
Baffin's Bay: B2 H
Baile de pandero: K(e.s.)
The bailiff's daughter of Islington: F3 L10
Bainyin: C12(f.)
Bak mir nit kayn bulkelech: R5(e.y.)
Le bal chez Boule <u>see</u> Boule's ball
Bald prangt, den morgen zu verkunden: G3(g.)
Il balen del suo sorriso: C9(e.i.) G4(e.i.)
The ball of Ballynoor: B8
ballad of <u>see first identifying word of title</u>
Ballatella (from Pagliacci) <u>see</u> Stridono lassu
Ballerina: E5
Balling the jack: E5
The balloon: W6
Balloon song: T6
A balmy afternoon in May <u>see</u> Una tarde fresquita de mayo
Baloo baleerie: C8
Baloo, lammy: S3
Balulalow: R
Bamba-lele: L2
Di ban: B7(e.y.)
Banana boat loader's song <u>see</u> Day, O
Banbury ale: T
Ban-chnuic Eireann O: O(e.ir.)
A band of birds: A2
The band played on: A B2 E3 E4 F6 F7 G3 R2 W3
Bangum and the bo': N
The bank of the Arkansaw: C L8
Ye banks and braes of bonnie Doon: B C8 G3
The banks of Newfoundland: L6
The banks of sweet Dundee: C6
The banks of sweet Loch Ray: F3
The banks of the Brandywine: C
The banks of the Genesee: C
The banks of the Ohio: B6 C <u>see also</u> We'll hunt the
    buffalo
The banks of the roses: C8
The banks of the Sacramento <u>see</u> Sacramento

The banks of the sweet primroses: C8
Bannity Dan: C7
Baquine: L2
Barbara Allen: B B4 D E3 E4 G3 I I3 L4 L6 L10
    N R2 S2 S7 S11
Barbara totally high: C7
The barber song (sea chantey) H
Barber, spare those hairs: L5
Barcarola see Agnese la zitella
Barcarolle: C9(e.f.) E2 F7 Belle nuit: G4(f.) Lovely
    night: W3 W8
The bard of Armagh: C8 I2
Barley harvesting see Mugi kari
Barnacle Bill the sailor: H
Barney: C7
Barnyard song: D L5
The barnyards of Delgaty: B7
Basher's round: K2
The basket of oysters: B8
Batson: L8
Batti, batti: G4(e.i.) S14(e.i.)
The battle-cry of freedom: E4 F4 F5 I3 S5 W3 W9
The battle hymn of the republic: A3 B B4 D E2 E4 F
    F4 F5 F8 G3 L3 P2 R2 S5 W3 W9
The battle of Bull Run: I3
The battle of Jericho see Joshua fit the battle of Jericho
The battle of New Orleans: T2
The battle of Saratoga: I I3
The battle of Shiloh (All you Southerners now draw near)
    S5
The battle of Shiloh Hill (Come all you valiant soldiers)
    L6 S5
The battle of the kegs: I I3 L5
Bay dem shtetl: R5(e.y.)
La Bayamesa: S4(e.s.)
Bayt-zhe mir oys a finf-un-tsvantsiger: R5(e.y.)
Be honest with me: T2
Be kind to the loved ones at home: W7
Be merry, be merry: R3

Be my little baby bumble bee: T8
Be quiet do! I'll call my mother: J
Be still, my soul: L4
O be thou not dismayed: H4
Be with me, Lord, where'er I go: L3
Bean an fhir ruaidh: O(e.ir.)
Beans, bacon and gravy: F8   H5
The bear in the hill: L7
Bear the news, Mary: L7
Beata progenies: G2(e.l.)
Beau soir see Peaceful evening
The beauteous day now closeth: L3
O, beauteous eyes: T
Beautiful: L7
Beautiful ballad of Waska Wee: G3
Beautiful, beautiful brown eyes see Beautiful brown eyes
Beautiful blue Danube: E2   F7
Beautiful brown eyes: R2   T2
Beautiful dreamer: B3   E2   F   F5   F7   G3   L4   R2   W3
Beautiful heaven see Cielito lindo
Beautiful isle of somewhere: F   L3
Beautiful isle of the sea: F5
Beautiful love: E5
O beautiful, my country: S6
Beautiful Waipio: G3
Beautiful yuletide: C2
Beauty sat bathing: G
Beauty's eyes: G3   W3
Beauty's queen see Gidene bak gidene
The Beaver Island boys: L8
Because (At night I sit alone and dream) G3
Because you're you: T7
Bed-time: W5
Bedelia (There's a charming Irish lady) B2
The bee (As Cupid in a garden strayed) D
Been in the pen so long: S13
Beer barrel polka: T3
The beezer: C7
Before dinner (Congolese song) T6

Before Jehova's awful throne: L3
Before worship: T6
Begin, my tongue, some heavenly theme: A3 L3
Begin the beguine: H3
Beginner's round: K2
Behold the lamb of God: L3
Behut dich Gott: G4(e.g.)
Bei mannern welche liebe fuhlen: G4(g.)
An beinnsin luachra: O(e.ir.)
Un bel di vedremo: C9(e.i.)
Belgian National Anthem see La Brabanconne
Believe me, if all those endearing young charms: B E2
    F F4 F7 G3 I2 L4 R2 W3 Z
Bell-bottomed trousers: B6 B8 J2
The bell doth toll: E3
The bell is ringing: P2
Bell trio (from Pinafore) Z
Bella figlia: E(e.i.) G4(i.)
Bella siccome un angelo: G4(e.i.)
Belle (Cajun song) L8(e.f.)
Belle nuit see Barcarolle
Belle O'Brien: G3
The belle of Long Lake: F3
Ah! bello a me ritorna: G4(e.i.)
The bells (Hear the sledges with the bells) Z
The bells, Song of (As the tolling, the tolling of the bells)
    P2
The bells of Aberdovey (Clychau Aberdyfi) C8(e.w.)
Bells of Nitra see Tie Nitrianske hodiny
The bells of Shandon: I2
Beloved comrade: H5
Beloved eyes see Ochietti amati
Ben Backstay: I3
Ben Bolt: B3 C E2 E3 F4 F5 F7 G3 I W3
Ben Franklin, Esq: R2
Bendemeer's stream: B4 C8 L4 P2 Z
Beneath a weeping willow's shade: S15
Beneath in the dust: T
Beneath the cross of Jesus: L3

La benedizione: E(e. i.)
Benny Havens, O: C
Berceuse (from Jocelyn) W3
La bergere: F(f.)
Bergere legere see O fickle shepherdess
Beryuzoviye kalechke: B7(e. r.)
Beside thy cradle here I stand (ich steh an deiner krippe
   hier) R S3(e. g.) Y
Bessie of Ballydubray: F3
The bestiary (Alligator, hedgehog, anteater, bear) I3
Betsy B: C6
Betsy Baker: C
Betty and Dupree: S13
Beulah land: A3 L3
Beyn n'har prat un'har chidekel: R5(e. h.)
The bibabutzeman: W5
Los bibilicos: B7(e. ld.)
Bible stories see Darky Sunday school
A bicycle built for two see Daisy Bell
Bid me to live: S15
Bidalia McCann: G3
Biddy, biddy (hold fast my gold ring) L8
Big bad John: T2
Big bamboo: A2
Big corral: P2 Z
Big fat woman: L8
Big Ola, dear Ola see Stor Ola, lill' Ola
The big red team: R2
Big rock candy mountain: B B6 E2 F5 G3 I3 L L6
   S11 W3
The big sunflower: B E4 G3
The Bigler: L L8
Bikurim: R5(e. h.)
Bile them cabbage down: B6 L6
Biljana platno belese: K(e. m.)
Bill Bailey, won't you please come home: A B E3 F4
   F6 G3 M
Bill Martin and Ella Speed: L7
The billboard: L5

Billie Magee Magaw: B6
Billy Barlow: L8 S5 Let's go a-hunting: I3 L6
Billy Boy: B6 C6 E3 F7 G3 I I3 L4 L7 R2 S2 W5
  see also My boy Billy
Billy broke locks: L6
Billy the Kid: I3 L6 L7
Bingo: G3 H4 L5
The birchbark song see Navervisan
The bird and the rose: W8
A bird in a gilded cage: B2
Bird in the cage see Kagome, kagome
Bird song ("Hi" says the blackbird) D L4 L5
Birkat am: R5(e.h.)
The birks of Aberfeldy: G3
The birth of the blues: H2
The birthday of a king: S3
Birthday presents (Japanese song) T6
Bist du bei mir: S16(e.g.) If thou art near: S15
Biztu mit mir broygez: R5(e.y.)
The Black Ball Line: H L7
Black Betty: L7
Black, black, black is the color see Black is the color
Black bottom: S10
Black, brown and white blues: H5 L6 S13
Black-eyed Susie: B6 B8 C7 L L7
Black gal: L6 see also The heavy-hipted woman
Black is the color of my true love's hair: B3 C6 L L6
  L10 R2
Black Jack Davy: L8
Black sheep: L6
Black tail range: F2
The blackbird's song see Aldapeko
The blackthorn tree see An draighnean donn
Blanche comme la neige: L8(e.f.)
The Blantyre explosion: F8
Blazhena stara-planina: K(e.bu.)
Bless 'em all: E5
Blessed assurance: A3 L3
Blessed be that lord: R3

Blessed land of love and liberty: J
Blessed may thou be: R3
The blessings of Mary see The seven joys of Mary
Blest be the tie that binds: A3 B6 F L3 W4
Blest is that man: S6
Blind man: D L6 L7
The blind man (Brazilian song) see Pobre cega
Blomman bland blommorna: K(e.sw.)
Blood on the saddle: C7
Blood red roses: L6
The blood-strained banders: L8
Bloody well dead: B6
Bloom, my tiny violet: W6
A blossom fell: T4
Blow, blow, thou winter wind: S15
Blow boys blow (A Yankee ship came down the river)
     C10 D E4 H
Blow, Gabriel, blow: H3
Blow high, blow low: S15
Blow on the sea shell: L9
Blow the candles out: B6 B7 L6
Blow the man down: B4 B6 C6 D G3 H I I3 L4 L7
     R2 S11
Blow the wind southerly: C7 C8 I3
Blow the wind southerly (round) Z
Blow thy horn hunter (by Cornysh) G2
Blow thy horn, thou jolly hunter: G2
Blow ye winds in the morning: F8 H I L
Blue see Old Blue
The blue and the gray: S5
Blue Bell: B2
The Blue Bells of Scotland: B4 C8 E2 F G3 L4 W3 W7
Blue bottle: L8
Blue Danube see Beautiful blue Danube
Blue gardenia: S8
The blue Juniata: C
Blue mountain lake: L
The blue room: H3
The blue tail fly: B4 B6 B9 F4 G3 H5 I I3 L4 L6
     R2 S2 S11

Bluebeard: B6
Blueberries: L2
The bluebird: W6
The blues ain't nothing: D S13
Blues in the night: S9
Blues like midnight: S13
Blues my naughtie sweetie gives to me: E5
The boar's head: R R3 S3 Y
A boat! A boat: T
Boat song (Im kahne) see In the boat
Boat song (O we are floating) W7
The boatman see Al pasar la barca
The boatman's dance: C C10
boatswain see bosun
Bobbing around: J
Bobby Shafto: I3 W5
Bodaj by vas: D2(e. sl.)
Body and soul: C5 H2
Ain boer wol noar zien noaber tou: K(e. d.)
Bohemia hall: B6
Boil that cabbage down see Bile them cabbage down
Bold Brennan on the moor see Brennan on the moor
A bold child see Leanbh an chlamrain
The bold Fenian men: C8
The bold fisherman: B9 C7
The bold grenadier: C6
Bold Jack Donahue: L6
The bold peddler: N
Bold Reynard: F3
The bold soldier: B6 C6 I
The Bold Trellitee see The Golden Vanity
The bold volunteer: B9
Boleraz: D2(e. sl.)
Bolivian National Anthem: S4(e. s.)
The boll weevil: B C10 D E4 F8 L L5 L7 S13 W
The boll weevil holler: L6
The bomb song: B6
Bon soir dames: L2
Bonhomme: K2(e. f.)

The bonnie banks of Fordie: N
The bonnie birdy: N
The bonnie blue flag: B F4 F5 G3 I3 L4 S5
Bonnie Dundee: B6 G3
Bonnie Eloise: C F4 F5 F6 S12 W3
Bonnie Farday: N
Bonnie George Campbell: B4
The bonnie laboring boy: C6
Bonnie sweet Bessie: W3
A bonnie wee lassie: I
The bonnie white flag: S5
bonny see bonnie
Boola boola: R2
Boolavogue: I2
Boomba: L2
Booth killed Lincoln: S5
Border trail: B6
Boreen: G3
Borrow love and go: S13
Bosan: W2(e.ja.)
The bosses are taking it on the chin: F8
Boston (From Boston harbor we set sail) H
Boston burglar: I2
The Boston come-all-ye: B4 C10 D L7 The fish of the
    sea: L6 Song of the fishes: H I I3
The Boston tea party see The tea party
The Boston tea tax: I I3 The tea tax: L5
Bosun John: C7
The bosun's story: H
Botany Bay: B F3
Boule's ball (Le bal chez Boule) Z(e.f.)
The boulevard of broken dreams: C5
Bound for the promised land: B L The promised land:
    D E4
The boundless expanse of the sea see Raskinulos more
    shiroko
Bourgeois blues: S13
The Bowery: A B2 B6 E3 F5 F6 F7 G3 R2 W3
Bowie, Bowerie: N

The boy and the cuckoo: W6
The boy guessed right: G3
A boy's best friend is his mother: E3 F6
O boys, carry me along: F4 G3 W3
Ach, boze moj: D2(e. sl.)
La Brabanconne: F(e. f. fl.) S4(e. f. fl.)
The braes of Yarrow: N
Brakeman's blues: S13
Brandolina: Z
Brandywine: N
The brass mounted army: L6 S5
The brats of Jeremiah: C6
A brave companion see Ogun gori na balkana
Brave Wolfe: C D L L6
Brazilian National Anthem: S4(e. pr.)
Bread and roses: F8
Bread of the world, in mercy broken: L3
Break forth, o beauteous light (Brich an, du schones
    morgenlicht) L3 P2 R S3(e. g.) S6
Break now my heart and die: G
Break the news to mother: B G3
Break thou the bread of life: A3 L3
Breakfast in my bed on Sunday morning: F6
The breaking waves dashed high: L3
Breast the wave, Christian: L3
Breathe on me, breath of God: L3
Breathless: E5
The breeze and I: E5
Breeze of night: G3
Brennan on the moor: B4 C6 I I2 I3 L8
Brethren in peace together: S6
Brian Boru: G3
Brich an, du schones morgenlicht see Break forth, o
    beauteous light
Bricks in my pillow: S13
Bridal chorus (Treulich gefuhrt) (from Lohengrin) E2
    F7 W8 Treulich gefuhrt: S14(e. g.)
The bridge: C
Bright and joyful is the morn: L3

Bright college years: R2
Bright moon (Korean song) T6
Bright morning stars are rising: S
Bright Phoebe: C6
Bright stars, light stars: S6
The bright sunny South: C6
Bright the moon, soft the tune see The serenaders
Brighten the corner where you are: L3
Brighter the sun seems: T
Brightest and best of the sons of the morning: L3 R W3
    W7 Star in the east: S
Brightly gleams our banner: L3
Brindisi (from Cavalleria Rusticana) see Viva il vino
    spumeggiante
Brindisi (from La Traviata) see Libiamo ne' lieti calici
Bring a torch, Jeannette, Isabella see Un flambeau,
    Jeannette, Isabelle
Bring back my bonnie to me see My bonnie lies over the
    ocean
Bring me little water, Sylvie: L2 L6 Sylvie: W
Bring me on my supper, boys: S12
Bringing in the sheaves: A3 L3
The British grenadiers: B4
A British tar is a soaring soul see Admiral's song
The broad and narrow paths see Es sind zween weg
The Broadway girl: G3
Broadway sights: J
Broke and hungry: S13 The cholly blues: L7
Broken reverie (Reverie interrompue) W3
Brooklet ever flowing see Tecie voda
Brooms for old shoes: T
Brother, can you spare a dime: H3
Brother Green: S5
Brother Jack see Frere Jacques
Brother John (union song, after Frere Jacques) F8
Brother, lift your flag with mine: S6
O brother man (fold to thy heart) S6
Brother man, awake: L3
Brother so fine: W6

Brother's revenge: N
Brown cheering song: R2
Brown college alma mater: R2
The brown girl: N S7
Brown October ale: F G3
Brown skin girl: A2
Bruderchen, komm tanz' mit mir: G4(e.g.)
B'tel chay: R5(e.h.)
Buachaill an chuil dualaigh: O(e.ir.)
An buachaill caol dubh: O(e.ir.)
Buckeye Jim: B C7 I3 L
Buck-eye rabbit: L6
Buckley's sleighing song: J
Des bucklich mennli: H4(e.pd.)
Buddy Bolden's blues: S13
Buenos reyes: B5
Buffalo boy: B7 L6
Buffalo driver's song: L2
Buffalo gals: B6 C C7 F4 F5 F7 G3 I L L2 L4 R2
    S11
The buffalo skinners: C F8 L L7 S11
Bugeillio'r gwenith gwyn see Idle days in summertime
Bugger Burns: L8
The bugle britches: N
Bulgaria mila, zemya na gheroi: S4
The bulldog on the bank: B6 C7 G3 L5
The bullgine run see Clear the track
The bully song: E4
Bunker Hill: D
An bunnan bui: O(e.ir.)
Burden down: P2
Burges: L7
Burgundian carol see The winter season of the year
The burial of the robin: W6
The Burman lover: D
Burmese National Anthem: S4(e.Burmese)
The burning of the granite mill: F3
El burro: B7(e.s.)
Bury me beneath the willow: F5 W
Bury me not on the lone prairie: D E4 F2 F7 G3 L L4

The dying cowboy: F5 P2 W3
Bury me out on the prairie see I've got no use for the
  women
Bushes and briars: K
O but I do: S9
Butsu, butsu mame: W2(e.ja.)
Buttercup Joe: C8
The buttercut meadow: W6
Buttercups and daisies: W6
Butterfly see Papillon
The butterfly's ball: W6
Buy a broom: J W5
Buy my dainty fine beans: T
Buy my violets (Como aves precursoras) F7(e.s.)
By and by see By'm by
By Killarney's lakes and fells see Killarney
By the camp fire: F5
By the light of the silvery moon: M T7
By the stream see Pri dunaju
By the well we saw her see U studiensky stala
Bye bye blackbird: M
By'm by (Stars shining) S12

C

C.C. Rider: S13
Ca, ca geschmauset: G3(g.)
Ca' the yowes see Call the ewes
La cachucha: W7
The cadet see Si algun cadete
Cadet Rousselle: V(f.)
Cailin deas cruite na mbo see The pretty girl milking
  her cow
Cainc yr odryddes: K(e.w.)
cain't see can't
Cairo: S5
Caisson song see Artillery song
Caitilin ni Uallachain: O(e.ir.)
The Calais disaster: F3

Calendar song: W6

Caleno custure me: B3

Calico pie: C7

California here I come: M

The California pioneers: J

California to the New York island see This land is your
    land

Call her back and kiss her: G3

Call me darling: J2

Call the ewes: B3 Z

Calling the cows (Tyrolese song) T6

Calm he rests: T

Calm on the listening ear of night: L3 S3

Calomel see Go call the doctor and be quick

La calunnia: C9(e. i.) G4(e. i.)

Calvary (Rest, rest to the weary) E2 F F7

Cambodian National Anthem: S4(e. f. cm.)

The cambric shirt see Petticoat lane

Came a-riding: Z

Cameroon National Anthem: S4(e. f.)

Caminito: C12(s.)

Caminito de tu casa: C12(s.)

Camino de Valencia: L9(e. s.)

The Campbells are coming: G3 L4

Camptown races: B4 B6 E4 F F4 F5 F7 G3 L4 L5
    R2 S11 W3

Can she excuse my wrongs: G

Can y melinydd: K(e. w.)

Can ye sew cushions: B9 C8 Z

Can you count the stars: L3

Can you find it in your heart: S8

Cana dulce: C12(s.)

O Canada: S4(e. f.)

Canaday-i-o: F8 L6

Canadian boat song: C

Canadian capers: T8

Cancao de berco: K(e. pr.)

Cancao de Natal: K(e. pr.)

can'cha see can't you

Cancion del marinero hondureno: C12(s.)

Candle and star: S6
Candy and cake: J2
A cannibal king: R2
Cannibalee: G3
Canoe song (Poi waka) (Maori song) T6
Canon of the mimes: S3
Can't get Indiana off my mind: J2
Can't I: E5
Can't we be friends: H3
Can't you dance the polka: B4 B8 H
Can't you do a friend a favor: S9
Can't you hear me calling Caroline: T8
Can't you line it: L L6
Can't you see I'm lonely: F5
Cantec soldatesc: K(e.rm.)
Cantec vechi: K(e.rm.)
Cantemos, cantemos: C12(s.)
Canticle to the sun: T6
Cantilena del maggio: K(e.i.)
Cantique de noel see O holy night
Canto do cysne: G3(pr.)
Canzone d'i zampognari: B5 Carol of the bagpipers:
    S3(e.i.)
Caoine Dhonnchadha Bhaile aodha: O(e.ir.)
Caoine magaidh: O(e.ir.)
Caoine na maighdine: O(e.ir.)
Cape Ann: L6
Cape Cod chanty see Cape Cod girls
Cape Cod girls: C7 D L5 L6 Australia: B6
A capital ship: B6 G3 L4 L5 R2 The walloping window
    blind: C7
El capotin: L9(e.s.)
Captain Jinks of the horse marines: C7 F4 L5
Captain Kidd: B D I L6
Captain Walker's courtship: C6
Caradoc calls his legions: P2
Caram baram see Maiden's initiation
Ay, caramba (Venezuelan song) L2
El carbonero: C12(s.)
The card song (from Carmen) see En vain pour eviter

Lu cardillo: E(e. i.) G3(i.)

The careful man: G3

Carefully on tip-toe stealing: G3

Careless love: B4 B6 D G3 H5 I I3 L L2 L4 L6
   L10 R2 S2 S11

Carissima: T7

Carme: E(e. i.) G3(i.) W3

Carmela: B3(e. s.) G3(s.)

Carmela mia: E(e. i.) G3(i.)

Carnation wreath: W3

Carnevale di Venezia: E(e. i.)

Caro mio ben: B3(e. i.) E(e. i.) G3(i.) W3 Ah, love of
   mine: S15

Caro nome: E(e. i.) G4(i.)

Carol, children, carol: W8

The carol of the bagpipers see Canzone d'i zampognari

Carol of the birds: Y

Carol of the flowers: S3

Carolina in the morning: S10

Caroline (Creole song) L2 L9(e. cr.)

Caroline of Edinburgh town: F3

The carpenter (Guatemalan song) T6

Carraig aonair: O(e. ir.)

El carretero see The cart-driver

Carry me back to old Virginny: B4 E3 F F5 F7 G3
   L4 W3 Z

The cart-driver (El carretero) Z(e. s.)

Carta del rey ha venido: L9(e. s.)

The cartin wife: N

Caruli: E(e. i.) W3

Casey Jones: B4 L L5 L6 T4

Casey Jones (union song) F8

Casey's social club: G3

A casinha pequenina: C12(pr.) The little cottage: Z(e. pr.)

Casta Diva: G4(e. i.)

Castanet song (from Carmen) G4 W8

Cathleen ni Houlihan see Caitilin ni Uallachain

Cats on the rooftops: B8

Caux carol: R

Il cavallo scalpita: G4(e.i.)
Cearc agus coileach: O(e.ir.)
Cease mine eyes: G2
El cefiro: G3(s.)
Celeste Aida: B3(e.i.) C9(e.i.) E(e.i.) G4(e.i.)
    S14(e.i.) Heavenly Aida: E2
O cessate di piagarmi: B3(e.i.) E(e.i.)
C'est l'aviron: L9(e.f.)
C'est un reve: G4(f.)
C'est une chanson d'amour: G4(f.)
Cet asile aimable et tranquille: G4(f.)
Ceylonese National Anthem: S4(e.sn.)
Cez Tisovec: D2(e.sl.)
Chacarera: C12(s.)
Chad gadya: R5(e.h.)
Chain gang blues: S13
Chairs to mend: T
Challenge: P2
Champagne Charlie: L5
Champagne song (from Die Fledermaus) G3
The chandler's wife: B8
Chang fu ch'u tang ping: C11(e.ch.)
Changing partners: E5
Chanson de danse et de quete de la petite mariee de Mai:
    K(e.wa.)
Chanson des scieurs de long: K(e.wa.)
Chant hindou see Song of India
Chantons les amours de Jean: B3(e.f.)
Chanukah: T6 see also Hanukkah
Chanuke, o Chanuke: R5(e.y.)
Charcoal man: D
Charles Guiteau: L6
Charleston: H2 S10
Charlie is my darling: C8 F4 F7 G3 L4 P2
Charlie Quantrell: L6
The charming young widow I met in the train: G3
El charro: L9(e.s.)
Chasing women: B6
Chattanooga choo choo: C4

Chatskele, chatskele: R5(e.y.)
Chcialo sie zosi jagodek: P(e.p.)
Ah! che a te personi iddio: G4(e.i.)
Che faro senza Euridice: C9(e.i.)
Che gelida manina: C9(e.i.) G4(e.i.)
Che puro ciel: C9(e.i.)
Chee lai: H5(e.ch.)
Cheer up, Molly: F5
The cheerful horn: B9
Cherokee: T4
Cherries are ripe: W5
Cherries ripe: W5
Cherry blossoms see Sakura, sakura
Cherry ripe: L10
The cherry tree carol: B6 C8 N S7
Cherubim song: Z
Chester: B D E4 F5 I I3
Le Chevalier du Guet: V(f.)
Chevaliers de la table ronde: B6(e.f.) V(f.)
Chi-baba chi-baba: J2
Chi mai, fra gl'inni e i plausi: G4(e.i.)
Chi mi dira (from Marta) G4(e.i.)
Chi mi frena (from Lucia) E(e.i.) G4(e.i.) Sextette: E2
Chicka hanka: L2
The chickens are a-crowing: D L6 Almost day: S
Chickery chick: J2
The child and the star: W5
A child has been born (Er is een kindetje geboren) C2(e.d.)
The child Jesus (El nino Jesus) S3(e.s.) The little Jesus:
    T6(e.s.)
The child of God: B5 S
A child this day is born: R S3 Y
O children, do not tarry see Ihr kinder, ihr verziegen
The children in the wood: F3
Children of different ways: S6
The children of far distant lands: S6
Children of the heavenly king: A3 L3 S W4
The children's angel: W7
Children's hosanna: W7

Child's dreamland: W7
Child's hymn: W7
Chilean National Anthem: S4(e.s.)
The chili widow: G3
Chilly winds: D L2 L8 S13
Chime again, beautiful bells: W7
Chiming bells of long ago: F5
Chimney pond trail: B6
Chin Chin Chinaman: G3
Chinatown, my Chinatown: T7
Chinese baby song: W5
Chinese lullaby: T6
Chinese National Anthem: S5(e.ch.)
Ching-a-ling-ling: G3
Chisholm Trail see The old Chisholm Trail
Chit chat: L5
The chivalrous shark see The rhyme of the chivalrous
    shark
Chizzum Trail see The old Chisholm Trail
Chlopek-ci ja chlopek: P(e.p.)
Chocbym ja jezdzil we dnie i w nocy: P(e.p.)
El choclo: E2
Chodi suhaj: D2(e.sl.)
Chodzilem po polu: P(e.p.)
Cholita: C12(s.)
The cholly blues see Broke and hungry
Chon kina: G3
Choose you a seat and set down: L8
Chopping the cane: L2
Choucoune: L2
Christ and Saint Mary: G2
Christ arose: L3
The Christ child's stable: T6
Christ day: C2
Christ, the Lord, is risen today: F L3 W4
Christ was born on Christmas day: L3 S3
Christian, dost thou see them: L3
Christians, awake, salute the happy morn: L3 R S3 Y
A Christmas antiphon (African song) T6

O Christmas babe (Zu Bethlehem geboren) C2(e.g.)
A Christmas carol <u>see</u> Kind Christmas comes but once
   a year
Christmas chimes: W3 W8
Christmas comes again (O Jul med din glede) C2(e.n.)
Christmas cradle song (Still and dark the night) R
Christmas day in the morning <u>see</u> I saw three ships
Christmas day in the morning (children's song) W5
Christmas Eve canon: S3
Christmas in Killarney: S8
Christmas in Mexico (Las posadas) T6
Christmas is coming: B5 B9 R S3 Z
Christmas is here (Joulu puu on rekennettu) C2(e.fi.)
Christmas song (Every year there comes to us) W8
Christmas song (Good day and welcome, dear Christmas
   tree) G3
Christmas spring: Z
The Christmas tree <u>see</u> O tannenbaum
Christmas voices: <u>W8</u>
Christopher Colombo: B8 B9 H
Chto ty zhadno gliadish na dorogu: R4(e.r.)
Ch'u t'ou ko: C11(e.ch.)
Chudobna dievcina: D2(e.sl.)
Chula: K(e.pr.)
Chula la manana: L9(e.s.)
Chums: T6
Ch'un hsin: C11(e.ch.)
Chung ch'iu kuei yuan: C11(e.ch.)
The church in the wildwood <u>see</u> The little brown church
   in the vale
The church's one foundation: A3 L3
Ciaze je to rolicka: D2(e.sl.)
Cie su to husky: D2(e.sl.)
Cie su to kone: D2(e.sl.)
Cielito lindo: B3(e.s.) C12(s.) E(e.s.) F(e.s.) F7
   S11(s.) W3 Z(e.s.) <u>Beautiful heaven:</u> E2
Cielo e mar: G4(e.i.)
Ciemnem borem nad wieczorem: P(e.p.)
Cigarettes will spoil your life: S12

Cinderella: W5
Cindy: B6 C7 D H5 L L6 S11
Ciobane: B7(e.rm.)
Ciribiribin: E(e.i.) E2 F4 F7(e.i.) G3 W3
The city blues: S13
The city rat and the country rat: W6
An clar bog deil: O(e.ir.)
The clean song: B8
Clear brook see Arroyo claro
Clear the kitchen: C7
Clear the track, let the bulgine run: H S5 The bullgine
    run: L6
Les clefs de la prison: L8(e.f.)
Clementine: B4 B6 C7 E2 F F6 L4 L5 R2 S11 W3
The cliff on the Volga see Utes
Climbing up the golden stairs: E2 G3 W3
Clinch Mountain see Rye whiskey
Clink, clink, clinkerty clink: W7
Clochette: W7
Clouds have risen over the city see Tuchi nad gorodom
    vstali
The clouds will soon roll by: T3
The clucking hen: W6
Clychau Aberdyfi see The bells of Aberdovey
Co budeme robit: D2(e.sl.)
Co-ca-che-lunk: G3 L5
Co si k nam neprisiel: D2(e.sl.)
Coaching song (from The Mascot) W8
The coal miner's child: L8
The coast of Peru: H
The coasts of High Barbary see High Barbaree
Cocaine Bill: B6 R2 see also Willie the weeper
Cock-a-doodle-doo: W5 see also Cocky doodle doodle doo
A cock and a hen see Cearc agus coileach
Cock Robin: C8 L6
Cock Robin and Jenny Wren: W6
The cockeyed mayor of Kaunakakai: E5
Cockles and mussels: B4 G3 I2 L4 P2 Molly Malone:
    L10 R2

Cocky doodle doodle doo: L8 <u>see also</u> Cock-a-doodle-doo
Cod liver oil: L8
Codiad yr hedydd <u>see</u> Rise, rise, thou merry lark
Coffee grows on white oak trees: L
The coffee song (They've got an awful lot of coffee in
    Brazil) E5
Cold is the morning: L3 S3
Cold rainy day: S12
Cole Younger: L6
Collector man blues: S13
Colleen Bawn: G3
Colombian National Anthem: S4(e.s.)
O Colombina (from Pagliacci) G4(e.i.) S14(e.i.)
The Colorado Trail: L6 P2 S12 <u>Weep, all ye little rains:</u>
    L10
Columbia (While freedom guides) G3
Columbia, God preserve thee free: W7
Columbia, the gem of the ocean: F F4 F5 G3 W9
    <u>The red, white and blue:</u> W3 W7
Come again (Sweet love doth now invite) B3 S15
O come all ye faithful <u>see</u> Adeste fideles
Come, all ye shepherds <u>see</u> Mesem vam noving
Come all you fair and tender ladies: L S11
Come all you worthy Christian men: K R
Come and go with me: L2
Come away, come sweet love: G
Come back, sweet May: W6
Come back to Erin: E2 G3 W3 W7
Come back to me: G3
Come back to Sorrento <u>see</u> Torna a Surriento
Come, Christians, join to sing: L3
O come, come away: W7
Come, come ye saints: B
Come, count the time for me: T
Come, fellow workers (Chinese song) H5
Come, fireflies <u>see</u> Hotaru koi
Come, follow to the greenwood tree: B6 T Z
Come, for thy love is waiting <u>see</u> Vieni, che poi sereno
Come heavy sleep: G

Come hither, Tom: T
Come, holy spirit, heavenly dove: W7
Come home, father: A B2 E3 Father, dear father, come
   home with me now: F4 F6
Come home, John: P2
Come into the garden, Maud: G3
Come, Josephine, in my flying machine: T4
Come, labor on: L3
Come, landlord, fill the flowing bowl: G3 R2 Landlord,
   fill the flowing bowl: B6
Come, lassies and lads: W7
Come, let us all a-Maying go: T
Come, life, Shaker life: L6
O come, little children: L3 P2 S3(e.g.) Ihr kinderlein,
   kommet: B5
O come love see O marenariello
Come my Celia: G
Come, my soul, thou must be waking: F L3
Come now, shepherds, come away: B5
O come, o come, Emmanuel (Veni emmanuel) B5 L3(e.1.)
   P2 S3(e.1.)
Come, o love see Shule aroon
Come on little Hovda: K2
Come out to play: T6
Come out, ye Continentalers: B9
Come per me sereno: G4(e.i.)
Come quickly, New Year see Hayaku koi koi oshogatsu
Come, ride with me (Ukrainian song) P2
Come, saints and sinners: B
Come scoglio: G4(i.)
Come, see the place where Jesus lay: L3
Come, sister dear see Vamos, Maninha
Come, son see Majka sina vice
Come take a little partner: W7
Come, thou almighty king: A3 L3 R2 W4
Come, thou fount of every blessing: A3
Come to the Sabbath school: L3
Come to the sea see Vieni sul mar
Come un bel di (from Andrea Chenier) G4(i.)

Come unto these yellow sands: S15
Come where my love lies dreaming: F5 F7 G3 W3
Come with the gypsy bride: G4
Come with your dancing see Salten y ballen
Come, ye disconsolate, where'er ye languish: L3
Come, ye faithful, raise the strain: L3
Come, ye redeemed of the Lord: H4
Come, ye thankful people: A3 F4 L3
Come ye to Bethlehem: P2
Come yourselves and see: I3
Coming in on a wing and a prayer: C4
Coming through the Rye: B3 E2 F F4 F7 G3 R2 W3
    W7
The commonwealth of toil: F8
Como aves precursoras see Buy my violets
Como una estrella fugaz: L9(e.s.)
The company of Jesus: T6
Compere Guilleri: V(f.)
Comrades (ever since we were boys) B2 E3 F5 F6 F7
    G3 W3 W6
Comrades, fill no glass for me: F7
Le Comte de Gruyere: K(e.f.)
Concerto militare (from Il Trovatore) E(e.i.) Song of the
    soldiers: W8 Squilli echeggi la tromba: G4(e.i.)
Confess Jehovah: D I
The conga passes: L2
Congo lullaby: T6(e.cg.)
Connais-tu le pays: C9(e.f.) G4(e.f.)
The Connecticut peddler: L7
Constancy (Hawaiian song) W3
Constante: L9(e.pr.)
The Constitution and the Guerriere: H I I3 L7
The continental: C5
The cool, sweet water see Isla devecka
Cool water: T2
Coplas: B7(e.s.)
Coquette: T5
Cordelia Brown: A2 L2
The cordwood cutter: C6

Corinna blues: L6 S13
The cork leg: G3
Corn rigs are bonnie: C8
Cornell alma mater see Far above Cayuga's waters
Cornfield holler: L7
Cornish May song: C3
Cornwallis country dance: I I3
Corrido de la canelera: L9(e.s.)
Corrido de Marcario Romero: L9(e.s.)
Corrido de Modesta Ayala: L9(e.s.)
Cortigiani (from Rigoletto) G4(i.)
Corydon and Caroline: F3
Costa Rican National Anthem: S4(e.s.)
Cotton eye Joe: I3 L7 L8
Cotton field song: L7
Cotton mill colic: L6 L8
Cotton needs picking: L6
Le coucou: V(f.)
Could I (Neapolitan song) see Vorrei
O could I speak the matchless worth: L3
The Count of Cabra see La viudita
The Countess of Laurel see La viudita del Conde Laurel
Counting song (Japanese song) see Kazoe uta
Counting the goats (Cyfri'r giefr) C8(e.w.)
Country sports are sweeter: T
The courting of Aramalee: N
Courting Susan Jane: C7
Cousin Jedediah: L5
Coventry carol: B4 B5 Y Lully lullay: L3 R R3 S3 W
The cow: W6
The cowboy: F2 P2 All day on the prairie: I3
The cowboy (O a man there lives on the western plain) F5
The cowboy and the lady: P2
Cowboy carol: R
Cowboy dance (Venezuelan song) L2
Cowboy Jack: G3 L4
Cowboy lullaby: B6
Cowboy to pitching bronco: L7
Cowboy's dream: B6 I3 L Cowboy's heaven: F2

Cowboy's getting-up holler: D L7 Wake up, Jacob: L6
Cowboy's heaven see Cowboy's dream
The cowboy's lament (My home's in Montana) F2 see also
   Bury me not on the lone prairie and The streets of
   Laredo
A cowboy's life (is a weary, dreary life) L6 Dreary life:
   F2
Cowboy's meditation: G3 L4
The cow's chant see Cronan na bo
Crabe dans calalou: L8(e. cr.)
Cradle hymn: S Hush, my dear, lie still and slumber:
   L3 S3
Cradle hymn (by Rousseau) W5
Cradle song (by Brahms) see Wiegenlied
Cradle song (by Gatty) W5
Cradle song (by Von Weber) F7 W5
Cradle song (Ed alavo) K
Cradle song of the poor (by Moussorgsky) S15
Cranberries and raspberries see Kalina, malina
Crawdad song: B B6 B9 I3 L L8 S11
Crazy: T2
Crazy rhythm: H3
Credo in un dio: G4(e. i.)
The crest and crowning of all good: S6
The cricket takes a wife see Hazasodik a tucsok
Cricket voices see Mushi no koe
The criminal cried: G3
Criole candjo: L7(e. cr.)
Cripple creek: L6
The crocodile song: I I3
Cronan na bo: O(e. ir.)
Croodin doo: I3
The crooked gun: L8
Crooked whiskey: J
The croppy boy: C8
Croquet: E4 L5
Crossing the bar: L3
Crossing the brook see Que bonita eres
The crow (Japanese song) see Karasu

The crow (Swedish song) Z
Crown him with many crowns: A3 L3
Crows in the garden: L7
Cruda, funesta smania: G4(e. i.)
The cruel brother: N
The cruel mother: N S7
The cruise of the dreadnaught see The dreadnought
The Cruiskeen lawn: C8 G3 I2
Crusher Bailey: B8
Cry of the wild goose: T2
The Cryderville jail: L7 Hard times: L6
The crying family: F3
El cuando: B4
Cuando al pie de tu ventana see Amor
Los cuatro generales: B4 H5(e. s.)
Las cuatro milpas: C12(s.)
Los cuatro muleros: B7(e. s.)
Cuatro palomitas blancas: L7(e. s.)
Cuba see Tu
Cuban National Anthem (La Bayamesa) S4(e. s.)
La cucaracha: B(e. s.) D(e. s.) F7(e. s.)
Cuckoo (by Gatty) W6
The cuckoo (is a funny bird) B9 K L6 W5
Cuckoo dear (Y gwcw vach) C8(e. w.)
The cuckoo, she's a pretty bird see The cuckoo (is a
    funny bird)
Cuckoos sing see Kukucka
Cucul: K(e. m.)
Cuddle up a little closer: T7
An cuimhin leat an oiche ud: O(e. ir.)
La cuisiniere: Z(e. f.)
Cuisle mo chroi: O(e. ir.)
The Cumberland and the Merrimac: S5
The Cumberland crew: C6 S5
Cumberland Gap: C C10 E4 L5 L6 L7 S5 S11
La cumparsita: C12(s.)
Cupan ui Eaghra: O(e. ir.)
Cupid and I: G3
Curious cures: G3

Curly locks: W5
The curtains of night: F7 L4
The cute little car: C7
Cutting down the pines: C6
The cutty wren: F8
Cyfri'r giefr see Counting the goats
Czarna rola bialy kamien: P(e. p.)
Czarskoselbskaya statuya see The statue at Czarskoe-Selo
Czechoslovakian National Anthem: S4(e. c. sl.)
Czekaj tu dziewczyno: P(e. p.)
Czemu ty placzesz: P(e. p.)
Cztery mile za Warszawa: P(e. p.)
Czterym latka: P(e. p.)

D

Da bhfaghainn mo rogha de thriur aca: O(e. ir.)
Da bi imal perje: K(e. sc.)
Daar nu het feest van Pasen is: K(e. d.)
Daar was een sneeuwwit vogeltje: K(e. d.)
Daddy (Take my head on your shoulder) W3 W6
Daddy shot a bear: L8
Daddy wouldn't buy me a bow-wow: A
Dad's a millionaire: E3
Dafydd y gareg wen see David of the white rock
Daisies won't tell: A E3 F4 F6 G3
The daisy (I'm a pretty little thing) W6
Daisy Bell: B E4 F5 F7 G3 R2 W3 A bicycle built
    for two: A E3 F F6
Dal labbro il canto: G4(i.)
Daleko, daleko: R4(e. r.)
Dalla sua pace: G4(e. i.) S14(e. i.)
Dame, get up and bake your pies: B5 W5
Dame, lend me a loaf: T
Une dame noble et sage: G4(e. f.)
Damn the Filipinos: L7
D'amor sull'ali rosee: G4(e. i.)
The damsel's tragedy: F3

Dan McGoogan's goat: G3
Dan paid for the oysters: G3
The Danbury mare: C7
Dance a baby diddy: W5
Dance a cachucha (from The Gondoliers) G3
Dance it see Tancuj
Dance me a jig: S5
Dance of the fairies: W7
Dance, Thumbkin, dance: W5
Dance to your daddy: B9
Dance up, dance down: P2
Dance with a dolly: T4
Dance, you maids see Pkiaste kopelles, sto choro
Dancing in the dark: H2
The dancing lesson (from Hansel and Gretel) W8
Dandoo: D
Dangerous woman: S13
Danish National Anthem see Der er et yndigt land and
    Kong Kristian
Dans cette etable see In that poor stable
Danville girl: B6
Dar star ett trad: K(e.sw.)
Darby and Joan: W3
The Darby ram: B8 B9 C7 O didn't he ramble: L2
    The ram of Darby: L8
Dare to be brave: L3
The daring young man on the flying trapeze see The man
    on the flying trapeze
The daring young man who provided the skis see The man
    on the flying skis
Dark as a dungeon: B6 F8 L6
Dark brown is the river: S6
The dark-eyed canaller: L8
The dark-eyed sailor: F3
Dark eyes (Ochy chornia) B3(e.r.) E2 F7 W3
The dark girl dressed in blue: G3
Dark is the night see Temnaia noch
The dark slender boy see An buachaill caol dubh
The darktown strutters' ball: T5

Darky Sunday school: B6 H L5 L7 Bible stories: C6
   The history of the world: C7 G3 J
Darling (If I'd a-known my captain was blind) S13
Darling (You can't love but one) see New River train
Darling Corey: B D I3 L L2 L8 S11 W
Darling, goodnight see Dobru noc, ma mila
Darling Nelly Gray: B C D E2 F4 F5 F7 G3 W3
Darogoy dal'noyu: B7(e. r.)
Dartmouth, our Dartmouth: R2
Dartmouth's in town again: R2
das (article) see next word of title
Datt wandlen wir die goldne schtrose: H4(e. pd.)
The daughter of Rosie O'Grady: T8
Daughter, will you marry see Maedli, witt du heire
O David: L6
David of the white rock (Dafydd y gareg wen) C8(e. w.)
David's lamentation: D
Davy Crockett (Now don't you ever want to know) C10
Davy Crockett, Ballad of: L7 T2
Dawn in Hawaii (Pili aoao) P2
Dawniej dziadowie: P(e. p.)
Day is dying in the west: A3 B4 L3
The day is gently sinking to a close: F L3
Day, O: L2 Banana boat loader's song: A2
A day of joy and feasting: S3
A day of joyful singing: S6
The day of liberty's coming: S5
O day of rest and gladness: L3
The day of resurrection: L3
Dayenu: B9(e. h.)
O the days are gone when beauty bright: G3
The days of '49: L
The days of spring (Fruhlingszeit) S15
Days of summer glory: W6
de (variant of "the") see next word of title
De aquel cerro verde see From yon mountain verdant
De blanca tierra see From the white earth
De Kalb blues: S13
De Mexico ha venido: D(e. s.)

De' miei bollenti spiriti: G4(e.i.)
Dear Evelina, sweet Evelina: F5 L4 P2 W3
Dear, if you change: G
Dear land of the south: J
Dear little boy of mine: T8
The dear little shamrock: I2
Dear Lord and father of mankind: L3 W4
Dear maiden, shall I with you go see Jungfraulein, soll
  ich mit euch gehn
O dear, what can the matter be: B3 C6 E3 F4 W5
Dearest Mae: C
The dearest spot on earth: G3
O death: D
Death, ain't you got no shame: L6 S12
Death hath deprived me: G2
The death of Geordie: N
The death of King Renaud see La mort du roi Renaud
The death of Mrs. Lydia Woodburn: F3
The death of Mother Jones: F8
The death of Queen Jane: N
The debutante: G3
The deceived girl: N
Deck of cards: T2
Deck the halls with boughs of holly: B4 B5 L4 R2 S3 S6
Dedication see Widmung
Deep blue sea: S11
Deep river: B6 D E2 F F4 F5 F7 G3 L4 L7 W3
  W7
Deep sea blues: S13
Deep under plain and mountain lie: S6
The deer see El venadito
The deer chase: L6
Deh vieni alla finestra: G4(e.i.) S14(e.i.)
Deh vieni, non tardar: G4(e.i.)
Deilig er den himmel blaa see O how beautiful the sky
Deirin de: O(e.ir.)
Delicado: S8
Dendenmushi: W2(e.ja.)
The dens of Yarrow: C6 The dowie dens of Yarrow: K

Deo gracias anglia (the Agincourt carol) G2
Departure see Li ch'ing
Depression blues: S13
der (article) see next word of title
Der er et yndigt land: F(e. dn.) S4(e. dn.)
des (article) see next word of title
O desayo: L2
dese see these
Deserto sulla terra: G4(e. i.)
Desperado: B6
La Dessalinienne: S4(e. f.)
Destroyer life: L7
Deta, deta: W2(e. ja.)
Deutschlandlied: S4(e. g.) German National Anthem: F(g.)
Un, deux, trois: L7(e. cr.)
The devil and the farmer's wife: C6 D I S11 W
    The farmer's curst wife: L6 N S7
Devilish Mary: C6 L6 L8 S11
The devil's nine questions: B9 I L6 N
The devil's questions see The devil's nine questions
Dhomhnuill, a Dhomhnuill: K(e. ir.)
di (article) see next word of title
Un di felice (from La Traviata) S14(e. i.)
Di mie discolpe: S14(e. i.)
Di pasta simile: G4(i.)
Di Provenza il mar: C9(e. i.) G4(e. i.) S14(e. i.)
Di quella pira: G4(e. i.)
Di tale amor: G4(e. i.)
Di tu se felele il flutto m'aspetta: G4(e. i.)
El dia que yo naci: C12(s.)
Diamond Joe: L8
Dich, teuere halle: G4(e. g.)
Dickory, dickory, dock see Hickory, dickory, dock
Did I remember: C4
Did you ever watch the campfire: S6
Didn't he ramble see The Darby ram
Didn't it rain: L6
Didn't my Lord deliver Daniel: D
Didn't old John cross the water on his knees: L8

die (article) see next word of title
Died for love: C8
Dies bildnis ist bezaubernd schon: G4(g.)
Dievca, coze to mas: D2(e.sl.)
Dievca, lastovicka: D2(e.sl.)
Dig a hole in the meadow: L6
Dig my grave (both long and narrow) L8
Din plaiurile romanei: B7(e.rm.)
Ding, dong, bell (pussy's in the well) F W5
Ding, dong, merrily on high: R Y
Dink's song: L L7 S11 Fare thee well, o honey: I3
    If I had wings like Nora's dove: S12
Dinky die: H5
The dipsycola: C7
Dir, hohe liebe: G4(e.g.)
Dir tone lob: G4(e.g.)
Dire-gelt: R5(e.y.)
Dirty Jack: W6
Dirty mistreating women: L7
Ditte alla giovine (from La Traviata) G4(e.i.)
Dives and Lazarus: N
Divinity is round us: S6
Dixie: B4 C12 D E2 E4 F4 F5 G3 L7 S5 W3 W7
    W9 Z
Dixieland (a parody) C7
Dixie's isle: H
Dnia jednego o polnocy: P(e.p.)
Do chuirfinn-se fein mo leanbh a chodla: O(e.ir.)
Do come back again: L8
Do-do, baby, do: W5
Do me ama: H
Do not awaken my memories see Ne probuzhdai
    vospominania
Do not deny my plea see Ne me refuse pas
O do not grieve: S16(e.r.)
Do not scold me see Ne korite menia, ne branite
Do slubejku jedziewa: P(e.p.)
Do they miss me at home: F5 G3 S5
Do they think of me at home: G3

Do you ever think of me: T5
Do you not know: G
Dobre mi: D2(e. sl.)
Dobru noc, ma mila: D2(e. sl.)
Dobrynia see Shto ne byelaya
Doctor Ironbeard see Doktor Eisenbart
Dr. Sean o Hairt (Dr. Hohn Hart) O(e. ir.)
The dodger: F8 H5 L8
Does true love ever run smooth: F6
The dog and cat: W6
Dog and gun: F3
The dog catcher's child: L5
The dog in the closet: F3
Doing nothing but sing: T6
Doktor Eisenbart: G3(g.) H4(e. pd.)
Dolina: D2
A dollar ain't a dollar any more: H5
A dollar and a half a day: D
Dolls' festival see Hina matsuri
Dolly and her mamma: W5
Dominican National Anthem: S4(e. s.)
Domovina: H5(e. j.)
Don Francisco: L2
Don Jose of Sevilla (by Herbert) G3
Don Ramon see Ramon del alma mia
Dona Ana: L9(e. s.)
Dona nobis pacem: B6(l.) S3(l.) S6(l.) T(l.)
Donald, O Donald see Dhomhnuill, a Dhomhnuill
Donde vas, Alfonso Doce: L9(e. s.)
Done laid around this old town too long: W
Doney gal: L6 L8
A donkey named Pete: C7
Donkey riding see Riding on a donkey
Una donna a quindici anni: G4(i.)
La donna e mobile: C9(e. i.) E(e. i.) G4(i.) Over the
    summer sea: W8 Woman is fickle: E2 W3
Donna Lombarda: K(e. i.)
Donna non vidi mai simile a questa: G4(e. i.)
Donne mie (from Cosi fan tutte) G4(i.)

Don't be cross (from Der Obersteiger) G3
Don't blame me: T5
Don't call me: B8
Don't cry Joe: S9
Don't fence me in: M S9
Don't get around much any more: C4
Don't go to strangers: E5
Don't let the stars get in your eyes: T2
Don't lie, buddy: L6 S13
Don't stub your toe on Friday: C7
Don't talk about it: L8
Don't you go, Tommy: J
Don't you hear the lambs a-crying: S
Don't you hurry worry with me: L8
Don't you leave me here: S13
Don't you like it: L8
Doodle doo doo: C4 T5
Dooligan's ghost: G3
Doon the moor: Z
Dormi, dormi, o bel bambin see Sleep, o holy child of
   mine
Dormi pur (from Marta) G4(e.i.)
D'ou viens-tu, bergere: B5 K(e.f.) V(f.)
Douce dame jolie: B3(e.f.)
Douman es lou prumie may: K(e.f.)
The dove see La paloma
The dove (Y deryn pur) C8(e.w.)
The dove has twin white feet: B3
Dove sono (from Le Nozze di Figaro) G4(e.i.)
The dowie dens of Yarrow see The dens of Yarrow
Down along the Mother Volga see Vniz po matushke po vol
Down among the sheltering palms: T5
Down and out: B6
Down by the bridge see A na tom zvolenskom moste
Down by the greenwood shady: C6
Down by the riverside: B7 B9 L2 (Ain't going to) study
   war no more: B6 F8 R2 S11 T6
Down by the riverside (A man and a maid went out rowing)
   G3

Down by the Salley Gardens: B3 C8 L10
Down by the station: R2
Down by the tanyard side: K
Down, down, down (miners' song) L L8
Down in a coal mine: C10 E4 F5 F7 F8
Down in a valley (Elizabethan song) G
Down in a valley, sing hallelu see Sing hallelu
Down in Charleston jail: S5
Down in the Lehigh Valley: C
Down in the valley: B4 B6 G3 I I3 L L4 L6 L7 P2
     R2 S11 Z
Down in the willow garden: L Rose Connelly: L6
Down in yon forest: B9 R
Down on Penney's farm: F8 L6 Hard times in the country:
     L8
Down on the green see Ej, na vrbovcovh
Down she sat see Sadla dole
Down that old ski trail: K2
Down the field: R2
Down the mountain see Tecie potok od krivana
Down the river: B9 C P2
Down the river of golden dreams: C4
Down the road see Going down the road feeling bad
Down the Volga River see Vniz po Volge reke
Down went McGinty: A E2 E3 F6 G3 L5
Down went the captain: G3
Down where the Wurzburger flows: B2
The downward road: L6
Doxology see Old hundred
Draftee's blues: S13
An draighnean donn: O(e. ir.)
The dreadnought: I I3 Cruise of the dreadnaught: H
A dream (Last night I was dreaming of thee love) F7 G3
Dream faces: F5 F7
The dreamer: S9
A dreamer's holiday: T4
Dreaming (of you sweetheart) F4 F6 G3
Dreaming (Love's own sweet message I'm bringing) E3
Dreaming (Traume, by Wagner) S15

Dreaming, dreaming (from Wizard of the Nile) G3
Dreams and imaginations: G
The dreary black hills: F3 I3 L6 L7
The dreary dream: N
Dreary life see A cowboy's life
Drenovare: K̄(e. a.)
Drik mir vin: K2(e. ic.)
Drill, ye tarriers, drill: B4 B6 E4 F8 I3 L6
   Tarrier's song: H5
Drink it down: S5 Here's to good old beer: B6 Pass
   around the good old beer: G3
Drink, puppy, drink: F
Drink to me only with thine eyes: B3 B4 C3 E2 F F4 F7
   G3 R2 W3 Z
Drinking song (How cool and fair this cellar) G3
Drinking song (My comrades when I'm no more drinking)
   R2
Drinking song (from Cavalleria Rusticana) see Viva il
   vino spumeggiante
Drinking song (from La Traviata) see Libiamo ne' lieti
   calici
Drive it on: L8
Driving on Bald Mountain: B7
Driving saw-logs on the Plover: C
Dropping pennies: L3
Drozyna: K(e. p.)
Druimfhionn donn dilis: O(e. ir.)
Druimin: O(e. ir.)
The drummer boy of Shiloh: S5
Drunk last night: B6 R2 Glorious, glorious: G3 One more
   drink for the four of us: L5
The drunkard's child: J
The drunkard's doom: L7
Drunkard's special: B6
The drunken sailor: B4 B6 H I R2 What shall we do
   with a drunken sailor: L5 S2
Drunten im unterland: G3(g.)
Du armste (from Lohengrin) S14(e. g.)
Du bist die ruh': B3(e. g.)

Du bist wie eine blume: B3(e.g.)
Du, du liegst mir im herzen: B6(g.) E2(g.) G(e.g.)
  K2(e.g.) L4(g.) You, you, in my heart living: B3(e.g.)
Du gamla, du fria: S4(e.sw.) Swedish National Anthem:
  F(e.sw.)
O du lieber Augustin: C3(e.g.) E2(g.) F(g.)
Du meydele du sheyns: R5(e.y.)
Duan chroi iosa: O(e.ir.)
Dubinushka: R4(e.r.)
Dublin Bay: G3
Ducks in the millpond: L8
Duncan and Brady: L8
Duncan Gray: G3
Dupree: L8
Duralaydeo: C7
The Durant jail: L
El durazno: L9
Durch die walder (from Der Freischutz) G4(e.g.)
Durch zartlichkeit und schmeicheln: G4(g.)
Dust pneumonia blues: S13
Dustbowl blues see Talking dustbowl blues
The dustman: W3 W5 W8
Dutch lullaby: C10
Dutch National Anthem see Netherlands National Anthem
Dutch warbler: G3 L5
Dve gitari: B7(e.r.) Two guitars: E2 F7 W3
Dwanascie listeczek: P(e.p.)
The dying Californian: D
The dying cowboy see Bury me not on the lone prairie and
  The streets of Laredo
The dying hobo: B6
The dying hogger: I3
The dying queen: N
The dying sergeant: F3
Dynom, danom: D2(e.sl.)

E

E allor perche (from Pagliacci) G4(e. i.) S14(e. i.)
E amore un ladroncello: G4(i.)
E il sol dell' anima: G4(i.)
E la Violeta: K(e. i.)
E l'amor mio (from Aida) S14(e. i.) <u>Ritorna vincitor</u>:
   G4(e. i.)
E lucevan le stelle: G4(i.)
Each is needed: S6
Each minute I look at you <u>see</u> A cada instante
Eadie: L8
Eamonn an chnuic: O(e. ir.)
Earl Brand: N
Earl Colvin: N
Early, early Sunday morn <u>see</u> A w niedziele porankiem
Early one morning: C6 C8
Earth arrayed in wondrous beauty: S6
East Colorado blues: L6
East of the sun: J2
East Virginia: H5 L8
Easter surprises (German song) T6
Easy rider: L S13
Eating goober peas <u>see</u> Goober peas
Ecco il mondo (from Mefistofele) G4(i.)
Ecco ridente in cielo: G4(e. i.)
Ecuadorean National Anthem: S4(e. s.)
Ed alavo: K(e. i.)
The Eddystone light: C7 W
Edgartown whaling song: H
Edi beo thu hevene quene: G2
Edmund of the hill <u>see</u> Eamonn an chnuic
Edward: I I3 L6 <u>N</u>
EE-LEE-AY-LEE-OH: B6
Eesti humn: S4(e. es.)
Eggs and marrowbone: B6
Egli e salvo: G4(i.)
Die ehre Gottes in der natur <u>see</u> The glory of God in nature
Ehre sei Gott <u>see</u> Glory to God

Ei, ukhnem see Song of the Volga boatmen
Eia, eia: S3
Eibhlain a Ruin: K(e. ir.)
Eight bells: B6
The eight hour day: F8
Eight hours (We mean to make things over) B
Eight little birds: W6
Eileen Aroon (Eibhlain a Ruin) K(e. ir.)
Eili, eili see Eli, eli
ein (article) see next word of title
eine (article) see next word of title
Eins, zwei, drei oder vier: H4(e. pd.)
Einsam in truben tagen: G4(e. g.) S14(e. g.)
Ej, na vrbovcovh: K(e. c.)
Ej nieraz, ja-ci nieraz: P(e. p.)
Ej, pada rosicka: D2(e. sl.)
Ej povedz, Katarinka: D2(e. sl.)
Ej! tys moja, dziewczyno: P(e. p.)
el (article) see next word of title
El Salvador National Anthem: S4(e. s.)
El-a-noy: B C D L6 Z
Eleazer Wheelock: B6 R2
Elegie (by Massenet) E2 F7(e. f.) S15
The elephant and the flea: D
Elephants: T
Eleven cent cotton: B F8
The elfin knight: N
Eli, eli (Hebrew song) E2 W3(e. y.)
Eli Yale: R2
Eliza's flight: C J
Elle a fui: G4(f.)
Ellen Bayne: F7 W3
Ellie Rhee: C
Elliptical skiers: B6
Elmenyek: K(e. hu.)
Elsie from Chelsea: B2
Embraceable you: H2
Emendemus in melius: G2(e. l.)
The emigrant's dying child: J

Emmet's cuckoo song: G3
Emmett's lullaby: E2 E3 F7 G3 <u>Go to sleep, Lena</u>
<u>darling</u>: F5 F6 W3 W5
En <u>Cuba la isla hermosa</u> <u>see</u> Tu
En fermant les yeux (from <u>Manon</u>) G4(f.)
En Habana: L9
En medio de esta noche <u>see</u> Serenata
En passant par la Lorraine: V(f.)
En revenant d'Auvergne: F(f.)
En todo el tiempo pasado: L9
En vain pour eviter (from Carmen) G4(e.f.) S14(e.f.)
En yndig og frydefuld sommertid: K(e.dn.)
L'enfant Jesus s'endort <u>see</u> While Jesus sleeps
The English Lady Gay: <u>N</u>
The enlisted men ride in a motor launch <u>see</u> Toorali
Enraptured I gaze: B F5
Entre le boeuf et l'ane gris: B5 <u>Oxen and sheep</u>: L3
S3(e.f.)
Entre Paris et Saint-Denis: K(e.f.)
Entreaty (California-Spanish song) L9
Entrei na roda: L9(e.pr.)
Eoghan Coir: O(e.ir.)
Ephasafa Dill: A
Er is een kindetje geboren <u>see</u> A child has been born
Eres alta: W(e.s.)
Eri tu: C9(e.i.) G4(e.i.)
The Erie Canal (I've got a mule, her name is Sal) B4 B6
D E4 L4 S2 <u>Low bridge, everybody down</u>: C10 F8
L7
The E-RI-E Canal (O the E-RI-E was arising and the gin
was getting low) B B6 B8 C7 I L L7 R2 S11
Erin, the tear and the smile is thine: G3
Erin's green shores: C6
An Eriskay love lilt: C8
Ermuntert euch, ihr frommen: H4(e.pd.)
Es hat die rose sich beklagt: B3(e.g.)
Es ist bestimmt in Gottes rat: G3(g.)
Es ist ein' rose entsprungen: B5 <u>I know a rose tree</u>
<u>springing</u>: R(e.g.) <u>Lo, how a rose e'er blooming</u>:
<u>L3 S3(e.g.)</u>

Es muss ein wunderbares sein see It must be wonderful
   indeed
Es ritten drei reiter zum tore hinaus: G3(g.)
Es schnayt un es blose: H4(e. pd.)
Es sind zween weg: H4(e. pd.)
The escape of old John Webb: I
L'esclave see The slave
Esli Volga razoletsia: R4(e. r.)
Esser mesto: G4(e. i.)
Esta noche es Noche Buena: K(e. s.)
Esta noche serena: C12(s.)
Estaba al pie de la cruz: K(e. s.)
Este raz hoja: D2(e. sl.)
Estilo: C12(s.)
Estonian National Anthem: S4(e. es.)
Estrellita see Little star
Et moi de m'encourir: V(f.)
Et tu lui diras (from Carmen) S14(e. f.)
Eten bamidbar: B7(e. h.)
Eternal father, strong to save: A3 L3
Eternal light! Eternal light: L3
Eternal spirit of the chainless mind: S6
Ethiopian National Anthem: S4(e. am.)
Eton boating song: G3
Euch luften, die mein klagen: S14(e. g.)
The evening bells see O how lovely is the evening
Evening glow see Yuyake, koyake
Evening hymn (glory to thee, my God, this night) W7
Evening prayer (from Hansel and Gretel) F F4 W3 W8
Evening prayer (As I lay me, weary, down to rest) W7
Evening song: W7
Evening star (from Tannhauser) E2 F7 W3 O star of eve:
   W8
Ever of thee: W3
Every bush new springing: G
Every day is ladies' day with me: T7
Every inch a sailor: G3 Jack was every inch a sailor:
   L4
Every little movement: T7

Every night in Central Park: G3
Every night when the sun goes in: B4 D L2 L7 S13 W
Every small inch of farm land (El pericon) T6
Every time I feel the spirit: L2 L4 W3
Every year there comes to us the dear Christ child: W8
Everybody has been wondering see Wszystkich to
    ciekawosc budzi
Everybody loves Saturday night: F8
Everybody's welcome: D
Everything I have is yours: T5
Everything is higher: H5
Everything is peaches down in Georgia: F5
Evil-hearted man: S13
Excelsior: J
The exile see Pa meme
Exquisite hour (L'heure exquise) S15
Exultation (Come away to the skies) S
Eyder ich leyg mich shlofn: R5(e. y.)
Eynem iz doch zeyer gut: R5(e. y.)
Ezekiel saw the wheel: B6 P2 R2 W3

F

Face to face: S8
The face upon the barroom floor: G3
The factory girl: L7
The faded coat of blue: S5
Fai ogoun: L2
Fain would I change that note: G
Fair and free elections: B9
Fair and tender ladies: L6
A fair beauty bride: L6
Fair Fannie More: F3
Fair Florella: F3
The fair flower of Northumberland: N
Fair Harvard: E2 R2
The fair hills of Eire see Ban-chnuic Eireann o
Fair, if you expect admiring: G

Fair in a morn: G
Fair John and the seven foresters: N
Fair Julian Bond: C6
Fair Margaret and sweet William: N
Fair Sally: S7
A fair wind's blowing: L2
A fair youth fell in love with a maiden see Pokochal sie...
Fairest Gwen (Mentra Swen) C8(e.w.)
Fairest Lord Jesus: A3 B4 F L3 L4 W4
O fairest maid: T
The fairy ring: W7
The fairy ship: W5
Fairy tales (from The Idol's Eye) G3
Fais do-do: C10
Faites-lui mes aveux (from Faust) S14(e.f.) Lovely
    flowers I pray: F7 W3 W8
Faith of our fathers: A3 L3 W4
Faith of the free: S6
The faithful comrade (Der gute kamerad) W6
The faithless sweetheart see Ar fall promesau
A fal-de-lal-day (I met a girl in Portland street) H
Falcon flying well see Preletel sokol
Falcon, spread your wings see Prelet sokol
The fall of Charleston: S5
Falls now the dew see Ej, pada rosicka
The false-hearted lover see Malhao
The false knight upon the road: N
The false lady: S7
Falt trom, trom dualach: K(e.ga.)
The famine song: I2 Over there: B The praties, they
    grow small: I
Fantaisie (from Lakme) G4(e.f.)
Fantje vasujejo: K(e.sl.)
Far above Cayuga's waters: F4 F5 Cornell alma mater:
    R2
Far away, far away see Daleko, daleko
Far away in old Judea: T6
Far from me: C3
Far from my mountains see Vo mine berge

Far from my native land see Que lejos estoy
Far in the sky see Vyletel vtak
Far is my love see Tuoll' on mun kultani
Fare thee well, babe: L7
Fare thee well, o honey see Dink's song
Fare ye well, my darling: L8
Fare you well (my own true love) C6
Farewell! But whenever you welcome the hour: C8
Farewell, little love see Adios con el corazon
Farewell, mine own sweetheart: T
Farewell my Lilly: G3
Farewell, my love see Adieu donc ma mie
Farewell to Carraig an Eide see Slan chun Carraig an Eide
Farewell to grog: L5 S5
Farewell to happiness see Proshchai radost
Farewell to the king's highway: G3
Farewell to the Maigue see Slan le Maigh
The farmer: W5
The farmer and the devil see The devil and the farmer's
    wife
The farmer and the shanty boy: F3 L6
The farmer comes to town see The farmer is the man
The farmer in the dell: E2 F7 W5
The farmer is the man: F8 H5 L6 S11 The farmer comes
    to town: D
The farmer-labor train: H5
Farmers' carol: R
The farmer's curst wife see The devil and the farmer's
    wife
A farmer's hymn (Moravian song) H4
Farmer's song (Chinese) see Ch'u t'ou ko
Farmland blues: S13
Farmyard song (by E. Grieg) W6
Fat baby sister (Wo chia yu ke p'ang wa) T6(e. ch.)
Father almighty, bless us with thy blessing: L3
Father and friend, thy light, thy love: L3
Father, blessing every seedtime: L3
Father, dear father, come down with the stamps: L5
Father, dear father, come home with me now see Come
    home, father

Father Grumble: L6 P2
Father O'Flynn: G3
Father, put the cow out: B6
Father, we thank thee for the night: L3
Father's a drunkard, and mother is dead: J
Father's whiskers: B6
Di fayerdige libe: R5(e.y.)
The feast of lanterns: W5
Feather your nest: C4
The Federal Constitution and liberty forever: J
Der feinste sport see Two boards upon cold powder snow
Feldeinsamkeit see Alone in the fields
Felix the soldier: L6
Fellowship of song: T6
The Fency King and the English King: N
Ferry, take me over see Prevez, prievoznicku
Fertile black soil and white field stone see Czarna rola
    bialy kamien
Ein feste burg see A mighty fortress is our God
Few days: L7
Fi la nana: K(e.i.)
O fickle shepherdess (Bergere legere) B3(e.f.)
Fiddle and I: W6 W8
Fiddle-de-dee: I L4 W5
Fiddle-i-fee (O I had a bird) L6
The fiddlers are playing see Na vulitsi skripka hrae
A fidler: B7(e.y.)
Fie, nay, prithee, John: T
Field artillery song see Artillery song
Fight for Cornell: R2
Fight on, Pennsylvania: R2
Fight the good fight: L3
La filadora: K(e.s.)
Filipino National Anthem see Philippines National Anthem
La fille de Parthenay: V(f.)
Fillimeeooreay see Paddy works on the (Erie) railroad
Finch'han dal vino: G4(e.i.) S14(e.i.)
Fine and dandy: C5
Fine knacks for ladies: G

The fine Lady Gay: N
The fine old Irish gentleman: G3 J
Finlandia: F(e.fi.) G3 P2
Finnegan's wake: D G3
Finnish National Anthem see Maamme
Fiore de lino: K(e.i.)
Fire down below: C7 H
Fire, fire: G
Firefly (Croatian song) T6
The fireman's band: B6
The fireman's song: J
The First Arkansas see Marching song of the First
    Arkansas
The first courier: T6
The first nowell (The first noel) A3 B4 B5 C2 F G3 L3
    L4 P2 R R2 S3 S6 W3 W8 Y
The first of May see Douman es lou prumie may
The fish of the sea see The Boston come-all-ye
Fishelech koyfn: R5(e.y.)
Fisherman's song (Weigh up - Susianna) A2
Five foot two, eyes of blue: T5
Five little dogs with curly tails: G3
Fivelgoer kerstlied: K(e.d.)
The flag, Song to: F5
The flag of our union forever: F5 J
Flag of the free: W7
Un flambeau, Jeannette, Isabelle: B5 V(f.) Bring a torch,
    Jeannette, Isabella: L3(e.f.) S3(e.f.) Jeannette,
    Isabella: B4
The flapjacks tree: C7
Flat River girl: C
The Flat River raftsman: C6
La fleur que tu m'avais jetee: G4(e.f.) S14(e.f.)
    Flower song: C9(e.f.)
Flight of doodles: S5
The flighty tailor see An tailliuir aerach
Fling out the banner: F5 L3
Florian's song: S15
Flow gently, sweet Afton: B4 C8 F4 F7 G3 W3

Flow my tears: G
The flower drum see Hua ku ko
Flower of flax see Fiore de lino
Flower song (from Carmen) see La fleur que tu m'avais
    jetee
Flower song (from Faust) see Faites lui mes aveux
Flowering hemp see Viragos kenderem
Flowers red and blue see Blomman bland blommorna
The flowers that bloom in the spring: F G3 W8
Flowing river see Rio-Rio
Fly, my affection see Vuela, suspiro
Flying birds: W6
Flying carp see Koi nobori
The Flying Cloud: L7
Ah, un foco in solito: G4(e.i.)
Fod: L6
The foggy dew (Over the hills I went one morning) C6
The foggy, foggy dew (When I was a bachelor) B4 B6 B8
    G3 I I3 L6 L10 R2 S2
Folks that put on airs: G3
Follow me, full of glee: W7
Follow me up to Carlow: I2
Follow the drinking gourd: B7 C10 L7 S5 W
Follow the gleam: L3
Follow thy fair sun: G
Follow Washington: B9
Follow your saint: G
Fooba wooba John: C7
Fool number one: T2
Fooled: S8
Foom, foom, foom: B5 S3(e.s.)
The foot traveller: P2
O for a closer walk with God: L3
O for a thousand tongues to sing: L3
For all the gifts of life: S6
For all the saints: L3
For bales: S5
For children: T6
For flowers: S6

For he is an Englishman: G3
For he's a jolly good fellow: E2 F F7 R2 W3 We won't
   go home until morning: G3
For I'm a true, loving wife: G3
For, lo, the winter is past: S6
For the beauty of the earth: F4 L3 S6
For the dear old flag I die: S5
For the first time: T4
For the summer's glowing pageant: L3
For thy mercy and thy grace: L3
Forbidden music see Musica proibita
Forests black near Krakow grow see Od Krakowa czarny
   las
Forget-me-not (Hawaiian song) G3
Forget-me-not (I look on thee, thou little flow'r) W3
Forgotten (you? Well, if forgetting be) F7 G3
Forn forstu fun mir avek: R5(e.y.)
Ah, fors' e lui: E(e.i.) G4(e.i.) S14(e.i.)
Forsaken (am I like a stone on the pathway) F7 W3 W7
Forty days and forty nights: L3
Forty-eight bottles: C7 Forty-nine bottles: G3
Found my lost sheep: S
The fountain in the park see While strolling through the
   park one day
Four-and-twenty tailors: W5
The four insurgent generals see Los cuatro generales
Four little white doves: C10
Four nights drunk see Our goodman
Four pence a day: F8
Four roads see Szanyvarosba
Four walls: T2
Four years have I see Czterym latka
The fourth day of July see The cuckoo (is a funny bird)
The fox (went out on a chilly night) B6 I L4 R2 S11 W6
Fra poco a me ricovero: G4(e.i.)
Frag', ob die rose: B3(e.g.)
A frangesa: E(e.i.)
Frankie and Johnnie (Frankie and Albert) B B6 D E2
   F6 G3 I3 L L6 L7 R2 S11

O Fred tell them to stop: E4
Free America (Free Amerikay) B9 E4 I I3
Free at last: S5
A free spirit: S6
O freedom (And before I'd be a slave) B F8 H5 L S5
Freedom is the finest gold: S6
Freiheit (Spaniens himmel breitet seine sterne) H5(e.g.)
Fremont campaign song: J
French cathedral: B6(f.)
The French partisan, Song of: H5(e.f.)
The Frenchman's ball: L8
Frere Jacques: B6(e.f.g.) F(f.) F4(f.) T(e.f.s.) V(f.)
    Brother Jack: W5
Fresh fish today: L2
The fretful baby see An leanbh aimhreidh
Friendless blues: D
The friendly beasts: B5 C2 S6
Friendly people: S6
Friends (I have some friends who like to play) S6
Friends and neighbors: C6
Friendship (My true love hath my heart) W8
Friendship song (All children who live in distant lands) T6
The frim fram sauce: E5
Frisch zum kampfe: G4(g.)
Frisky Jim: C7
Frog he would a-wooing go see Frog went a-courting
Frog song see May Irwin's frog song
Frog went a-courting: B6 D F4 F5 I I3 L5 L7 S2 S11
    W5
The frog's flute see Kaeru no fue
From all that dwell below the skies: S6
From beyond the hills see Tam poza gory
From California to the New York island see This land
    is your land
From every land: S6 T6
From every stormy wind that blows: A3
From France I come to you see Od Francyji jade
From Greenland's icy mountains: A3 L3 W3 W4
From heaven above (From heaven high) see Vom himmel
    hoch

From leaflet to leaflet <u>see</u> Od listka do listka
From Lucerne <u>see</u> Vo Luzarn
From Mexico there's just come a strange new decree <u>see</u>
    De Mexico ha venido
From the cold sod that's over you <u>see</u> Taim sinte ar do
    thuama
From the eastern mountains: L3 S3
From the valleys and hills: G4
From the white earth (De blanca tierra) Z(e. s.)
From yon mountain verdant (De aquel cerro verde) Z(e. s.)
Frosted panes: S6
The frozen girl: B9
The frozen logger: L6 W <u>Logger lover</u>: B6
Fruhlingszeit <u>see</u> The days of spring
Fruits and vegetables: T6
Fuair mise poigin: O(e. ir.)
Fuhl ich zu dir so suss mein herz entbrennen: G4(e. g.)
    S14(e. g.)
Fum, fum, fum (Catalan carol) <u>see</u> Foom, foom, foom
Funem sheynem vortsl aroys: R5̄(e. y.)
Funiculi funicula: B4 B6 C3(e. i.) E(e. i.) E2 F4(e. i.)
    F7(e. i.) G3 L4 R2 W3 W7 <u>A merry life</u>: P2
Funny (Not much) T4
Funny how time slips away: T2
Una furtiva lagrima: C9(e. i.) E(e. i.) G4(e. i.)
The future Mrs. 'Awkins: G3 W3

G

The gal I left behind me <u>see</u> The girl I left behind me
A gal in calico: S9
The gal with the balmoral: L5
The gallows tree: F3
The gambling suitor: L6
Game farm: C7
The gaol of Clonmel <u>see</u> Priosun Chluain meala
Garden hymn (The Lord into his garden) P2
The garden where the praties grow: I2

Gardenia flower (Hawaiian song) Pua sadinia) G3
The garland (The pride of ev'ry grove I chose) B3
Garryowen: I2
Gates and doors: P2
Gather ye rosebuds: B3
Gaudeamus igitur: G3(l.) R2(l.)
A gay ranchero: E5(e.s.)
A gay Spanish maid: F3
Gaze on his face: G3
Gebet an den heiligen Christ see Prayer to the child Jesus
Die gedanken sind frei: F8(e.g.) W(e.g.)
Gee, but I want to go home see I don't want no more army
Geese flying high see Lecialy gesie
A geisha's life: G3
Geliebter, komm (from Tannhauser) G4(e.g.)
'Gelique O see Angelique O
Gentille bateliere: V(f.)
Gentle Annie: B3 F5 G3 W3
Gentle fair Jenny: L6
Gentle Jesus, meek and mild: L3
Gentle mother see Yasashii okasan
Gentle Nettie Moore: C
The gentle shepherd leads his sheep: S6
A gentleman came to our house see Aunt Sal's song
A gentleman of Exeter: F3
Gently, Johnny, my jingalo: B6 C8 L10
Gently unveil her, unveil her see Pomalu ja rozbierajcie
Genzelech: R5(e.y.)
Geography song: W7
Geordie: N
Georgia boy: L8
Georgia camp meeting see At a Georgia camp meeting
Georgia land: L8
Georgie Porgie: F W5
German cradle song: W5
German National Anthem see Deutschlandlied
Gerry's rocks see The jam on Gerry's rocks
Gertie from Bizerte: T3
Get along cayuse, get along: C10

Get along, little dogies: E2 F2 G3 I3 L L6 L7 W9
  Whoopee ti yi yo: B4 B6 F5 L4 W3 see also Run
  along, you little dogies
Get happy: C5
Get off the track: J
Get out of Mexico: J
Get the money: S12
Get thee behind me, Satan: F8 H5 S13
Get up and bar the door: N
Get up, Jack: L6
Get up, my ox see Arre, buey
Get your head above the crowd: G3
Ghanaian National Anthem: S4
Ghost song: B6
Gia i sacerdoti adunansi: G4(e. i.)
Gia il sole dal Gange see Sunrise on the Ganges
Gia mi pasco ne' tuoi sguardi: G4(e. i.)
Gia nella notte: G4(e. i.)
Gibn dir mayn tochter: R5(e. y.)
Gidene bak gidene: K(e. r.)
Di gilderne pave: R5(e. y.)
Gilu hagalilim: R5(e. h.)
gimme see give me
Gin-sling see In good old colony times
Giovanottina che vieni alla fonte: K(e. i.)
gipsy see gypsy
The girl friend: H3
Girl, I advise you see Nevydavaj
The girl I left behind me: F7 G3 I2 L6 L7 R2 S5 W3
Girl I love to see see Este raz hoja
Girl, once I loved you well see Mal som ta dievca rad
The girl that keeps the peanut stand: G3
A girl was sauntering by a mill see Szla dziewczyna kolo
  mlyna
The girl with the flaming red hair: P2
Girls and boys come out to play: W5
Girls by Danube see Na Dunaji
The girls of Coleraine: I2
git see get

Give it back, girl see Vrat mi, mila
Give me a night in June: S10
Give me back my shilling: A2
Give me that old time religion see Old time religion
Give me the sweet delights of love: T
Give my regards to Broadway: B2
Give thanks (for the corn and the wheat that are reaped) S6
O give thanks (a round) Z
Give us a flag: S5
Glad am I see Pochvalen bud pan jezis
Glad news: C2
The glad sun: S6
Glee reigns in Galilee: B4
The Glendy Burk: C P2
Gloire immortelle (from Faust) S14(e.f.) Soldiers' chorus:
    W8
Gloria (by Taverner) G2(e.1.)
Gloria all' Egitto (from Aida) S14(e. i.)
Gloria in excelsis deo see Angels we have heard on high
Glorious beer: B6
The glorious fourth: F5
Glorious glorious see Drunk last night
Glorious things of thee are spoken: A3 L3
Glory for Dartmouth: R2
Glory, glory for Columbia: R2
The glory of God in nature (Die ehre Gottes in der natur)
    S15
The glory of love: T3
Glory, praise to thee be given: H4
Glory to God (Ehre sei Gott) S3(e.g.)
Gloucestershire wassail: S3 Wassail, wassail, all over
    the town: R
Glow worm: B
Go call the doctor and be quick: J
Go crystal tears: G
Go down, Moses: B4 B6 D E2 F F8 G3 H5 L L4
    P2 R2 S5 S6 W3
Go down, old Hannah: L6 L8
Go down, you little red rising sun: L8

Go forward, Christian soldier: L3
Go from my window: B
Go get the axe: D
Go no more to Brainford: T
Go on home: T2
Go on, you little dogies see Get along, little dogies
Go tell Aunt Nancy see Aunt Rhody
Go tell it on the mountain: B5 B6 C2 K2 L4 P2 S S3 W
Go to bed sweet muse: G
Go to Joan Glover: B3 T
Go to sleep, Lena darling see Emmett's lullaby
Go to sleepy: D
Go way from my window: I3 L2 L7
The gobble duet: W6
God be with you till we meet again: A3 L3
O God, beneath thy guiding hand: A3
God bless our native land: F5
God bless the master of this house: R
God defend New Zealand: S4
God don't like it: L8
God in heaven see Ach, boze moj
God in springtime see Gott im fruhling
O God, in whom we live and move: L3
God knows all: W7
God moves in a mysterious way: L3
God moves on the water: L8
The God of Abraham praise: L3
God of all (Jewish song) T6
O God of love, O King of Peace: L3
God of our fathers: A3 F5 L3 L4 P2
God of the earth, the sky, the sea: S6
O God, our help in ages past: A3 B L3 S12 W4
God rest you merry, gentlemen: A3 B4 B5 C2 F4 G3
    L3 L4 R R2 S3 W3 W8 Y
God save America: J
God save our president: F5
God save the King: B4 E2 F S4
God save the people: S12
O God, send down thy power see O Gott, schick runner
    deine kraft

God, that madest earth and heaven: L3
God, the all-powerful: A3 God the omnipotent: L3
God the omnipotent see God, the all-powerful
God, though this life is but a wraith: S6
God, who made the earth: L3
God will take care of you: L3
Godamighty drag: L8 see also Great God-a'mighty
God's going to set this world on fire: S12
God's world (Polish song) T6
Going down the road feeling bad: D F8 H5 I3 L P2
    Down the road: F7
Going home: L7
Going home on a cloud: Z
Going (gwine) to Alabamy: D
Going to Boston: L7 Z
Going to get a home by and by: H
Going to harness in the morning soon: L7
Going to leave old Texas see Old Texas
Going to shout all over God's heaven see Heaven, heaven
Going to study war no more see Down by the riverside
Going up the river: D
The gold band: S5
The golden boat song: W5
The golden city: S6
Golden harps are sounding: L3
The gold rule: W7
Golden slippers see O them golden slippers
The golden sun: W6
The Golden Vanity: B4 B6 H I I3 L6 The Bold
    Trellitee: C6 The Sweet Trinity: N see also Turkish
    Revery
The goldenrod has lighted its candles: S6
The goldfinch see Lu Cardillo
Goldfish vendor see Kingyo
The gollycully: C7
La golondrina: C12(s.) E2 The swallow: F7(e.s.) W3
Goober peas: B9 I3 S5 Eating goober peas: L4 L5
Good Christian men, rejoice: A3 B4 B5 L3 R Y see
    also In dulci jubilo

Good day, Sir Christmas: R3
Good King Wenceslas: B4 B5 G3 L3 L4 R R2 S3 W3
    W8 Y
Good kings see Buenos reyes
Good morning (from The Fortune Teller, by Herbert) G3
Good morning (I say good morning to the wren) S6
Good morning, blues: L6 S13
Good morning, Carrie: E3 F6 G3
Good morning, daffodils: S6
Good morning, merry sunshine: W6
Good morning, Mr. Zip-Zip-Zip: F5
Good news (Liberian song) T6
Good night (going home, going home) W5
Good-night (slumber sound) Z
Good-night and good morning: W6
Good night, Irene see Irene, goodnight
Good night ladies: E2 F F4 F7 G3 M R2 W3
Good night sweetheart: F7
Good night, wherever you are: T3
The good old man see Our goodman
Good old mountain dew: B6 L7
The good old rebel: L6 L7 S5
Good sweet ham: G3 L5
Good-bye (by Tosti) see Addio
Good-bye Broadway, hello France: F5
Good-bye Mother: L7
Good-bye, my lover, good-bye: B6 G3 L4 R2
Good-bye, old paint: C10 D F2 L7
Good-bye, pretty Mama: L7
Good-bye, sweetheart, good-bye (by Hatton) F7
Good-bye Venezuela: L2
Goody Bull: L5
Goosey, goosey, gander: W5
Oj gorol-ci jo gorol: P(e.p.)
Gory, gory (Rockclimbers) B6
Gory, gory (Skiers) B6
The gospel train: D P2 W9
Got them blues: S13
Got to travel on: T2

Got up one morning see Tee roo
Gott im fruhling: S16(e. g.)
O Gott, schick runner deine kraft: H4(e. pd.)
gotta see got to
Grace (For health and strength and daily food) Z
Grafted into the army: J S5
Grandfather's clock: B6 E2 E3 F5 F7 G3 I R2 W3
   W7
Grandma Grunts: L4
Granny and the golden ball: N
The grasshopper and the ant see Il grillo e la formica
Grasshoppers three: P2
The grave of Washington: C
The great bells of Osney: T
A great big sea: L6
Great big stars: S
Great day (The union's marching) F8
Great getting-up morning see That great getting-up
   morning
Great God-A'mighty: L7 see also Godamighty drag
Great-granddad: B9 F2 L5
Great is the sun, and wide he goes: S6
Great Tom is cast: T
The great tradition: S6
Greek National Anthem: F(e. gk.) S4(e. gk.)
Green are the gardens see Ludzkie ogrody sie zazielenily
The green bushes: C8 I2
The green grave: N
Green grow the lilacs: B4 B9 L4 P2 Green grows the
   laurel: L6
Green grow the rashes, O: B8 C8
Green grow the rue and juniper see Zielona ruta jalowiec
Green grow the rushes, O: B4 B6 B9 Z
Green grows the laurel see Green grow the lilacs
The green little shamrock: G3
The Green Mountain Yankee: J
Green years: S8
Greenbacks: J
Greenfields: B

The Greenland whale fishery: B6 L6 L8 W The whale:
  H I I3 When the whale get strike: L8
Greenland's National Song: S4(e. dn.)
Greensleeves: B6 B7 C8 F I I3 L4
Greer County bachelor: I3
Gretchen Pumpernickle: B6
The grey goose (Last Sunday morning, Lord, Lord, Lord)
  I I3 L L7
Gridiron king: R2
Il grillo e la formica: K(e. i.)
Ground hog: D I3 L L6 L7
Grumbling Joe: W6
The grumbling mother-in-law see T'an ch'in chia
Gruss (Leise zieht durch mein gemuth) B3(e. g.)
Guabina chiquinquirena: C12(s.)
The guaracha: L2
The guaranteed wage, Song of: F8
Guarare: C12(s.)
Guarda, amor mio (from Pagliacci) S14(e. i.)
Guardian angels (by Schumann) W7
Guatemalan National Anthem: S4(e. s.)
Guelder rose, my guelder see Kalina, kalina
Guess what I've got: L2
Guest from heaven: C2
Guide me, O thou great Jehovah: B4 L3
Gumbo chaff: C
Der gute kamerad see The faithful comrade
Guy Reed: F3
Gvardeiskaia polka: R4(e. r.)
gwine see going to
The gypsy laddie: L10 N
Gypsy love song: B2 F G3
Gypsy song (from Carmen) see Les tringles des sistres
  tintaient
The gypsy's warning: F5 G3

H

Ha, ha, thisaway: B9
Ha! welch' ein augenblick: G4(e.g.)
Habanera (from Carmen) C9(e.f.) E2 S14(e.f.) S16(e.f.)
   W3 L'amour est un oiseau rebelle: G4(e.f.)
Had a little fight in Mexico: L8
Had I wings see Da bi imal perje
Hail, Columbia: B B9 E2 E4 F F4 F5 G3 I3 W3 W7
Hail, guest (Welsh song) T6
Hail, hail, the gang's all here: E2 F5 F6 W3
Hail, Mary, full of grace (mother in virginity) R3
Hail, Pennsylvania: R2
Hail, the hero workers: S6
Hail to the chief: G3
Hail to the month: P2
Haitian National Anthem see La Dessalinienne
Hajej, nynej, jezisku: B5
Hajji Baba: S8
Halay: K(e.t.)
Half an hour past twelve o'clock: T
Halico, calico: G3
Halka had a rooster: P2
hallelujah see also alleluia
Hallelujah! (Sing hallelujah and you'll shoo the blues away)
   H3
Hallelujah, I'm a bum: B4 B6 D E2 F8 L7 R2
Hallelujah, I'm a-traveling: H5
Halte la (from Carmen) G4(e.f.) S14(e.f.)
Hambone am good: B6
The hammer song: L7 S2 S11
Han della porpora: G4(e.i.)
Han skal leve hojt: Z(dn.)
Hana'ava babanot: B7(e.h.)
The hand cart song: I I3
Hand me down my walking cane: B6 E2 F4 G3 W3
A handful of earth: E3
A handsome lad is Paudeen see Is deas an buachaill Paidin
Handy Andy: C7

Hanging Johnny: H
The hanging tree: S8
The hangman: N Hangsaman: D The hangsman's tree: S7
Hans und Lisel: G3(g.)
Hanukka candles: S6
Hanukkah hymn see Rock of ages, let our song
Hanukkah song: B4 B5 see also Chanukah
Hapless, O how hapless see Tylez-ty, tyle ty
Happy be thou, heavenly queen (Edi beo thu hevene quene)
    G2
The happy child: F3
O happy day: A3
Happy I see Dobre mi
The happy kitten: W6
A happy new year see The old year now away has fled
Happy new year (for you, for me) T6
Happy times: S8
The happy wanderer: E5
Hard, ain't it hard: B6 L6 W
Hard times see The Cryderville jail
Hard times come again no more: G3 W3
Hard times in Dixie: S5
Hard times in the country see Down on Penney's farm
Hard times in the mill: F8
Hard to get: S8
Hard traveling: F8 H5 L6 S11 W
Hard trials: L7
The hard-working miner: L7
Hardly think I will: L7
Hares on the mountains: C8
Hark all you ladies: G
Hark, hark, my soul: L3 W3
Hark! Hark! the dogs do bark: W5
Hark, hark, the lark: E2 F7 G3 W3 W7
Hark how all the welkin rings see Hark the herald angels
    sing
Hark, ten thousand harps and voices: L3
Hark, the bell is ringing: T
Hark, the bonny Christ-Church bells: T

Hark, the cock crows see A'l chiante 'l gial
Hark the herald angels sing: A3 B4 B5 C2 F F4 G3 L3
    L4 R R2 S3 W3 W8 Hark how all the welkin rings: Y
Hark! tis the breeze: W7
Hark to the cuckoo see Kaki se kukkuu
The harp that once thro' Tara's halls: E2 F4 F7 G3 W3
The Harrison song: J
Harry Bridges, Ballad of: H5
The hart he loves the high wood: I T
The Hartford wreck: F3
Haru ga kita: W2(e. ja.)
Harvardiana: R2
Harvest home: F4
Harvey Logan: L8
Has sorrow thy young days shaded: I2
Has your mother any more like you: F6
The hasty crab barber see Awate dokoya
Hat man nicht auch: G4(e. g.)
Hatikvah: B4 E2(h.) R5(e. h.) S4(e. h.)
Hato popo: W2(e. ja.)
Hattie Belle: L6
Haul away, Joe: B4 B6 C7 H H5 I I3 S2
Haul away, my rosy: L8
Haul the bowline: H
Have thine own way, Lord: L3
Have you any work for a tinker: T
Have you ever been lonely: T3
Have you heard (Calypso song) A2
Have you seen but a white lily grow: B3
Have you struck ile (oil) C J
Hawaiian butterfly: C4
Hawaiian farewell song: W3 W7 see also Aloha oe
Hawaiian war chant: T5
Hayaku koi koi oshogatsu: W2(e. ja.)
Haymaking song: W7
Haynt iz Purim, brider: R5(e. y.)
Hayo, haya: R5(e. h.)
Hazasodik a tucsok: K(e. hu.)
Hazel Dell: F5

He came from his palace grand: S12
He carved his mother's name upon the tree: F6
He didn't have a bend in his knees: K2
He didn't think: W6
He don't know where he's at: G3
He is born, little infant king see Il est ne, le divin enfant
He is Irish: G3
He leadeth me: A3 L3
He liveth long: L3
He never said a mumbaling word see Never said a
     mumbling word
He shall feed his flock: S3
He smiles within his cradle: R Y
He that will an alehouse keep: G2 T
He venido a despedirme: C12(s.)
Healing waters: L7
Hear, hear, o ye nations: S6
Hear, o shepherds (Oj pastiri) S3(e.sc.)
Hear the waltz (from Waltz Dream) G3
Hear them bells: G3
Hear thou my prayer: T
Heard from heaven today: S
The hearse song: B6 L5 L7
Heart of oak: I
Heartaches by the number: T2
Heartbreak hotel: T2
Heave and ho, rumbelow: T
Heave away: D L7
Heave away cheerily: H
Heave away my Johnnies (we're all bound to go) H
Heaven bell ring: S
Heaven, heaven: E2 F5 F7 G3 R2 All God's children
     got wings: E4 W7 Going to shout all over God's
     heaven: C3 I got a robe (I got shoes) B6 W3
Heaven is my home: W3
Heaven protect the working girl see The poor working girl
Heavenly Aida see Celeste Aida
Heavenly father, send thy blessing: W4
O ye heavens: C2

The heavy golden curls see Falt trom, trom, dualach
The heavy-hipted woman: L7 see also Black gal
Hedge rose see Sah ein knab' ein roslein stehn
Hefo deio i dywyn see To see Swainson
Heidenroslein see Sah ein knab' ein roslein stehn
heigh-ho see also hi ho
Heigh-ho (nobody home) B6 F8 H5 R2 T Z
Heil, Konig Heinrich: G4(e.g.)
Heir of all the ages, I: S6
hej see also hey
Hej, haj, zeleny haj: D2(e.sl.)
Hej, ked sa Janicko na vojnu bral: D2(e.sl.)
Hej, na Presovskej turni: D2(e.sl.)
Hej! od Krakowa jade: P(e.p.)
Hej pada pada: B7(e.sl.)
Hej, pod Krivanom: D2(e.sl.)
Hej Slaveni: S4(e.j.)
Hej! zabujaly biale labedzie: K(e.p.)
Hell and heaven: L7
The hell-bound train: L6
Hell in Texas: L7
Hello central, give me heaven: A E3 F6 G3
Hello! Hello! (We are glad to meet you) P2
Hello! my baby: F5 F6
Hello, Susie Brown: C7
Hellow walls: T2
Help me, Lord almighty see Wesprzyj-ze mnie boze
Hen wlad fy nhadau: S4(e.w.) Welsh National Anthem:
    C8(e.w.)
Hennery White, Ballad of: C7
Henry Green, Ballad of: C
Henry K. Sawyer: F3
Henry Martin: I K
Henry Orrison: F3
Her bright smile haunts me still: F5
Her golden locks time hath to silver turned: G
Her kommer dine arme smaa see They little ones, dear
    Lord, are we
Her name was Lil: B8

Her reputation: A2
Heraclio Bernal see Tragedia de Heraclio Bernal
The herd of the pet cow see Aeire cinn bo ruin
The herdsmaid see Vallkulla
Herdsmaid's song see Hjuringsvise
The herdsman's call see Le ranz des vaches
Here a little child I stand: L3
Here am I, a shepherd see Ja som baca velmi stary
Here are my boots: K2
Here away, there away: G3
Here come three merchants a-riding: D
Here flat on her back: T
Here is the little door: R
Here lies a woman: T
Here we come a-wassailing see Wassail song
Here with the ass and oxen mild see Entre le boeuf et
     l'ane gris
Here's a how-de-do: G3
Here's to good old beer see Drink it down
Here's to good old Brown: R2
Here's to romance: E5
Here's to the maiden: F G3
Here's to the trail and the mountain tops: B6 K2
Here's your mule: S5
The hermit: B8
Heroes (Fair is their fame) S6
O Herr, schenk mir mehr gnaden: H4(e.pd.)
He's a fool: H5
He's gone away see Who's going to shoe your pretty
     little foot
Het kwezelken see Little hypocrite
Het singelshuis: K(e.fl.)
L'heure exquise see Exquisite hour
hey see also hej
Hey, diddle diddle (the cat and the fiddle) F I W5
Hey-diddle-diddle! when man is in love (from The Geisha)
     G3
Hey dum diddle um day see Sourwood Mountain
Hey ho, nobody home see Heigh-ho (nobody home)

Hey ho, to the greenwood: G T
Hey ho, what shall I say: T
Hey! Zhankoye: H5(e.y.)
hi see also heigh
Hi ho jerum: C6 C7
Hi Jenny, ho Jenny Johnson: G3
Hi, waiter! a dozen more bottles: F4
Hickory, dickory, dock: W5 Dickory, dickory, dock: F
Hide and seek see Kakurembo
Hie away home: L5
Hier im ird'schen jammertal: G3(g.) G4(e.g.)
Hier soll ich dich denn sehen: G4(g.)
High above the starlit mountains: K2
The high and the mighty: S8
High Barbaree: B6 H I L4 L8 S7 The coasts of high
    Barbary: B4 P2
High, Betty Martin: C10
High in the heavens: L3
High is the blue sky (Tsing tien kao) T6(e.ch.)
High on a mountain: K2
O high on Preshov's tower see Hej, na Presovskej turni
High price blues: S13
High Skalitza's tower see Skalicka veza
High stands the green hill see Horicka zelena
The high-toned southern gentleman: S5
High you shine see Vysoko zornicka
A highland lad my love was born: C8 G3
The highly educated man see I was born about a thousand
    years ago
Hill and gully: A2
The hills of Glenshee: C6
Hilo, my Ranzo way: H
Der himmlische ackersmann: K(e.g.)
Hina matsuri: W2(e.ja.)
Hind horn: N
Hinky-dinky, parley-voo see Mademoiselle from
    Armentieres
Hiraita, hiraita: W2(e.ja.)
His boarding house not far away: G3

His funeral's tomorrow: G3
His heart was true to Poll: G3
His name is Patrick Brannigan: G3
The history of the world see Darky Sunday school
Hjuringsvise: K(e.n.)
Ho for the Kansas plains: J
Ho-la-hi! Ho-la-ho: B6(g.)
Ho ro my nut-brown maiden see Nut-brown maiden
Ho! westward ho: J
Hob ich a por oksn: R5(e.y.)
Hob ich mir a kleynem michalke: R5(e.y.)
Hob y deri dando see Joy upon thy bright cheek dances
Hobaderry danno see Joy upon thy bright cheek dances
The hobby horse: W5
Hobellied (from Der Verschwender) G3(g.)
Hochie slalom: K2
Hoe laat is 't: K(e.d.)
Hog drovers: B9 L6
The hog-eye man: H
Hog rogues on the Harricane: L8
The hog-thorny bear: F3
Hoggedee boggedee how now: C7
Hojita de guarumal: C12(s.)
Hold me: T5
Hold, men, hold: S3
Hold the fort (for I am coming) A3 S5
Hold the fort (union song) F8 H5 S11
Hold the wind: L6
Holidays (children's song) W6
Der holle rache: G4(g.)
The holly and the ivy: B5 H5 R S3 Y Z
The holy baby: L6 S
The holy boy: S3
The holy city: F G3
Holy Ghost (If this ain't the Holy Ghost, I don't know) L8
Holy, holy (by Gaul) P2
Holy! Holy! Holy! (Lord God almighty) A3 L3 W3 W4 W7
O holy night (Cantique de noel) F S3(e.f.) W3 W8
    Cantique de noel: E2 R2

Holy night, peaceful night (by Gruber) W8
Holy spirit, truth divine: L3
The holy well: Y
Home again (from a foreign shore) G3
Home, home, can I forget thee: W7
Home in that rock: W
A home on the mountain wave: H
Home on the range: B4 B6 C3 C12 E2 E4 F F2 F5 F7
    G3 L L4 M R2 S11 W3 W9 Z
Home song (You ask me why the tears arise) G3
Home, sweet home: B4 C3 E2 F F4 F5 F6 F7 G3 L4
    S5 W3 W7 W9
Home to our mountains see Ai nostri monti
The homespun dress: S5
Homeward bound: G3 H
Honduran National Anthem: S4(e.s.)
Honest John Jones: G3
Honey: C4
Honey-babe: S8
O honey, I'm going down the river: C
Honey, take a whiff on me see Take a whiff on me
Honeycomb: J2
Honeysuckle rose: J2
Hop! hop! dzis, dzis za kominem: P(e.p.)
Hop! mayne homntashn: R5(e.y.)
Hop up, my ladies: L8
Hopsha diri: W(j.)
Horch was kommt: K2(e.g.)
Horicka zelena: D2(e.sl.)
The Hornet and the Peacock: I I3
The horse named Bill: L6 S12
The horse trader's song: L6
The horse with a union label: H5
The horses run around: B6
The horticultural wife: J
Hosanna (Blessed is he that comes) (Moravian song) H4
Hosanna (Calypso song) A2 L2
Hosanna (Un homme est mort) F(e.f.)
Hot cross buns: T W5

Hot tamale alley: G3
Hotaru koi: W2(e. ja.)
The hound dog song: L6
The hour of prayer: W7
The Housatonic Valley: C
The house carpenter: B6 F3 L6 N S7
House of the rising sun: S11 S13 W The rising sun blues:
    L6 L8
Houses of worship: T6
The housewife's lament: L6
Hovda is the ski for me: K2
How am I to get me a wife see Uchi ma, maycho, nayuchi
How are you greenbacks: J
How are you, John Morgan: S5
O how beautiful the sky (Deilig er den himmel blaa)
    C2(e. dn.)
How brightly shines the morning star (Wie schon leuchtet
    der morgenstern) A3 L3 S3(e.g.)
How can I leave thee (Thuringian song) F7 G3 W3 W7
How could you use a poor maiden so: I3
Ho do you do: P2
How far is it to Bethlehem: C2
How firm a foundation: A3 B L3
How gentle God's commands: W7
How happy is the child: W7
How happy the soldier: I I3 L5
O how he lied: B6 R2
O how I love Jesus: A3
How I wish I could have see Zebym ja tak miala
How long blues: L6 S13
O how lovely is the evening (O wie wohl ist's mir am abend)
    B6 R2 S3(e.g.) The evening bells: B(e. g.) Lovely
    evening: E3
O how lovely is the maiden see O wie lieblich ist das
    madchen
How many miles to Bethelehem: S
How much is that doggie in the window: J2
How often, o how often see Ej nieraz, ja-ci nieraz
How old are you, my pretty little miss: L6

How sad is true love: P2
How shall I fitly meet thee (Wie soll ich dich empfangen)
    S3(e.g.)
How should I your true love know: B3 L10
O how sweet (is our singing) Z
How sweet the name Jesus sounds: L3
How sweet you are: S9
How'd you like to be the iceman: A
Hsiao ho shang: C11(e.ch.)
Hsiao pai ts'ai: C11(e.ch.)
Hua ku ko: C11(e.ch.)
Hudson River steamboat: L6
The Hudson side: C
Hugh McCue: G3
Hullabaloo belay: I I3
Hulyet, hulyet, kinderlech: B7(e.y.)
The humming top: W6
Humoresque (by Dvorak) E2 When the moon is shining:
    W3
Humoresque (parody: Passengers will please refrain) B8
Humpty Dumpty: E2 F F7 W5
A hundred years ago: H
Hungarian National Anthem: S4(e.hu.)
The hunters of Kentucky: B6 C D I I3
Hunter's song: W6
Hurrah for Baffin's Bay see Baffin's Bay
Hurrah, lie: L6
Husband goes to war see Chang fu ch'u tang ping
The husbandman see Der himmlische ackersmann
Hush little baby (don't say a word) I3 L8 P2 W
Hush little girl, don't cry: G3
Hush, my dear, lie still and slumber see Cradle hymn
    (Hush my babe)
Hush, the waves are rolling in see Old Gaelic lullaby
Hushabye (don't you cry) B7
Hush-a-bye (Swedish song) see Vyssa lulla
Husheen: G3
Husker du i hoest see Little Karen
A hymn for the spinning sisters: H4

Hymn of praise (The sun shines in splendor) T6
A hymn of thanks for daily food (Moravian song) H4
Hymn of thanksgiving: B9

I

i (article) see next word of title
ILGWU Anthem: F8
I ain't going to grieve my Lord no more: B6 R2
I am a courtier: G3
I am a cuckoo: J
I am a little child, you see: H4
I am a poor wayfaring stranger see The wayfaring
    stranger
I am a rover of the sea: G3
I am leaving Krakow see Hej! od Krakowa jade
I am so glad each Christmas Eve (Jeg er saa glad hver
    Julekveld) C2(e. dn.)
I am the monarch of the seas: G3
I been a bad, bad girl: L8 see also The bad girl
I believe in miracles: C4
I came home late one evening see Jeg lagde mig saa silde
I came to this country in 1865: L8
I can whip the scoundrel: S5
I cannot sing the old songs: E2 F7 G3 W3
I can't do the sum: T7
I can't make up my mind: L5
I care not for these ladies: G
I catcha da plenty of feesh: D
O I come from the highlands see Og gorol-ci jo gorol
I could not find my baby-o: S12
I couldn't bend my knees: K2
I couldn't hear nobody pray: L4 L6
I cover the waterfront: C5 H3
I cried for you: T5
O I did climb a tree-top see Ich wollt' ein baumlein steigen
I did not know you see Aysem
I didn't sleep a wink last night: K2

I didn't slip, I wasn't pushed, I fell: S8
I don't believe she'd know me: S13
I don't care (what they may think of me) F4 T7
I don't know enough about you: E5
I don't know why (I just do) T5
I don't like no railroad man: S12
I don't love nobody: A
I don't want no more army: L5 Gee, but (Mom) I want to
    go home: B9 L
I don't want to be buried in the stawm: S12
I don't want to get adjusted: W
I don't want to play in your yard: A B2 E3 F5 F6 F7
    G3 W3
I don't want your millions, mister: F8 H5 L6
I double dare you: T4
I dreamt that I dwelt in marble halls: G4 W8
I envy the bird: G3
I fall to pieces: T2
I feel like my time ain't long: L8
I forget how you smiled, how you talked: G3
I found a million dollar baby: C5 M
I gave my love a cherry see The riddle song
I get a kick out of you: H2
I go before my darling: G2
I goes to fight mit Sigel: S5
I got a kiss see Fuair mise poigin
I got a letter from Jesus: S12
I got a robe see Heaven, heaven
I got shoes see Heaven, heaven
I got to roll: L6 L8
I guess I'll get the papers and go home: E5
I guess I'll have to telegraph my baby: E3 F4 F6 G3
I had a little nut tree: F W5
I had but fifty cents: G3
I handed it over to Riley: G3
I have a song to sing, o (from Yeomen of the Guard) W8
    Z
Ah! I have sighed to rest me: E2 W3
I hear the soft note: Z

I heard a sound of voices: L3
I heard the bells on Christmas Day: L3 S3
I heard the sound of a sickle see Sichelein rauschen
I heard the voice of Jesus say: L3
I heard you cried last night: E5
I know a rose tree springing see Es ist ein' rose
    entsprungen
I know my love (by her way of walking) B3 C6 I2 I3 L10
I know that my redeemer liveth: F(e.g.)
I know that you know: H2
I know where I'm going: B3 I2 I3 W
I kto evo znaet: R4(e.r.)
I lay with an old man: T
I lived in a town: D
I love a parade: H3
I love little pussy: F W6
I love little Willie: L4 L7
I love Louisa: H3
I love my baby: T4
I love the Blue Mountains: H
I love the summer-time: W6
I love thee (by Grieg) see Ich liebe dich
I love thee (by Herbert) G3
I love to tell the story: A3 L3 W3
I love you in the same old way: B2
I love you truly: B2 F
I met a girl in Portland Street see A fal-de-lal-day
I missed me: T2
I must and I will get married: D
I need thee every hour: A3 L3
I never will marry: L6 S11 W
I once saw fair Mary in the grist mill see Widzialem
    Marysie...
I only have eyes for you: C5
I pray you, good mother: T
I prethee, send me back my heart: B3
I ride an old paint: B6 D F2 S11 Old paint: I3 L W
I saw my lady weep: G
I saw three ships: B5 L3 R S3 W5 Y Christmas day
    in the morning: S see also The three ships

I shall buy you ribbons see Przywioze z miasteczka
O I should like to marry: J
I speak to the stars: S8
I taut I taw a puddy-tat: S8
"I thank you, ma'am" says Dan: I2
I think when I read that sweet story: A3 L3 W4
I thought I saw a pussy-cat: S8
I told them that I saw you: G3
I walk the unfrequented road: S6
I walked the road again: C6
I want to be happy: H3
I want to be ready: P2
I want to see my dear old home: G3
I want what I want when I want it: T7
I was born about a thousand years ago: B6 L The highly
    educated man: L7 I was there: C6 A long time ago: H
I was once your wife: G3
I was there see I was born about a thousand years ago
I will give my love an apple: B9 L6 see also The riddle
    song
I will labor see Ich will streben
I will sing a lullaby: W5
I wish I had a girl: F5 F6
I wish I had died in my cradle: T3
I wish I had the shepherd's pet (lamb) C8(e. ga.) I2 Is
    trua gan peata an mhaoir agam: O(e. ir.)
I wish I was a mole in the ground: L7
I wish I was a single girl: C6 Single girl: D L6 When I
    was single: L7
I wish I was single again: B6 C6 R2 When I was single:
    I L L7
I wish I were a crank: C7
I wish I were a little sugar bun: B6
I woke at dawn see Accordei de madrugada
I wonder as I wander: S16
I wonder what you think of me: G3
I wonder what's become of Sally: M
I wonder when I shall be married: C6
I wonder where my buddies are tonight: F5

I wonder where she is tonight: A
I wonder who's kissing her now: B E5(e.f.)
I would be true: L3 P2
I would that my love (Ich wollt' meine liebe) W7 W8(e.g.)
Iarraidh na ngamhna: O(e.ir.)
Icelandic National Anthem see Lofsongur
Ich bin der musikant: B6(e.g.)
Ach, ich fuhl's (from Die Zauberflote) G4(g.)
Ich hob ge-akert un gezeyt: R5(e.y.)
Ich liebe dich (by Beethoven) B3(e.g.)
Ich liebe dich (by Grieg) B3(e.g.) E2 F(e.g.) G3
    I love thee: F7 W3
Ach ich liebte (from Die Entfuhrung aus dem Serail) G4(g.)
Ich steh an deiner krippe hier see Beside thy cradle here
    I stand
Ich will streben: H4(e.g.)
Ich wollt' ein baumlein steigen: K(e.g.)
Ich wollt' meine liebe see I would that my love
Icubak: T
I'd like to hear that song again: A
I'd put you myself, my baby, to slumber see Do
    chuirfinn-se fein mo leanbh
Ida May: C
Ida, sweet as apple cider: B
Idaho: J
Idir chaiseal agus durlas: O(e.ir.)
Idle days in summertime (Bugeilio'r gwenith gwyn)
    C8(e.w.)
If (Italian song) see Se
If (they made me a king) T3
If a poor girl is born see Chudobna dievcina
If a skier meet a skier: K2
If all the world were paper: W5
If ever hapless woman: G
If he'd be a buckaroo: L8
If I could be with you: S10
If I got my ticket, can I ride: L8
If I had a-listened what my mother said see Prison moan
If I had a son for each star in old glory: F5

If I had my pick of the three see Da bhfaghainn mo...
If I had the wings: Z
If I had wings like Nora's dove see Dink's song
If I only could blot out the past: F4
If love were what the rose is: F7
If my complaints: G
If people said the things they mean: G3
If there is someone lovelier than you: H3
If they made me a king: T3
If thou art an honest friend: T
If thou art near see Bist du bei mir
If thou longst so much to learn: G
If you love me (Se tu m'ami) S15
If we can't be the same old sweethearts, we'll just be the
     same old friends: F6
If you are near see Bist du bei mir
If you hit me: L2
If you love me truly: G3
If you want to go a-courting: D
If you want to know where the privates are: L5 L7
If you were the only girl: T8
If your foot is pretty, show it: J
Ihr kinder, ihr verziegen: H4(e. pd.)
Ihr kinderlein, kommet see O come, little children
il (article) see next word of title
Il est doux (from Herodiade) G4(e. f.)
Il est ne, le divin enfant: B5 V(f.)
Il etait une bergere: C3(e. f.) V(f.)
Il etait une fois a la cour d'Eisenach: G4(f.)
Il pleut, bergere: V(f.)
I'll always be in love with you: T4
I'll be a sergeant: S5
I'll give my love a light and friendly kiss see Je
     caresserai la belle par amitie
I'll give my love an apple see I will give my love an apple
I'll give you a paper of pins see A paper of pins
I'll not have you, Katie see Oj nie chce cie Kasiu
I'll place it in the hands of my attorney: G3
I'll play something for you: B9

I'll pray for you: S9
I'll see you again: S10
I'll sing thee songs of Araby: E2
I'll take you home again, Kathleen: B3 E2 E4 F5 F6 F7
    M W3
Illinois: C
Ils gials cumainzan a chantar: K(e. ro.)
I'm a beggar from Lobzow see Jestem dziodek z Lobzowa
O I'm a good old rebel see The good old rebel
I'm a-leaving Cheyenne: L6
I'm a-looking for a home: H5
O I'm a peasant gay see Chlopek-ci ja chlopek
I'm a pilgrim: F
I'm a poor stranger: I2 see also The wayfaring stranger
I'm a-rolling: P2
I'm a roving cowboy see Black tail range
I'm a stranger here: L8 S13
I'm a tinker see Ja som dobry remeselnik
I'm all out and down: L6
I'm always chasing rainbows: T5
I'm bound to follow the longhorn cows: F2 L6
I'm broke and hungry: D
I'm called little Buttercup: F G3 W3 W8
I'm forever blowing bubbles: T8
I'm going away to Texas: L6
I'm going back to Dixie: E3 F5 F7 P2 W3 W7
I'm going down the road see Going down the road feeling
    bad
I'm going to leave old Texas now see Old Texas
I'm going to lock my heart: T3
I'm going to sing (when the spirit says "sing"): L4
I'm going to sing me a love song: S13
I'm happy at Maxim's: G3
I'm just a poor, wayfaring stranger see The wayfaring
    stranger
I'm just wild about Harry: S10
Im kahne see In the boat
I'm looking over a four leaf clover: M S10
I'm nobody's baby: T5

I'm not strong, sir: T

I'm on my way: H5

I'm on one bank, you the other see Ja za woda, ty za
   woda

I'm sad and I'm lonely: D I

I'm seventeen come Sunday: C6 C8 K As I roved out:
   B7 As I walked out one May morning: B9

I'm sitting on top of the world: F5

I'm sorry I made you cry: C4

I'm thankful: S6

I'm the boy: B9 L6

I'm the most original: G3

I'm troubled: L6

I'm worried now, but I won't be worried long: L8

Im wunderschonen monat Mai: B3(e.g.)

Imbabura: C12(s.)

Immortal love, forever full: L3

Immortal love, within whose righteous will: L3

Imogene Donahue: G3

In a cellar made of brick see W murowanej piwnicy

In a gondola: P2

In a little Spanish town: C4

In a manger: S3

In a shanty in old shantytown: C5

In a thatch-roofed little cottage see Sloma krytej...

In an old Dutch garden: C5 H3

In darkness let me dwell: G

In der heimat: K2(e.g.)

In der kuznye: R5(e.y.)

In des lebens fruhlingstagen: G4(e.g.)

In diesen heilgen hallen: G4(g.)

In dreamland (from Wizard of the Nile) G3

In dulci jubilo: B L3 R S3 see also Good Christian men,
   rejoice

In einem kuhlen grunde: G3(g.)

In fair Andalusia: G3

In fernem land (from Lohengrin) G4(e.g.) S14(e.g.)

In freedom we're born see The liberty song

In Glendalough lived a young saint: I2

In glory breaks the golden morn: G3
In good old colony times: B L6 Z <u>Gin-sling</u>: G3
In good Queen Bess's days: G3
In happy moments day by day (from Maritana) W8
In heavenly love abiding: L3
In Holland stands a house <u>see</u> Het singelshuis
In Kansas: L6
O in love I've fallen <u>see</u> Zakochalem-ci sie
In my merry Oldsmobile: T7
In old Madrid: E2 G3
In olden times <u>see</u> En todo el tiempo pasado
In Podolia on a white rock <u>see</u> Na Podolu bialy kamien
In quelle trine morbide: G4(e.i.)
In Sherwood lived stout Robin Hood: G
In Skalitza <u>see</u> Pri Skalici
In spring the day is early: S6
In that poor stable (Dans cette etable) R(e.f.) <u>In this
stable</u>: C2(e.f.)
In the baggage coach ahead: G3
In the bleak mid-winter: R
In the blue of evening: T3
In the boat (Im kahne, by Grieg) S15 W8
In the cellars of old Standish Hall: K2
In the chapel in the moonlight: T3
In the cross of Christ I glory: A3 L3
In the dawn: S6
In the days of '76: L6
In the days when we went gold-hunting: J
In the evening by the moonlight: A B6 E3 E4 F4 F5
F6 F7 M W3 <u>Southern memories</u>: R2
In the fair hamlet of Fancy: G3
In the field so early: C7
In the garden: L3 S6
In the garden of my heart: T7
In the gloaming: B3 E2 F5 F6 F7 G3 R2 W3
In the gloaming (version for children) W7
In the good old summertime: B B2
In the gypsy's life (from The Bohemian Girl) G4
In the hour of trial: L3

In the lonely glens of Yarrow: N
In the meadow flowers glisten see Tam na bloniu
   blyszczy kwiecie
In the meadow stood a little birch tree see Vo pole
   berezynka stoiala
In the meadowland see Na srodku pola
In the pines: S13
In the shade of the old apple tree: T7
In the spring (how they sing) W6
In the sweet by and by: A3 B L3 Sweet by and by: F4
   F5
In the tea room: W6
In the time of roses: W7
In the town: S3
In the valley see Sredi doliny rovnyia
In the vinter see In the winter time
In the wilderness: L6
In the winter time: B9 S12
In thee is gladness: Y
In this stable see In that poor stable
In this street see Nesta rua
In those twelve days: Y
In Vossevangen: Z
In wondrous lovely May see Im wunderschonen monat Mai
In wood embowered: Z
In yonder graveyard see Tam na cmentarzu
Inaffia l'ugola: G4(e. i.)
India: C12(s.)
The Indian Christmas carol: I I3
The Indian flute: L9
Indian National Anthem see Jana gana mana
Indiana (Back home again in Indiana) T4
India's burning sands: F3
Indonesia raya: S4(e. in.)
Indroysn geyt a drobinker regn: R5(e. y.)
Indroysn iz a triber tog: R5(e. y.)
Inghean an Phailitnigh: O(e. ir.) The Palatine's daughter:
   I2
The ingle side: G3

Inneggiamo il Signor non e morto: G4(e.i.)
Inno di mameli: S4(e.i.) Italian National Anthem: F(i.)
Innu Malti see Maltese hymn
Integer vitae: P2(e.l.)
The interfering parrot: G3
Into the garden see So statt'a l'ortu
Into the night: S16
Into the woods my master went: L3
The investigator's song: H5
Io t'amo (from L'amico Fritz) G4(e.i.)
Iranian National Anthem: S4(e.pe.)
Ireland must be heaven: C4
Irene, goodnight: L6 S11 W
Irish carol (Christmas day is come, let's all prepare for
    mirth) S3
An Irish folk song (You wander far and wide, dear) G3
The Irish girl: K
The Irish jaunting car: G3
The Irish jubilee: E3 G3
The Irish lady: L8
An Irish love song (O the time is long, mavourneen) G3
The Irish mail robber: F3
Irish National Anthem see Amhran na bhfiann
The Irish poker club: G3
The Irish spree: G3
The Irish wedding: G3
Is deas an buachaill Paidin: O(e.ir.)
Is Maud in: G3
Is there for honest poverty see A man's a man for all that
Is trua gan peata an mhaoir agam see I wish I had the
    shepherd's pet
I'se see I'm
O Isis und Osiris (from Die Zauberflote) C9(e.g.) G4(g.)
Isla devecka: K(e.c.)
Isla marina: D2(e.sl.)
The island of Jamaica: C2
Islands fair see Sihote, zelene sihote
Islo dievca pre vodu: D2(e.sl.)
O isn't it nice: W7

Israel romps ta chaine: G4(e. f.)
Israeli National Anthem see Hatikvah
Istiklal marsi: S4(e. t.)
It ain't going to rain no more: F4 F7 P2
It came upon the midnight clear: A3 B5 C2 E2 F F4
    G3 L3 L4 R S3 S6 W3 W8 Y
It can't be wrong: S9
It could be a wonderful world: F8
It don't seem like the same old smile: A
It had to be you: S10
it is see also tis
It is blithe May Day: T
It is spring: B9
It makes a long-time man feel bad: L6 S13
It must be wonderful indeed (Es muss ein wunderbares
    sein) S15
It snows and it blows see Es schnayt un es blose
it was see also twas
It was a dream see Ah! tis a dream
It was a lover and his lass: G
It was four miles out of Warsaw see Cztery mile za
    Warszawa
It was May Day in the morning: B9
It was not to be so: W3
It was on a bright morning: T
It was winter and blue Tory noses: L5
It will never do to give it up so: C
Italian National Anthem see Inno di mameli
Ite caldi sospiri: G(e. i.)
Itiskit, itasket: D W5 A-tisket a-tasket: F4 T5
It's a me, o Lord: F5 F7 Standing in the need of prayer:
    B6 L4
It's a way we have at old Harvard: R2
It's advertised in Boston see Blow ye winds in the
    morning
It's all in the game: S8
It's an old southern custom: E5
It's delightful to be married: E5
It's hard on we poor farmers: L8

It's love-love: J2
It's magic: S9
It's my union: H5
It's only a paper moon: H3 M
It's the same old shillelagh: T3
It's the same the whole world over: B B8 D L5
It's very true (L'e ben ver) B3(e. i.)
It's your time, now: S13
Ivan Petrofsky Skevar see Abdul the Bulbul Ameer
I've a longing in my heart for you, Louise: A E3 G3
I've a threepenny bit see Yeu ei chi sou
I've been roaming (where the meadow dew is sweet) S15
I've been skiing down the mountain: K2
I've been to gay Paree: G3
I've been working on the railroad: B4 E3 F F4 G3 L4
   W3 Working on the railroad: B6
I've got a feeling I'm falling: J2
I've got a pocketful of dreams: J2
I've got no use for the women: B6 I Bury me out on the
   prairie: G3
I've got rings on my fingers: T7
I've rambled this country both early and late: L8
I've waited, honey, waited long for you: A W3
I've worked eight hours this day: A E3 G3
Iwwer dem Jardon: H4(e. pd.)

J

Ja-da (ja-da, jing, jing, jing) F5
Ja som baca velmi stary: D2(e. sl.)
Ja som dobry remeselnik: D2(e. sl.)
Ja, vi elsker dette landet: S4(e. n.) Norwegian National
   Anthem: F(e. n.)
Ja za woda, ty za woda: P(e. p.)
Jack (Poor little Jack lay on his back) W6
Jack and Jill: E2 F F7 W5
Jack and Joan: G
Jack, boy, ho: T

Jack Frost: W6
Jack of diamonds: L8 see also Rye whiskey
Jack Spratt: W5
Jack was every inch a sailor see Every inch a sailor
Jack Wrack: L7
The jacket so blue: C6
Jackie Rover: C6
Jack's the boy (from The Geisha) G3
Jacob's ladder: B B6 L4 L6 Z We are climbing Jacob's
   ladder: P2
J'ai perdu mon Eurydice: G4(f.)
Jak jechalem z Ameryki: P(e.p.)
Jak pojdziemy do kosciola: P(e.p.)
The jam on Gerry's rocks: B C6 F3 L Gerry's rocks:
   L7
James Harris: N
James MacDonald: F3
Jamie Raeburn's farewell: B7
Jamie's on the stormy sea: J
Jan was a gypsy bold: G3
Jana gana mana: S4(e.be.)
January, February: S
Japanese National Anthem see Kimigayo
Jardin d'amour: V(f.)
Jarsey Jane: C7
Jas konika poil: P(e.p.)
Jasio konie poil: P(e.p.)
The Jaycee Line: C7
Je caresserai la belle par amitie: L8(e.f.)
Je dis que rien ne m'epouvante: G4(e.f.) S14(e.f.)
Je me suis louee a la Saint-Jean: K(e.f.)
Ah, je ris de me voir (from Faust) G4(e.f.) S14(e.f.)
   Jewel song: C9(e.f.)
Je suis encore tout etourdie: G4(f.)
Je suis seul (from Manon) G4(f.)
Je suis Titania: G4(e.f.)
Je veux vivre (from Romeo et Juliette) G4(e.f.)
Je voudrais bien savoir (from Faust) G4(e.f.)
Jeanie with the light brown hair: B4 D E3 F F4 F5 F6
   G3 L4 R2 W3 Z

Jeannette, Isabella see Un flambeau, Jeannette, Isabelle
Jeannette, ou irons-nous: V(f.)
Jechal jeden Polak: P(e.p.)
Jedna druhej riekla: D2(e.sl)
Jedzie, jedzie rycerz zbrojny: P(e.p.)
Jedzie woz po pod woz: P(e.p.)
Jeepers creepers: C5
Jeff in petticoats: L5 S5
Jefferson and liberty: B9 D E4 F3 F8 H5
Jefferson and the common man: S6
Jeffery, James, and John: F3
Jeg er saa glad hver julekveld see I am so glad each
     Christmas eve
Jeg lagde mig saa silde: K(e.n.)
Jehovah hallelujah (The Lord will provide) S
Jemina (There was a little girl, and she had a little curl)
     W6
Jennifer gently: C6
Jenny Jenkins: C7 I3 L L8
The Jenny Lind mania: J
Jerry (song about a mule) S13
Jerry, go and oil that car: F8 L6
Jerusalem the golden: L3 W3 W4 W7
Jesous ahatonnia (American Indian carol) B5
Jesse James: B B6 D F2 I3 L L6 L7 S11
Jestem dziodek z Lobzowa: P(e.p.)
Jesu Cristes milde moder: G2
Jesu is crying: L2
Jesu, joy of man's desiring: L3
Jesu, lover of my soul see Jesus, lover of my soul
La Jesucita: B4
Jesus born in Bethlea: S S2
Jesus, call thou me: H4
Jesus calls us over the tumult: A3 F L3
Jesus came on Christmas day: S6
Jesus Christ is risen today: A3 L3 W3
Jesus Christ's mild mother: G2
Jesus, hear our prayer: H4
O Jesus, I have promised: L3
Jesus is born (Jesous ahatonnia) B5

Jesus is tenderly calling: A3
Jesus, keep me near the cross: A3
Jesus, lover of my soul: A3 B E2 F L3 W3 W7
Jesus loves even me: A3
Jesus loves me! This I know: A3 L3
Jesus, saviour, pilot me: A3 B4 L3
Jesus shall reign where'er the sun: L3
Jesus, tender shepherd, hear me: L3 W4
O Jesus, thou art standing: L3
Jesus, thou divine companion: L3
Jesus wants me for a sunbeam: L3
Jesus went walking through the fields see Chanson de
    danse et de quete
The jewel of Asia: G3
Jewel song (from Faust) see Ah, je ris de me voir
The Jew's daughter: F3
Jiffery, James, and John: F3
Jig along home: W
Jim along Jo: C7
Jim Brown: C
Jim Crow blues: H5 S13
Jim Fisk: E4 F3
Jimmy Randall see Lord Randall
Jimmy Valentine: T7
Jimmy Whalen see The lost Jimmie Whalen
Jingle bells: B5 F F4 F7 G3 S3 W3 W7 W9
Jinny get around: C7 L8
Joan, come kiss me now: B3 T
Job (O Job, Job, o, what you reckin?) L8
Joc: K(e. rm.)
Jock O'Hazeldean: G3
Jockey hat and feather: J
Joe Bowers: D I I3 L6 L7 S11
Joe Hill: B4 F8 H5
Joe Thomas: C
Joe Turner blues: D L2 S13
Joel Baker: F3
John Adkins' farewell: S12
John Anderson, my jo: G3

The John B. sails: B6 L6 S12 The wreck of the John B:
   W
John Barleycorn: F3
John Bramble see Lord Randall
The John Brown song (not John Brown's body) S5
John Brown's body: B4 D E2 F8 G3 I3 L L7 P2 S5
   S11
John done saw that number: L8
John Francois (Boney was a warrior) H
John Gilbert is the boat: L6
John Hardy: D L L6 L7
John Henry: B4 C10 D E4 F8 G3 H5 I3 L L4 L6
   L7 L8 S2 S11
John Jacob Jingleheimer Schmidt: B6
John, John Crow: H
John O'Dwyer of the glen see Sean O Duir a' ghleanna
John of Hazelgreen: N
John Peel: B4 B6 F R2
John Riley: L6 L8 L10
John the revelator: L6
John was a-writing: L8
John was watering horses see Jasio konie poil
John Whipple's mill: C6
Johnie see Johnny
Johnnie see Johnny
Johnny Appleseed: D S2 S6
Johnny Booker: C7 H Knock John Booker: L6
Johnny bought a ham: L8
Johnny Cock: N
Johnny come down to Hilo: L7
Johnny Doyle: F3
Johnny get your gun: F4
Johnny get your oatcake done: H
Johnny Graw: C7
Johnny had a little dog: W6
Johnny has gone for a soldier: B4 C I I3 L L6
Johnny, I hardly knew you: B7 I2
Johnny is my darling: S5
Johnny McCardner: L8

Johnny Riley: C6
Johnny Sands: G3
Johnny Schmoker: H4(e.pd.) J L5 P2(e.g.)
Johnny slumbered in the meadow see Zasnal Jasio na
    murawie
Johnny Stiles: L8
Johnny Vorbeck: B6
Johnny will: T2
Johnny, won't you ramble: L6 L8
The Johnson boys: L6 W
Johore National Anthem see Lago bangsa Johore
Join into the game: W
Join the circle see Entrei na roda
Join us in this festive carol see W tej koledzie kto dzis
    bedzie
The jolly boatswain: C6
The jolly huntsman see Three jolly hunters
Jolly Irishmen: J
The jolly lumbermen: D
The jolly miller: W6
Jolly shepherd: G
The jolly stage driver: C6
The jolly tester: W5
The jolly thrasher: C6
The jolly tinker: B8
The jolly wagoner: D
Jonah and the whale: G3
Jongo: L2
Jordanian National Anthem: S4(e.ar.)
Joseph and Mary see The cherry tree carol
Joseph, lieber Joseph: B5 Joseph, dearest Joseph:
    B(e.g.) R
Josephine: T5
Josephus Orange Blossom: L5
Joshua fit the battle of Jericho: B4 B6 D G3 H5 L L4
    R2 S11 Z
Joulu puu on rekennettu see Christmas is here
Joy of my heart see Caro mio ben
Joy to the world: A3 B4 B5 C2 F G3 L3 L4 R2 S3
    W3 W8

O joy upon the earth: H5
Joy upon thy bright cheek dances: C8(e.w.) Hobaderry
   danno: Z
Joyful, joyful, we adore thee: L3
A joyful thing: T6
The joys of love see Piacer d'amor
The joys of Mary see The seven joys of Mary
Juanita: B(e.s.) B6 C3 E2 F F7 G3 L4 M W3 W7
Jubilee (Swing and turn, jubilee) L6
Jubilo see Kingdom coming
Judas: N
Judas and Jesus: N
The judge's song (from Trial by Jury) G3
Judy drownded: A2
O Judy, my Judy: N
Le jugement de Paris: G4(f.)
O Jul med din glede see Christmas comes again
Julie Ann Johnson: L7
The Julie Plante: L6
July song: W6
Jump Jim Crow: B E4 L5
Jumping Judy: L6 L7
Jungfraulein, soll ich mit euch geh'n: B3(e.g.)
Jungle drums: E5(e.s.)
The juniper tree: B9
Just a little bit south of North Carolina: E5
Just a memory: H3 S10
Just a-wearying for you: B2 F
Just after the battle: S5
Just as I am, without one plea: A3 L3
Just because she made them goo-goo eyes: A E3 F6 G3
Just before the battle, Mother: B E2 F5 S5
Just listen to America: S6
Just one girl: B2 G3
Just one of those things: C5 H2
Just plain folks: F5
Just tell them that you saw me: A B2 E3 F5 F6 G3
   T2 W3

K

'k heb mijn wagen volgeladen <u>see</u> See my wagon, it's
   full-laden
K-K-K-Katy: F5
Kacer na doline: D2(e.sl.)
Kadar kata: K(e.hu.)
Kaeru no fue: W2(e.ja.)
Kafoozalum: B8
Kagda ya pyann: B7(e.r.)
Kagome, kagome: W2(e.ja.)
Kak mnogo devushek khoroshikh: R4(e.r.)
Kaki se kukkuu: K(e.fi.)
Kakurembo: W2(e.ja.)
Kalina, kalina: P(e.p.)
Kalina, malina: D2(e.sl.)
Kalinka: R4(e.r.)
The kangaroo: C7 L6
The Kansas emigrants, Song of: C
Kapala mnie mama we wodzie: P(e.p.)
Karabli: B7(e.r.)
Karasu: W2(e.ja.)
Kari: W2(e.ja.)
Kate and her horns: C6
Kate Kearney: G3
Katey Morey: C6 Katey Dorey: L8
Katharine Jaffray: F3
Kathleen (There was a lord in Ireland) F3
Kathleen Aroon: B3 G3
Kathleen Mavourneen: B3 E3 G3 W3
Katiusha: R4(e.r.)
O Katka, tell me <u>see</u> Ej povedz, Katarinka
Katty, darling: G3
Katy <u>see</u> Katey
Kazoe uta: W2(e.ja.)
Kde domoj muj <u>see</u> Czechoslovakian National Anthem
Kde si bola: D2(e.sl.)
Ach, keby som bola: D2(e.sl.)
Ked pojdes cez horu: D2(e.sl.)

Ked sa drotar: D2(e. sl.)
Ked som isiel: D2(e. sl.)
Ked som travu kosil: D2(e. sl.)
Keep a-inching along: L6
Keep in the middle of the road: P2
Keep it a secret: T4
Keep moving: P2
Keep them golden gates wide open: G3
Keep your hand on the plow: L L8
The keeper (did a-hunting go) B6 S11 W Z
The keeper of the Eddystone light: B6 C7 W
The keeper of the London zoo: B6
Kegn gold fun zun: R5(e. y.)
Kelly, the boy from Killann: I2
Kemo-Kimo: I
Kentucky babe: B2 G3 R2
Kentucky moonshiner: D
Kentucky! O Kentucky: S5
Kenya, land of the lion: S4
Kermesse (from Faust) see Vin ou biere
Kerstlied: K(e. fl.)
Kevin Barry: B C8 F8 H5
The keys of Canterbury: B9 I3
The keys of the jail see Les clefs de la prison
Khoros tou Zalongou: K(e. gk.)
Ki tavo-u el ha-arets: R5(e. h.)
The kicking mule: L6
Kilgary Mountain: C8 I2
Killaloe: G3
Killarney (By Killarney's lakes and fells) E2 F4 F7 G3
    W3 W7
Killin's hill of faery see Ur-chnoc chein mhic cainte
Kimigayo: S4(e. ja.) W2(e. ja.)
Kind are her answers: G
Kind Christmas comes but once a year: W8
The kind old man (Yr hen wr mwyn) C8(e. w.)
Kinder, mir hobn simches toyre: R5(e. y.)
Kinder yoren: B7(e. y.)
King Alcohol: E4 J

The king and the bishop: N
King Arthur: W5
King Henry Fifth's conquest of France: F3 N
King Jesus hath a garden: R
King John and the bishop: N S7
The King of France (marched up the hill) W5
The king of love my shepherd is: L3 W7
The king of the cannibal islands: G3
The king of the main: G3
King of the river: L2
The king will take the queen see A toast
King William was King George's son: L8
King William's son: N
Kingdom coming: F4 F5 F7 G3 L5 S5 W3 Jubilo: B9
    Year of Jubilo: D
The kings (Die konige) S3(e.g.)
The king's children see Zwei konigskinder
Kingyo: W2(e.ja.)
Kirya y'feyfiya: R5(e.h.)
Kisha: W2(e.ja.)
The kiss see Il bacio
Kiss duet (from Waltz Dream) G3
Kiss me again: T8
Kiss ye the baby see Cancao de natal
Kisses sweeter than wine: S11 W
Kissing song: L5
Kitty, kitty casket: L8
Kitty of Coleraine: G3
Kitty Tyrrell: G3
Kitty White: W5
Der kleine sandmann bin ich: G4(e.g.) see also The
    little sandman
Knick knack Cadillac: C7
The Knickerbocker Line: C6 C7
The knight and the shepherd's daughter: N
Knit, girls, knit: F5
Knock John Booker see Johnny Booker
Knocked them dead in the old Kent Road: W3 What cher:
    G3

K'o lien ti Ch'iu Hsiang: C11(e.ch.)
Kogannemushi: W2(e.ja.)
Kogda ia na pochte: R4(e.r.)
Koi nobori: W2(e.ja.)
Koimatai to moroutzko mou: K(e.gk.)
Kol nidre: E2
Kommt ein schlanker bursch gegangen: G4(e.g.)
Kommt ein vogerl geflogen: G3(g.)
Komoriuta: W2(e.ja.)
Kong Diderik og Hans Kaemper: K(e.dn.)
King Kristian: S4(e.dn.)
Die konige see The kings
Kookaburra: B6 R2 Z
Kookie, kookie: S8
Korean National Anthem: S4(e.k.)
Der krahwinkler landsturm: G3(g.)
Kretchma: B7
Kru-im anu: R5(e.h.)
Ktoredy Jasiu pojedziesz: P(e.p.)
Ku Kluck Klan: D
Kuckuk, kuckuk ruft aus dem wald: G3(g.)
Kui mina alles noor veel olin: K(e.es.)
Kukucka: D2(e.sl.)
Kukuleczko, gdziezes wtenczas byla: P(e.p.)
Kukulienka: D2(e.sl.)
Kukuvaca: K(e.sc.)
Kum aher, du filozof: B7(e.y.) R5(e.y.)
Kum bachur atzel: W(h.)
Kumbaya: W
Kutsu ga naru: W2(e.ja.)
Het kwezelken see Little hypocrite

                              L

l' (article) see next word of title
la (article) see next word of title
La ci darem la mano: C9(e.i.) G4(e.i.) S14(e.i.)
La tra foreste vergini (from Aida) S14(e.i.)

Labbra di foco: G4(i.)
Il lacerato spirito (from Simon Boccanegra) C9(e.i.)
Laceri miseri: G4(e.i.)
Lad beloved see Mily, kade chodis
Laddie, come early see Pridi ty, suhajko
Laddy, they're beating me see Suhajko biju mna
Ladies in the dining room: L8
The ladies' man: B6
Lady Alice: N
The lady and the gypsy: N
The lady and the shepherd: N
Lady, come down and see: T
Lady fair and gentle see Douce dame jolie
Lady Gay: L6 S7
The lady in crape: G3
The lady in red: C5
Lady Isabel and the elf-knight: L6 N
Lady Ishbel and her parrot: N
Lady Maisry: N
Lady Margot and Love Henry: N.
Lady Margot and sweet Willie: N
Lady Moon: W6 Z
The Lady of Carlisle: L8
Lady of Spain: E5
The Lady of York: N
Lady Washington's lamentation: F3
The lady who loved a swine: L8
Lago bangsa Johore: S4(e.ml.)
The Laird of Lauderdale: F3
Laisse-moi (from Faust) G4(e.f.) S14(e.f.)
The Lake of Ponchartrain: F3
The lakes of Col Fin: F3
Lama sukka zu: R5(e.h.)
Lamb, lamb, lamb: A E3
Lamb of God see Agnus dei
The lambkin: W6
The lame soldier: L8
Lament for Donough of Ballea see Caoine Dhonnchadha
Lament of the blessed virgin see Caoine na maighdine

Lament to love: E5
The lamentation over Boston: F3
Lamfin: N
L'amour est un oiseau rebelle see Habanera
L'amour, toujours l'amour: H3
The lamplighter (Latin-American song) see Yo soy
   farolero
Land of sunshine: P2
The land of the Lassen: B6
The land of the leal: G3
O the land that we love: G3
The landing of the pilgrims: F4 F5
Landlord, fill the flowing bowl see Come, landlord,
   fill etc.
Langt udi skoven: K(e. dn.)
Lanigan's ball: G3
Laotian National Anthem: S4(e.Laotian)
Lardy dah: L5
Laredo: B7(e. s.) see also The streets of Laredo
Largo (by Handel) W3
Largo al factotum della citta: G4(e. i.)
The lark in the clear air: C8 I2
The lark in the morning: K
Larry Moore: G3
las (article) see next word of title
The lass of Roch Royal: N
The lass with the delicate air: G3
Lassie, little bird mine see Dievca, lastovicka
Lassie, what have you there see Dievca, coze to mas
Lassie, won't you see Umocil ma dazdik na dvore
Last fair deal gone down: S13
Last night (the nightingale woke me) G3 S15 W3 W7 W8
Last night as I lay on the prairie see Cowboy's dream
Last night I had the strangest dream: W Strangest dream:
   S11
The last rose of summer: B3 E2 F(e. i.) F4 F7 W3
   W7 W8 Qui sola vergin rosa: G4(e. i.) Tis the last
   rose of summer: G3 L4
The last rumba: L2

Last week I took a wife: G3
Last winter was a hard one: C6
Lather and shave: C6
Latvian National Anthem: S4(e.lv.)
Laudate nomen: T(l.)
Laugh, clown, laugh: S10
The Lauterbach maiden: G3
Lavender cowboy: I3
Lavender's blue: C6 C8 J2 L4 R2
Lavender's blue (children's version) W5
lawd see lord
The lawyer outwitted: F3
Lay this body down: L7
Layla, layla: B7(e.h.)
Laytishe mazoles: R5(e.y.)
The lazy cat: W5
Lazy Mary, will you get up: E2 W5
Lazy moon: B
le (article) see next word of title
L'e ben ver see It's very true
Lead, kindly light: A3 E2 F7 L3 W3
Lead on, o king eternal: L3
Lead us, o Father: L3
Leaf by leaf the roses fall: F5
An leanbh aimhreidh: O(e.ir.)
Leanbh an chlamrain: O(e.ir.)
Leaning last night: S6
Leaning on the lamb: C7
The leather-winged bat: C6 I3 L
Leave alas this tormenting: G2
Leave her Johnny, leave her: F8 H I3
Ah, leave me not: Z
O leave your sheep: R
Leaves (Hungarian song) S6
Leaving blues: S13
Lebanese National Anthem: S4
Lecela husicka: K(e.sl.)
Lecialy gesie: P(e.p.)
Leezie Lindsay: B3 C8

The legend of the bell (From Chimes of Normandy) W8
Legende (from Lakme) see Ou va la jeune indoue
La legende de Saint Nicolas: V(f.)
Legeres hirondelles: G4(e.f.)
Lehn' deine wang' an meine wang': B3(e.g.)
Lei poni moi (Wreath of carnations) G3
O Lemuel! go down to the cotton field: F4 W3
Lenski's aria (from Eugen Onegin) C9(e.g.)
les (article) see next word of title
Let all mortal flesh keep silence: L3
Let all the world (in every corner sing) T6
Let Erin remember the days of old: C8 I2
Let go the reefy tackle: H
Let her go: B6 She's gone, let her go: G3
Let her sleep under the bar: B6
Let me explain (from Waltz Dream) G3
Let me go, Melda Marcy: A2
Let me shake the hand that shook the hand of Sullivan: G3
Let not thy hands be slack: L3
Let Simon's beard alone: I T
Let the bulgine run see Clear the track
Let the deal go down: L6
Let the lower lights be burning: A3 L3
Let the rest of the world go by: M T8
Let there be love: T4
Let us all speak our minds: F8 J
Let us with a gladsome mind: L3
Let's be sweethearts again: E5
Let's dance: E5
Let's do it: S10
Let's give three cheers: G3
Let's go a-hunting see Billy Barlow
Let's have a peal: T
Let's have another round: C6
The letter edged in black: E2 E3
A letter from the king see Carta del rey ha venido
A letter is a gypsy elf: S6
Letter scene (from Eugen Onegin) C9(e.g.)
Letter song (from La Perichole) see O mon cher amant

The letter that never came: E3
Ah! leve-toi, soleil: G4(e.f.)
Levee camp holler (we get up in the morning so dog-gone
    soon) L7
The levee song (variation of I've been working on the
    railroad) B9
The Lexington murder: L8
Li ching: C11(e.ch.)
Liberian National Anthem: S4
The liberty ball: S5
The liberty song: B D E4 I I3 In freedom we're born:
    B9
Libiamo ne' lieti calici: G4(e.i.) S14(e.i.) Brindisi:
    C9(e.i.) Drinking song (from La Traviata) W3
Libyan National Anthem: S4(e.ar.)
Lieber Augustin see Du lieber Augustin
Liebes madchen, hor' mir zu: B3(e.g.)
Liebestraum (by Liszt) E2 F7
Liechtenstein National Anthem: S4(e.g.)
Lies: T3
Lietuvos Himnas: S4(e.lt.)
Life has loveliness to sell: S6
Life is a toil: F8
Life let us cherish: W7
Life of ages, richly poured: S6
Life on the ocean wave: G3 L4
A life on the Vicksburg Bluff: C
O life that maketh all things new: S6
Lift every voice and sing: H5
The light see Ogonek
Light as a swallow: L9
Light of ages and of nations: S6
Light of ages, shed by man: S6
Lightly row: W7
Lights in the quarters burning mighty dim: L8
Lights out: T3
Like a shooting star see Como una estrella fugaz
li'l see little
Lilac tree see Boleraz

Lili Marlene: B4
Lilli Burlero: C8
The lily and the nightingale: G3
Lily Dale: G3
Lily Munro: I3 L6 L8
The lily of Laguna: G3
The lily of the West: S12
Limehouse blues: H2 S10
Limerick is beautiful: I2
Lincoln (He came when days were perilous) S6
Lincoln and liberty: B9 D L6 S5
Lincoln campaign song: S12
Ay! linda amiga see Ah! lovely lady
Lindy Lowe: H
Linger awhile: C4
Link O'Day: D
Linstead market: L2
The lions' den: F3
Lippai: S3(e.ty.)
Lipstick on your collar: J2
Lisette: B3(e.f.)
List to the bells: Z
Listen, Mister Bilbo: H5
Listen, my boy, love me you must see Sluchaj chlopcze...
Listen to the angels shouting: P2
Listen to the bells: B9
Listen to the lambs: Z
Listen to the mocking bird: B D E2 F F5 F7 G3 W3
    W7
Lithuanian National Anthem see Lietuvos himnas
Little Alabama boy: G3
Little Annie Rooney: B2 E2 E3 F5 F6 F7 G3 W3
Little ball: W5
The little ball of yarn: B8
The little bell see Odnozvuchno gremit kolokolchik
The little bird (Came a birdie a-flying) W6
Little bird, go through my window: L8
A little bit of blowing: S6
A little bit of heaven: T8

A little bit off the top: G3
Little bitty baby: S
A little bitty tear (let me down) T2
The little black ant: W6
The little black train: L8
Little Bo Peep: E2 F F7 W5
Little Bonny: L8
Little Boy Blue: E2 F7 W5
The little brown bulls: L6 L8
The little brown church in the vale: A3 B G3 P2
   The church in the wildwood: L3
The little brown girl see   El ole
Little brown jug: B B6 D F F4 F5 F6 F7 G3 L5 L7
   M R2 W3
The little brown thrush: W6
The little bunch of roses see An beinnsin luachra
Little cabbage see Hsiao pai ts'ai
The little cabin boy: C6 S7
Little Charley went a fishing: J
A little child on the earth has been born: R
The little cock-sparrow: W6
The little cottage see A casinha pequenina
The little cradle rocks tonight in glory see The child of
   God
Little David: D W9
The little dead boys: N
A little doll with China eyes (from Tales of Hoffman) W8
Little Dolly Daydream: G3
Little drops of water: L3
The little drownded girl: N
The little drummer: W6
Little Dutch mill: J2
The little fib: W6
Little fishermaiden: W6
Little gal at our house: L7
The little gal who winked at me: G3
Little girl (Little girl, don't lie to me) S11
Little girl, where have you been: W6
O little girl who has come to the fountain see
   Giovanottina che vieni alla fonte

Little girl's good-night: W6
Little grove, all in green: Z
The little hatchet see Machadinha
The little hunchback see Des bucklich mennli
Little hypocrite (Het kwezelken) B(e.d.)
Little Jack Horner: E2 F F7 W5
The little Jesus (El nino Jesus) see The child Jesus
Little Jesus, sweetly sleep: R S6 Rocking: S3 Y
Little John Henry: L6 My little John Henry: L7
Little jumping Joan: W5
Little Karen (Husker du i hoest) B3(e.sw.)
Little Katy: J
The little lamb: W6
Little Liza Jane: B3 B6 F5 L4 Liza Jane: L2 L5 L7
The little lost child: B G3
Little maid, pretty maid: W5
Little man and maid: W5
Little Matthy Groves: L6 N
Little Miss Muffitt: F W5
The little Mohee: B9 F3 I L7 S2
Little monk see Hsiao ho shang
A little more cider: G3
Little Moses: G3
Little Musgrave and Lady Barnard: N
The little old red shawl my mother wore: F4 F6 That
    little old red shawl: G3
The little old sod shanty: I I3 L6
Little partridge see Perdikitza
The little patriot's salute: W7
The little pigs: C7
Little red bird see Ushag veg ruy
The little red fox: C8
The little red hen: C7
Little robin red-breast: W6
The little sailor's song: W5
Little Sally Sand: D
Little Sally Waters: W5
The little sandman: C3(e.g.) see also Der kleine
    sandmann bin ich
The little saucepan (Sospan vach) C8(e.w.)

The little Scotch girl: C6
The little sparrow: C6
Little star (Estrellita) W3
The little strawberry girl: J
Little things: W5
The little tin soldier: W6
Little Tommy Tucker: F W5
Little Topsy's song: J
O little town of Bethlehem: A3 B4 B5 C2 F G3 L3 L4
    P2 R R2 S3 S6 W3 W8 Y
Little tyke: B7
Little wee dog: G3
Little wheel a-turning in my heart: W7
The little wide bridge a burden bears now see Szeroki
    mosteczek ugina sie
The little widow Dunn: G3
Little Willie's my darling: L8
The little woman: W5
The little wood: C7
Little yellow bird: F4
The Liverpool girls: H
Liza Jane see Little Liza Jane
Lizzie May: N
Llwyn on see The ash grove
Lo, how a rose e'er blooming see Es ist ein' ros'
    entsprungen
Lo, the earth is risen again: Z
Lobet und preiset see Praise and thanksgiving
Das lobsang (Amish song) H4(e.pd.)
Loch Lomond: B4 C3 F4 F7 L4 R2 S16 W3 Z
Locked out after nine: G3
Locks and bolts: D
Lofsongur: S4(e.ic.)
The lofty giant: C7
Logger lover see The frozen logger
The logger's boast: C
Logie O'Buchan: G3
Loinneog Oireamh: O(e.ir.)
O Lola (from Cavalleria Rusticana) G4(e.i.)

Lollipop: E5
Lolly-too-dum: B6 C6 I I3 L L8 <u>Rolly trudum</u>: S12
Lomir ale zingen - a zemerl: R5(e. y.)
London Bridge (is falling down) W5
Londonderry air: F7 G3 <u>Would God I were the tender</u>
 <u>apple blossom</u>: E2 F <u>W3</u>
The lone fish-ball: G3 L5 <u>One fish-ball</u>: B6
The lone green valley: L6
The lone prairie <u>see</u> Bury me not on the lone prairie
The lone rock <u>see</u> Carraig aonair
Lonely a linden stands <u>see</u> Medzi horami
Lonely accordion <u>see</u> Odinokaia garmon
Lonely street: T2
Lonesome blues: S13
The lonesome cowboy: F5 W3
The lonesome grove: D
Lonesome house blues: S13
Lonesome road <u>see</u> Look down that lonesome road
Lonesome traveller: W
Lonesome valley: L P2 S6 Z
Long ago, my laddy <u>see</u> Povedal si
Long gone <u>see</u> Long John
Long-handled shovel: S13
Long John: L2 L6 <u>Long gone</u>: L7
Long-line skinner blues: <u>S13</u>
Long lonesome road: L8 <u>see also</u> Look down that
 lonesome road
Long, long ago: B3 E2 F G3 W3 W7
Long summer day: L8
The long tail blue: C7
A long time ago (I remember it well) <u>see</u> I was born
 about a thousand years ago
A long time **ago** (Once there was a little kitty) L6 L7 W6
The longest train: L6
Looby loo: W5
Look away to Bethlehem: S
Look down that lonesome road: B6 L8 L10 <u>Lonesome</u>
 <u>road</u>: B4
Look over yonder: D L2

Looking for the calves see Iarraidh na ngamhna
Lookit here: C7
Looky there now: C7
Lord Banner: F3
Lord Bateman: N
Lord, blow the moon out: B6
Lord Dillard and Lady Flora: N
Lord dismiss us with thy blessing: A3 L3
Lord God of hosts, whose purpose, never swerving: L3
Lord God, we worship thee (Moravian song) H4
Lord, guide and bless (Moravian song) H4
O Lord, have mercy see Pieta signore
O Lord how long: L7
Lord, I want to be a Christian: Z
O Lord, I went up on the mountain: L8
O Lord, increase my faith: G2
The Lord is my light: F
The Lord is my shepherd: E2 P2
Lord, it's all, almost done: L8
Lord Jeffrey Amherst: B6 R2
Lord Lovel: B4 L6 L10 N S7
Lord of all being, throned afar: L3
The Lord of Lauderdale: F3
Lord of our life: L3
Lord Orland's wife: S7
Lord Randal: I L10 N R2 Jimmy Randall: N John
    Bramble: S2
Lord, send grace from thy mercy seat see O Herr,
    schenk mir mehr gnaden
Lord Thomas and fair Elinore: I N
O Lord, turn not away thy face: G2 T
Lord, we do all adore thee: P2
Lord William's death: N
The lords of creation men we call: L5
The Lord's prayer: E2 W3 W7
Die Lorelei: B6(g.) E2 F7 G3 W3 W7
Lorena: B3 S5
los (article) see next word of title
The lost chicken: W6

The lost chord: E2 F F7 G3 W7
The lost doll: W6
Lost he wanders: T
The lost Jimmie Whalen: L7
Lost love: W3
Die lotosblume: B3(e.g.) The lotus flower: S15
Louisiana girls: L7 see also Buffalo gals
Louisiana hayride: C5 H3
Lousy miner: L6
Love came down at Christmas: R
Love divine, all loves excelling: A3 L3
Love has eyes: S15
Love is a bauble: G
Love is a simple thing: J2
Love is pleasing: L6
Love is the sweetest thing: H2
Love me and the world is mine: T7
Ah, love of mine (by Giordani) see Caro mio ben
Love remains the same: G3
Love somebody, yes I do: B3
The love that I had see El amor que te tenia
Love that is hoarded: S6
Love that no wrong can cure: G3
O love that will not let me go: A3 L3
Love thoughts (Hawaiian song) W3
Lovel the robber: F3
A lovelorn youth: S2
Lovely appear: T6
O lovely appearance of death: L8
Lovely carnations see Sliczne gwozdziki
Lovely cricket: A2
O Lovely day, o happy day: W7
Lovely evening see O how lovely is the evening
Ah! lovely lady (Ay! linda amiga) B3(e.s.)
Lovely lilac time see Le temps des lilas
Lovely maiden, hear me see Liebes madchen, hor' mir
    zu
Lovely May: W6
Lovely night (from Tales of Hoffmann) see Barcarolle

The lovely Ohio see We'll hunt the buffalo
Lovely secret gardens grow: S6
Lovers' farewell: N
Lovers, mother, I'll have none: J
The lovers' quarrel see Drozyna
Love's golden dream: F5
Love's lament in mid-autumn see Chung ch'iu kuei yuan
Love's old sweet song: B3 B6 E2 F F7 G3 L4 W3 W8
Love's the tune: W3
Loving Hannah: L6
The low-backed car: G3 I2
Low bridge, everybody down see The Erie Canal
Low down chariot: L8
The low-down, lonesome low: L8
The lowest trees have tops: G
Lowlands: B4 C10 D H L see also Mobile Bay and
    Roll the cotton down
Lowly Bethlehem (Nicht Jerusalem, sondern Bethlehem)
    D(e. g.)
Lu cardillo: E(e. i.) G3(i.)
Lubly fan: D
Lucky day: S10
Lucky Jim: G3
Lucy Locket: W5
Ludzkie ogrody sie zazielenily: P(e. p.)
O, Lula: L
Lulajze jezuniu see Polish lullaby
Lullaby (by Elliot) W5
Lullaby, Emmett's see Emmett's lullaby
Lullaby (from Jocelyn, by Godari) E2 F7
Lullaby (from Erminie, by Jakobowski) E2 W3 W5 W8
Lullaby (by Mozart) S15
Lullaby (Suo gan, a Welsh song) C8(e. w.)
Lullaby, baby (by Sullivan) W5
Lullaby song (Lullaby, lullaby, dearest baby do not cry)
    W5
Lullaby to the Christ child (Armenian song) T6
Lullay, lullay (As I lay on a Yuleis night) R3
Lullay, lullow (I saw a sweet and seemly sight) R3

Lullay, my child: R3
Lullay my liking: R
Lullay, thou little tiny child see Coventry carol
Lulloo lullay see Coventry carol
Lully, lullay (O sisters too, by Haydn) S3
Lully, lullay, thou little tiny child see Coventry carol
Lulu: L6 L7
Lulu is our darling pride: F4 F7
The lumberman in town: L
Lumberman's song (Minum kultani) B3(e.fi.)
Luna nova: E(e.i.)
O lusty May: G
Lutheran lad see Suhajko luteran
Luxembourg National Anthem (Ons hemecht) S4(e.lx.)
Lydia Pinkham: L5
Lynchburg town: L6 L8

                          M

Ma dall' arido: G4(e.i.)
Ma guitare et moi: B7(e.f.)
Ma mere je la vois: G4(e.f.)
Ma Normandie: V(f.) My Normandy: W3
O ma tendre Musette: B3(e.f.) V(f.)
Ma Teodora: L2
Ma tu, re (from Aida) S14(e.i.)
Maamme: S4(e.fi.)
Maca dievca konope: D2(e.sl.)
Macario Romero, Corrido de: L9(e.s.)
McCarthy's widow: G3
McFadden's uptown flat: G3
Machadinha: L9(e.pr.)
Mack the knife: S8
MacPherson's lament: B7
McSorley's twins: G3
Madamina (from Don Giovanni) G4(e.i.)
Ein madchen oder weibchen: G4(g.)
Madeline (My Madeline she climbs right well) C7

Madelon: T8(e.f.)
Mademoiselle from Armentieres: D E2 L R2 Hinky
     dinky, parley-voo: F4 F7 G3 L5 L7 M
Madle, ruck, ruck, ruck: G3(g.)
Madre, madre (from La Forza del Destino) G4(i.)
Madrigal and gavotte (from Ruddigore) W8
Maedli, witt du heire: H4(e.pd.)
Mae'r durtur ber: K(e.w.)
Maggie by my side: G3
Maggie, the cows are in the clover: A
Maggie's pet: W6
The magic tom-tom (Congolese song) T6
The magic vine: S6
The magnet and the churn: G3
A magnet hung in a hardware shop: W8
Der Mai ist gekommen: G3(g.)
The maid and the palmer: N
The maid freed from the gallows: N S12
The maid from the mountains see Drenovare
The maid of Amsterdam see A-roving
The maid of Slievenamon: I2
The maid of the sweet brown knowe: I2
The maid on the mountain's brow: C6
The maid on the shore: C6 L6
The maid she went a-milking: T
Maiden of the dark brown hair see Nighean dubh's a
     nighean donn
The maiden with the dreamy eyes: B2
Maiden's initiation: L2
Maiden's prayer: G3
Maikai Waipio see Beautiful Waipio
Maili San Seoirse: O(e.ir.)
Maimuna see Adieu to Maimuna
Maine stein song see Stein song
Majeran: D2(e.sl.)
Majka sina vice: K(e.j.)
Make me a garment: L8
Make we joy: R3
Make we mirth: R3

Making maple sugar: T6
Mal reggendo (from Trovatore) E(e.i.) G4(e.i.)
Mal som ta dievca rad: D2(e.sl.)
Malaguena: E5(e.s.)
Malaguena salerosa: B7(e.s.)
Malay National Anthem: S4(e.ml.)
Malbrouck s'en va-t-en guerre: B(e.f.) C3(e.f.) V(f.)
Malhao: K(e.pr.)
Maloney and the brick: G3
Maltese Hymn (Innu Malti) S4(e.mt.)
Malt's come down: T
mama see also mamma
Mama, find me a husband see Mariez-moi, ma petite
    maman
Mama from the train: S8
Mama Inez: C12(s.) E5(e.s.)
Mama send me: L2
Mambru se fue a la guerra: L9(e.s.)
Di mame iz gegangen: R5(e.y.)
Mamenyu, Lyubenyu: R5(e.y.)
Mamie's blues: S13
mamma see also mama
Mamma, mamma (Well, it's mamma, mamma, o Lawd)
    L8
Mamma, quel vino: G4(e.i.)
Mamma's gone to the mail boat: L8
Mammy, will you let me go to the fair see A mhaithrin,
    a' leigfea
Mam'selle: T5
A man and his dream: J2
Man going round (taking names) L7
The man in the moon (came down too soon) W5
The man in the moon's ball: G3
Man is the earth upright and proud: S6
Man lives not for himself alone: S6
Man may long: G2
The man on the flying skis: B6 The daring young man
    who provided the skis: K2
The man on the flying trapeze: A B B6 E4 F4 F6 G3
    L5 L7 M P2 W3

Man smart, woman smarter: A2
The man that waters the workers' beer: F8
The man who broke the bank at Monte Carlo: A B2 E2
    E3 F4 F6 G3 W3
The man who fights the fire: F6
The man with the mandolin: J2
A man without a woman: B6 R2
Mandolinata: G3
Mandoline: S16(e.f.)
Mang Chiang Ngu: C11(e.ch.)
The manger throne: Y
Mangos: E5
Mangwani mpulele: B7(e.z.)
Manhattan: E5
El manisero: C12(s.)
Manitou listens to me: T6
Ein mannlein steht (from Hansel and Gretel) G4(e.g.)
Ah! Manon (mi tradisce) G4(e.i.)
A man's a man for all that: F8 G3 S6 Is there for honest
    poverty: C8
The mansion of aching hearts: A F4 G3
Manx National Anthem: S4(e.mx.)
Many a time: G3
Many thousand gone: B4 L6 L7 S5 No more auction
    block for me: F8
The maple leaf forever: G3 S4
Maple leaf rag: B2
Maple sweet: C10
M'appari tutt' amor (from Martha) E(e.i.) G4(e.i.)
    Ah, so pure: E2 W8
March of the Cameron men: G3
The march of the kings see La marche des rois
March of the men of Columbia: F5
March of the men of Harlech see Men of Harlech
March of the toys: T7
La marche des rois: B5 March of the kings: S3(e.f.)
Marche Lorraine: B4
Marching along: B9 S5
Marching along together: F5

Marching game: W5
The marching song (This is the way we march) W5
Marching song of the First Arkansas (Negro) Regiment:
   S5
Marching through Georgia: E2 F S5 W7
Marechiare: E(e.i.)
O marenariello: E(e.i.) G3(i.)
Margarido, ma mio: K(e.f.)
Margarita (Italian song) E(e.i.) W3 Take me home: G3
Margarita Punzo: C12(s.)
Margery, serve well the black sow: T
Margherita (from Faust) W3
Maria (On a fence in a garden a little Tom cat sang) G3
Maria auf dem berge see Mary on the mountain
Maria della glisch: K(e.ro.)
Maria durch ein dornwald ging see Maria wandered
   through a wood
Maria-la-o: L2
Maria, Mari: E(e.i.) E2 F4(e.i.) F7(e.i.) G3(i.) W3
Maria wandered through a wood: S3(e.g.)
Marianina: B6 L4 Z
Marianna (Italian song) E(e.i.) G3(i.)
Mariez-moi, ma petite maman: L9(e.f.)
The mariner (El marinero) (Chilean song) Z(e.s.)
El mariner (Spanish song) K(e.s.)
El marinero see The mariner
El marinero hondureno see Cancion del marinero
   hondureno
Mariner's hymn (Hail you! and where did you come from)
   S
The Marines' hymn: E3 F G3
Maringa: C12(pr.)
Mariska: D2(e.sl.)
Marjoram see Majeran
Market on Saturday night: G3
Marlene (went walking down the street) C7
The marriage of Sir Gawain: N
Married man going to keep your secret: L8
Married me a wife: L8

Married to a mermaid: H
The Marrowbone itch: L8
Marrying blue yodel: S13
La Marseillaise: B4 E2(e.f.) F(e.f.) F8(e.f.) G3
   H5(e.f.) S4(e.f.) V(f.)
Marta: E5(e.s.)
Martern aller arten: G4(g.)
Marthy had a baby: L8
Martian love song see My true love
Mary and Martha: L4
O, Mary and the baby, sweet lamb: S
Mary and Willie: F3
Mary Ann (Calypso song) A2
Mary Ann (Canadian song) L6
Mary Ann, I'll tell your ma: G3
Mary Black from Hackensack: G3
O Mary, don't you weep: B6 H5 L4 S11
Mary had a baby: S
Mary had a little lamb: E2 F F7 W5
Mary had a William goat: B6
Mary had the little baby see Ain't that a rocking all night
Mary Hamilton: N S7
Mary Kelly's beau: G3
The Mary L. MacKay: L6
Mary on the mountain (Maria auf dem berge) S3(e.g.)
Mary was a red bird: L8
Mary, what you going to name that pretty little baby: S
O Mary, where is your baby: S
Mary wore three links of chain: S12
Maryland, my Maryland: E2 F5 G3 S5 W3
Mary's lamb (parody on Mary had a little lamb) C7
Mary's lullaby (Japanese song) T6
Massa's in the cold, cold ground: B6 E2 F F4 F5 F7
   G3 W3 W7
O master, let me walk with thee: A3 L3
Master's in the cold ground see Massa's in the cold,
   cold ground
Masters in this hall: B4 R S3
Matarile: L9(e.s.)

The mate to a cock: T(e.l.)
Matilda (Calypso song) A2
Matulu, tatulu: P(e.p.)
Maui girl: G3
La maumariee: V(f.)
The May carol: B9
A May Day carol: C8 L10
May Day in the morning: B9
May-day song: W6
May Irwin's bully song: E3 G3 The bully song: E4
May Irwin's frog song: E3 G3
The May Queen's plaint: T
May snow: S6
May song see Cantilena del maggio
A May song (May, the maiden violet laden) W8
Maybe: T5
Maying song see Schoon lief, hoe ligt gij hier
Mayn yingele: R5(y.)
Me and my captain (don't agree) S13
Me father's a lawyer in England: L6
Me gustan todas: G3(s.)
Me Johnny Mitchell man: D
Me voici dans son boudoir: S16(e.f.i.)
Meadowlands see Poliushko-pole
Mechuteneste mayne: R5(e.y.)
Medzi horami: D2(e.sl.)
Meerschaum pipe: G3
Meet me by moonlight: F5
Meet me in St. Louis, Louis: B2
Meeting of the waters: G3
Megan's fair daughter: C8(e.w.)
Megeve: K2(e.f.)
Mein glaubiges herze, frohlocke: F(e.g.)
Mein Herr und Gott (from Lohengrin) S14(e.g.)
Mein kind, musst beten: B7(e.g.)
Mein lieber Schwann see Nun sei bedankt
Mein madel hat einen rosenmund: B3(e.g.) S16(e.g.)
Melinda: G3
Melissa: L2

Melody in F see Welcome, sweet springtime
Melody of love: T4
Memories (Dreams of love so true) M T8
Memories of Vienna: W3
Memory lane: H2 S10
Men of Dartmouth: R2
Men of Harlech: B B6 C8(e.w.)
Men of the soil: F8
The men of the West: I2
The menagerie: L5 P2
Mentra Gwen see Fairest Gwen
Menuet d'exaudet: V(f.)
Mephisto's serenade see Vous qui faites l'endormie
Merch Megan see Megan's fair daughter
La Mere Michel: V(f.)
The mermaid: B6 G3 H L4 L8 N
The merman: H
The merman's bride see Wassermann's braut
Merrily, merrily sing: W7
Merrily we skip along: W7
Merry Christmas: S3 T6
Merry is the morning see Chula la manana
A merry life see Funiculi-funicula
Merry widow waltz: E2 F7 W3
Mesem vam noving: B5
The message see A pombinha voou
Meu limao, meu limoeiro: C12(pr.)
Mexican Christmas procession: C2
Mexican National Anthem: F(e.s.) G3(e.s.) S4(e.s.)
Mexicanos al grito de guerra see Mexican National
    Anthem
Di mezinke oysgegeben: R5(e.y.)
Mi caballo blanco: W(e.s.)
Mi carino: C12(s.)
Mi chiamano Mimi: C9(e.i.) G4(e.i.)
Mi dicha lejana: C12(s.)
Mi mama me aconsejaba: L9(e.s.)
Mi par d'udire ancora: E(e.i.)
Mi pollera: C12(s.)

Mi tradi quell' alma ingrata: G4(e. i.)
Mi yivne hagalil: R5(e. h.)
Mi y'malel: B9(h.) R5(e. h.) W(h.)
Micaela's aria see Je dis que rien ne m'epouvante
Michael Finnigin: C6 C7
Michael, row the boat ashore: S11 W
Michael Roy: C G3
Michie Banjo see Mister Banjo
Michie Preval: L2 L7(e. cr.)
Michigan water blues: S13
Mid a nodl, on a nodl: R5(e. y.)
Mid twilight shadows see W pogodny wieczor
Midnight on the ocean: C7
Midnight, sleeping Bethlehem: S3
The midnight special: B B6 H5 I3 L L2 L7 S11 S13
    W
The midshipmite: G3
Midsummer morn see Je me suis louee a la Saint-Jean
Might I be the wooded fernbrake see Que ne suis-je
    la fougere
Mighty day: T6
A mighty fortress is our God: A3 B(e. g.) B4 C3(e. g.)
    F L3 L4 S6 W3 W4
Mighty like a rose: B2
Mike McCarty's wake: G3
Milking song see Cainc yr odryddes
Milkweed seed: S6
The mill was made of marble: F8
The mill-wheel: W6
The miller's song see Can y melinydd
The miller's three sons: F3
Mily, kade chodis: D2(e. sl.)
Mimes, Canon of see Canon of the mimes
O Mimi tu piu non torni: G4(e. i.)
A mince pie or a pudding: S
Mind your bittnet: L2
A miner's life (is like a sailor's) F8
Minha esperanca: G3(pr.)
Minka: W3

The minstrel boy: B4 E2 G3 W3
Minum kultani see Lumberman's song
O mio babbino caro (from Gianni Schicchi) C9(e.i.)
O mio Fernando: G4(e.i.)
O mio rimorso (from La Traviata) G4(e.i.)
Il mio tesoro (from Don Giovanni) C9(e.i.) G4(e.i.)
   S14(e.i.)
Mir schwimme iwwer der Skulkill: H4(e.pd.)
Mira, o Norma: G4(e.i.)
Miserere (from Il Trovatore) E(e.i.)
Miserere nostri domine: T(l.)
Miss Bailey's ghost: B6 I
Miss Jenny Jones: W5
Miss Mary Jane: L6
Miss you: J2
Missie Mouse: C6
The mission of a rose: W8
Missouri mule: I3
The mist grows deeper see Pala magla
Mister and Mississippi: T3
Mr. and Mrs. Brown: J
Mister Banjo: B L5 L9(e.f.) S2(e.f.) Michie Banjo: L2
Mister Congressman: H5
Mr. Froggie went a-courting see Frog went a-courting
Mister golden beetle see Kogannemushi
Mister, here's your mule: L5
Mister MacKinley: L6
Mr. Pierce's experience: F3
Mister rabbit: I3 L L4
Mrs. Bond: W5
Mrs. Craigin's daughter: G3
Mrs. McGrath: B7 C8 I2
Mistress Mary, quite contrary: F W5
Mistress mine: G L10
Mrs. Murphy's chowder: B6 see also Who threw the
   overalls in Mrs. Murphy's chowder
Mrs. Patrick Casey's swell pink tea: G3
Mit gewitter und sturm: G4(e.g.)
Mix a pancake: W5

Miya-sama (from The Mikado) G3
Mlody panie nasz: P(e.p.)
Moaning (The trumpet sounds it in my soul) L7
Mobile Bay: H see also Lowlands and Roll the cotton
   down
Mociute mano: K(e.lt.)
Mock lament see Caoine magaidh
Modesta Ayala, Corrido de: L9(e.s.)
Mogst du, mein kind: G4(e.g.)
O moj rozmarynie, rozwijaj sie: P(e.p.)
Ach moj wianku rozmarynie: P(e.p.)
Molad'ti: R5(h.)
Molly and I and the baby: G3
Molly Brannigan: C8 I2
Molly darling: F5
Molly Malone see Cockles and mussels
Molly O: A E3 G3 W3
Molly St. George see Maili San Seoirse
Un momento (from Il Trovatore) G4(e.i.)
Mon ami Pierrot see Au clair de la lune
O mon cher amant (from La Perichole) G4(f.) Letter
   song: C9(e.f.)
Mon coeur s'ouvre a ta voix: C9(e.f.) G4(e.f.) My heart
   at thy sweet voice: E2 W3
Monaco's National Anthem: S4(e.f.)
The monastery bells: G3
Monday, Tuesday: C8
Money am a hard thing to borrow: J
Money is the meat in the cocoanut: S12
The money rolls in: B8
Mongoose dead O: A2
The monkey palanquin see Osaru no kagoya
The monkey's wedding: C7 G3
Monotone (Ein ton) S15
Monsieur Banjo see Mister Banjo
Moody river: T2
The moon is blue: J2
The moon is coming out see Deta, deta
The moon-lighter: G3

The moon shines bright: R
Moonbeams: T7
Moonlight bay: M T8
Moonshiner: B7 L6
Moosehead Lake: L6 L8
More: T4
Morgen (by Strauss) see Tomorrow
Morgenlich leuchtend: G4(e.g.) The prize song: C9(e.g.)
Morir! si pura e bella (from Aida) G4(e.i.)
The morning hangs a signal: S6
Morning song: S6 W7
Morning star (Moravian song) H4
Morning thanks (Westphalian tune) W4
The morningside of the mountain: S8
Morro (from Ballo in Maschera) G4(e.i.)
La mort du Roi Renaud: K(e.f.)
O mortal man, remember well: R
Moscow: B4
Moscow nights see Podmoskovnye vechera
M-o-t-h-e-r: C4
O mother dear, Jerusalem: L3
Mother horse and colt see Ouma
Mother Machree: M T7
Mother, may I go out to swim: W5
Mother of men: R2
Mother pin a rose on me: A E3 F6 G3
Mother, shall I now relate (Ah, vous dirai-je, maman)
    B3(e.f.)
Mother was a lady: B G3
Mother's kisses: W6
Mother's prayer (by Godard) W7
Mot'l: B7(e.y.)
Mountain monkey see Oyama no osaru
Mountain song: F3
Mountains: S6
The Mountains of Mourne: C8
The Mountains of Pomeroy see Renaldine
Mourn for the thousands slain: T
The mower see An spealadoir

Mowing the barley: L10
Mowing the hay: W7
Mu asapru: B7(e.y.)
Mucama: G3(pr.)
Mud pies: W7
Mude bin ich: H4(e.pd.)
The muffin man: W5
Mugi kari: W2(e.ja.)
Mul ha'ohel: B7(e.h.)
The mulberry bush: W5
Mule skinner blues: L6 S13
The mule song: C6
Mule train: T2
The Mulligan Guards: E4 L5 W3
Mura matsuri: W2(e.ja.)
The murder of Sarah Vail: F3
The murdered boy: N
The murdered brother: N
Murdered by a brother: F3
Musetta's waltz: C9(e.i.)
Mush, mush: B6 G3 W3
Mushi no koe: W2(e.ja.)
The music goes round and round: J2
O music, sweet music: T
Musica proibita: E(e.i.)
Musical alphabet: J W7
Musing: G
Muss i denn: B4(e.g.) B6(g.) C3(e.g.) G3(g.) K2(e.g.)
Must I go bound: L10
Mustang gray: L7
My Angeline: G3
My beauty was lost in the mountains: K2
My birchbark canoe: C
My blue heaven: C4
My bonnie lies over the ocean: B3 B6 E2 F R2 W3
    Bring back my bonnie to me: G3
My boy Billy: B9 My boy Willie: C8 see also Billy Boy
My buddy: M
My children are laughing behind my back: B7

My coal black lady: A
My country is the world: S6 T6
My country, so fair to see: S6
My courtyard see El patio de mi casa
My Creole Sue see Creole Sue
My dad's the engineer: A E3
O my darling Clementine see Clementine
My darling's little shoes: J
My days have been so wondrous free: D F5 I
My devotion: J2
My doll (Watashi no ningyo) T6(e. ja.)
My dolly: W6
My dove: C7
My dream is yours: S9
My dreams are getting better all the time: J2
My ducksie has fled: C6
My every thought: Z
My faith looks up to thee: A3 B4 L3 L4 W3 W4 W7
My father gave me a lump of gold: L8
My father gave me an acre of ground: N
My Father, how long: S5
My father's a lawyer in England see Me father's a lawyer
    in England
My foolish heart: J2
My gal is a high born lady: A E3 E4 F4 G3
O my garland of rosemary see Ach moj wianku
    rozmarynie
My gentle harp: B4
My God, how endless is thy love: L3
My God, how the money rolls in see The money rolls in
My God, I thank thee: L3 P2
My good old man: B6 Where have you been, my good old
    man: L8
My grandfather had some very fine ducks: J
My heart see Kak mnogo devushek khoroshikh
O my heart (it is so sore) G2
My heart at thy sweet voice see Mon coeur s'ouvre a ta
    voix
My heart ever faithful, sing praises see Mein glaubiges
    herze, frohlocke

My heart is palpitating: G3
My heart is sair for somebody: G3
My heart, once light as a feather: T
My heart stood still: H3 S10
My heart's in the highlands: G3 L4
My homeland (Till osterland) (Swedish song) T6
My hope is built: A3
My horses ain't hungry: L4 S11 Z Rabble soldier: S12
My isle of golden dreams: T8
My Jesus, as thou wilt: L3
My lady: F7
My lady wind: W6
My lady's garden: W5
My last cigar: G3
My last old dollar: L6
My little dog: W6
My little grass shack in Kealakekua Hawaii: T5
My little John Henry see Little John Henry
O my liver and my lungs: L8
My Lord, what a morning: B4 L4 P2 Z When the stars
   begin to fall: L6
O my love (lov'st thou me) B3 T
My love in garden spot is dwelling see L'amour de moi
My love is a rider: L6
My love is gone to sea: B3
My love is like a dewdrop: C6
My love is like a red, red rose: B3 C8 G3
My love was just a day dream: G3
My lovely Celia: S15
My loving gal Lucille: S13
My mother bathed me in clear water see Kapala mnie
   mama wodzie
My mother's advice see Mi mama me aconsejaba
My mother's bible: F5 J
My name is Yon Yonson: B6
My native land (Gesang Weylas, by Wolf) S15
My Nelly's blue eyes: F6 F7
My Normandy see Ma Normandie
My old cabin home see The old cabin home
My old coon dog: I3

My old Dutch: F6 F7 G3 W3
My old Kentucky home: B C D E2 F F4 F5 G3 R2
   W3 W7 W9 Z
My old true love: L8
My own dear one see Caro mio ben
My own true love: S8
O my papa (O mein papa) T4
My Pearl's a Bowery girl: A
My pony: W6
My prayer (when the twilight is gone) T3
My pretty little maid: C6
My Red Cross girlie: F5
O my rosemary plant see O moj rozmarynie, rozwijaj sie
My ship and I: W6
My sweetheart see Akh ty, dushechka
My sweetheart's the man in the moon: B2 E3 F4 F5 F6
   F7 G3 W3
My sweetheart's the mule in the mines: F8 L6
My true love (Martian love song) W
My truly, truly fair: J2
My trundle bed: J
My two front teeth: S9
My wild Irish rose: F G3 M
My yellow gal: L7

                                    N

Na dolinie zawierucha: P(e. p.)
Na Dunaji: D2(e. sl.)
Na haste do castanheiro: K(e. pr.)
Na Krakowskiem zamku: P(e. p.)
Na lei o Hawaii see Song of the islands
Na Podolu bialy kamien: P(e. p.)
Na srodku pola: P(e. p.)
Na vulitsi skripka hrae: K(e. r.)
Na zelenej lucke: D2(e. sl.)
Nachtwachterruf: K(e. g.)
Naci en la cumbre: C12(s.)

Nad tatru sa blyska see Czechoslovakian National Anthem
Nad woda wieczornej porze: P(e. p.)
Namo namo matha: S4(e. sn.)
Nancy Lee: G3 H
Nancy Till: C
Nangminek erinalik: S4(e. dn.)
Nantucket point: H
Nar Juldagsmorgon glimmar see When Christmas morn
   is dawning
Nassau bound: A2
Nasty man: E5
A nation once again: I2
The national debt: G3
Natural-born easman: L7
Natural history: W5
Naughty Clara: G3
Navajo happy song: L4
Navervisan: K(e. sw.)
Navy blue and gold see Navy victory march
The Navy goat: F5
Navy victory march: F5
Ne korite menia, ne branite: R4(e. r.)
Ne me refuse pas: S16(e. f.)
Ne mesyats to svetit: K(e. r.)
Ne permettrez-vous pas (from Faust) S14(e. f.)
Ne pleure pas, Jeannette: V(f.)
Ne probuzhdai vospominania: R4(e. r.)
Ne slyshno shumu gorodskovo: R4(e. r.)
Neapolitan cradle song: W5
Neapolitan serenade see Serenata Napolitana
Neapolitan song (The summer wind blows off the shore) G3
Near a Krakow castle see Na Krakowskiem zamku
Near Belgrade city see Pod Belehradom
Near Preshporok see Pri Presporku
Near the old tower see Przy wielkiem zamku
Nearer, my God, to thee: A3 B E2 F I L3 W3 W4 W7
Nedzne zycie czeladnika: P(e. p.)
Negara ku: S4(e. ml.)
Nellie see Nelly

Nelly Bly: B E2 F4 G3 W3
Nelly was a lady: C E2 F F4 F5 F7 G3 W3
Nem aroys a ber fun vald: R5(e.y.)
Nemico della patria (from Andrea Chenier) C9(e.i.)
Nepalese National Anthem: S4(e.np.)
Nesta rua: L9(e.pr.)
Netherlands National Anthem: F(e.d.) S4(e.d.)
Never get a licking till I do down to Bimini: L8
Never let a man: T
Never no more hard times blues: S13
Never said a mumbling word: D L L7 W3
Never take the horse-shoe from the door: G3
Never weather-beaten sail: G
Nevydavaj: D2(e.sl.)
The new-born baby: S
New England, New England (my home by the sea) C10
New every morning is the love: L3
A new Jerusalem: F8
New moon see Luna nova
New oysters: G2
New river train: P2 S11 Darling (you can't love but one):
    L7
New stranger's blues: S13
A new wind a-blowing: D
New Year carol: W6
New Year song (Upon this first day of the year) W6
New York City (I'm in New York City, gonna lay my line)
    S13
New York, o what a charming city: C J S12
New York town: S13
The New York volunteer: S5
New Zealand's National Song (God defend New Zealand) S4
The Newburgh jail: C6
Newfoundland National Anthem: S4
Newspapermen: H5
Next Monday morning: F3
Niagara falls: C
Nicaraguan National Anthem: S4(e.s.)
The nice young man: J

Nicht Jerusalem, sondern Bethlehem see Lowly
  Bethlehem
Nicodemus: I Wake Nicodemus: B
Nicodemus Johnson: G3
Oj nie chce cie Kasiu: P(e.p.)
Nie dla psa kielbasa: P(e.p.)
Niema-ci to, nie ma: P(e.p.)
Nighean dubh's a nighean donn: K(e.ga.)
Night and day: C5 H3
Night herding song: D F2 L4 L6 Z
The night shall be filled with music: J2
Night watchman's song see Nachtwachterruf
The nightingale: T
Nightingale (Slovak song) see Spievaj si, slavicku
The nightingale and the rose: G3 S15
Nina (Italian song) E(e.i.) G3(i.) W3
Ninas hermosas: L9(e.s.)
Nine hundred miles: L
Nine men slept in a boarding house bed: B6
Nine miles to the junction: S5
Nineteen birds: W5
Nineteen hundred and eight: G3
Ninety and nine: L3 W3
El nino Jesus see The child Jesus
Nitra, mila Nitra: D2(e.sl.)
Nkosi sikelel'i Africa: S4(e.z.)
No hay arbol: L9(e.s.)
No hiding place: B6 L2
No hips at all: B8
No home, no home: J
No Irish need apply: F8
O no, John: B6 C8 R2
No moon at all: E5
No more auction block for me see Many thousand gone
No more booze: D
No! No! a thousand times no: F6 T5
No, no, Turiddu: G4(e.i.)
No room in the inn: S3
No rose of such virtue: R3

No shadows yonder: W3

No sir (Tell me one thing) W3

No sounds from the city are heard see Ne slyshno shumu
    gorodskovo

No tree but has a shadow see No hay arbol

Noah's ark see One more river to cross

The noble Duke of York: C7

The noble sku-ball: F3

Nobody: L5

Nobody knows the trouble I've seen: B4 B6 E2 E4 F F4
    F5 F7 G3 I3 L4 R2 W3 W7

Nobody knows you when you're down and out: S13 W

Les noces du papillon: V(f.)

Noel noel (Tis the day, the blessed day) Y

Noel nouvelet: B5 V(f.)

Noel sing we: G2 R3

Nokoreach see Cambodian National Anthem

Nola: E5

Non e ver: E(e.i.)

Ah! non giunge uman pensiero: G4(e.i.)

Non la sospiri (from Tosca) G4(i.)

Non mi dir (from Don Giovanni) G4(e.i.) S14(e.i.)

Non mi resta che il pianto edil dolore: G4(e.i.)

Non piu andrai (from Le Nozze di Figaro) C9(e.i.) G4(e.i.)

Non siate ritrosi: G4(i.)

Non so piu cosa son: G4(e.i.)

Non ti rammenti: G3(i.)

None but the lonely heart: F(e.g.) F7(e.g.) G3 W3
    Nur wer die sehnsucht kennt: B3(e.g.)

Noriu miego: Z

The north wind (When the north wind keenly blows) W6

The north wind doth blow: W5

North wind whistles see Na zelenej lucke

Norwegian National Anthem see Ja, vi elsker

Not alone for mighty empire: Z

Not for dogs is sausage see Nie dla psa kielbasa

Not gold, but only men: S6

Nothing but the blood of Jesus: A3

Nothing like grog: L5

Nothing, really nothing see Niema-ci to, nie ma
Nous n'irons plus au bois: V(f.)
Nova, nova: G2 R3
Now all the heavenly splendor: S6
Now all the woods are sleeping: Z
Now God be with old Simeon: G
Now God be with us, for the night is closing: L3(e.l.)
Now he is my own: G3
Now I am married: T
Now I lay me down to sleep: W7
Now in joy or sorrow (from The Bartered Bride) W8
Now is the month of Maying: S15
Now it is Christmastime (Nu ar det Jul igen) S3(e.sw.)
Now kiss the cup, cousin: T
Now let me fly: B4
Now make we joy: R3
Now our meeting's over: L7
Now peep, bo peep: G
Now, Robin, lend to me thy bow: T
Now sing we of the brave of old: S6
Now thank we all our God see Nun danket alle Gott
Now that the spring: T
Now the day is over: A3 F L3 W3 W4 W7
Now the laborer's task is o'er: L3
Now the rose is red see Totenlied
Now there is frost: S6
Now there once was a young girl: S12
Now they stop at her house see Przed dom przyjechali
O now this glorious Eastertide see Daar nu het feest van
    pasen is
Now we are met: T
Now we'll make the rafters ring: T
Now well may we mirth make: R3
Now we're on our way to church see Do slubejku
    jedziewa
Now what is love: G
Now, when the dusky shades of night: L3
Now while we sing our closing psalm: L3
Now winter nights enlarge: G

nowell see noel

Nu ar det Jul igen see Now it is Christmastime

O nuit d'amour (from Faust) G4(e.f.)

Number four, second floor: G3

Number 12 train: S13

Nun danket alle Gott: H4(e.g.) Now thank we all our God:
    A3 L3(e.g.) P2

Nun sei bedankt (mein lieber Schwann) G4(e.g.) S14(e.g.)

Nun zirade: K(e.b.)

Nunc dimittis (by Tomkins) G2

Nuns in frigid cells: S3

Nur du: B4(e.g.)

Nur wer die sehnsucht kennt see None but the lonely
    heart

The nurse pinched the baby: S12

Nut brown maiden: B6 C8 G3 W3

                                  O

o see next word of title

O.P.A. ditty (We'll roll back the prices) S12

The oak and the ash: C8

Oaken leaves: G2 T

Oath of friendship (Chinese song) T6

Oats, peas, beans and barley grow: W5

Obeissons (from Manon) G4(f.)

L'occasion manquee: V(f.)

Occhietti amati: B3(e.i.)

Ocean, thou mighty monster: G4

Ochy chornia see Dark eyes

October song: W6

Od Francyji jade: P(e.p.)

Od Krakowa czarny las: P(e.p.)

Od listka do listka: P(e.p.)

Od mora, od mora: K(e.j.)

Od Ostrova: D2(e.sl.)

Ode on science: D

Ode to the Fourth of July : D

Odinokaia garmon: R4(e. r.)

Odnozvuchno gremit kolokolchik: R4(e. r.)

O'Donnell Aboo: C8

O'Dwyer caught a cold: G3

Of a rose sing we: R3

Of all the birds: G

Of speckled eggs the birdie sings: S6

Oft to Philadelphia: G3 I2

The officers of Dixie: S5

Oft in the stilly night: C8 F7 G3

The Ogallaly song: C

'Oganaigh oig: O(e. ir.)

Ogonek: R4(e. r.)

O'Grady's goat: G3

Ogun gori na balkana: K(e. bu.)

oh see next word of title

O'Hara's cup see Cupan ui Eaghra

O-HI-O see We'll hunt the buffalo

O'Hoolighan: G3

Oil on the brain: L5

Les oiseaux dans la charmille: G4(f.)

oj see next word of title

Ol' kaunis kesailta: K(e. fi.)

Ola Glomstulen: K(e. n.)

Aa Ola, Ola, min eigen onge: K(e. n.)

Olafur og Alfamaer: K(e. ic.)

Olban see The white captive

Old Abe Lincoln (came out of the wilderness) B B9 D
   S5 S12

The old ark's a-moving: B6 L6

The old bachelor: L7

Old Bangum: L6 L8 N S7 Z

Old Bill: L7

Old black Joe: E2 F F4 F5 F7 G3 R2 W3 W7

Old Blue: B6 I I3 L L4 L6 L8

Old brass wagon: C10

Old Butler's: C

The old cabin home: W3 W7 My old cabin home: C

The old Chisholm Trail: B B6 D E4 F2 F8 G3 I3 L
   L4 L6 L7 S2 Z

Old colony times see In good old colony times
Old Dan Tucker: B̄ C̄7 C10 D E4 I L L7 S11
Old dog Tray: E2 F4 G3 W3 W7 W9
Old England forty years ago: F3
Old faithful: T4
Old fashioned garden: H3 T8
Old fashioned mother: G3
The old-fashioned well by the way-side: G3
Old fisherman see Pan ch'iao tao ch'ing
The old folks at home: B4 C C3 C12 E2 E4 F F5 F7
    G3 L4 R2 S11 W3 W7 Z
Old Gaelic lullaby (Hush, the waves are rolling in) Z
The old granite state: J
The old gray goose see Aunt Rhody and The grey goose
    and The old grey goose
The old gray mare: E2 F4 F5 F6 F7 G3 R2 W3
The old grey goose (Monday was my wedding day) B
    see also Aunt Rhody and The grey goose
The old grey mare see The old gray mare
Old grumbler: B9
Old hag, you see manny: L8
Old Hewson, the cobbler: F3
Old Hundred: B B4 F7 I W3 W7 Doxology: L4
    Praise God, from whom all blessings flow: F L3
Old Ironsides: F5
Old Joe Clark: B6 C7 D I3 L L5 L7 S11
Old King Cole: B6 B9 C7 F G3 W5
Old King Cole (army parody) L8
The old lamp-lighter: T3
The old lord by the northern sea: N
Old Ma Bell: F8
Old MacDonald had a farm: F G3 R2
Old maid: B6
The old maid's lament: C6
The old maid's song: F3 L10
The old man see An seanduine
The old man and the door: N
The old man clothed all in leather: W5
The old man in the wood: Z

Old man Mose: G3 J2
Old man Noah: G3
The old man of Kilcockan see Seanduine Chill Chocain
The old man's lament: L6
Old marse John: L6
The old miner's refrain: E4
Old Mother Hare: L7
Old Mother Toad: W6
Old mountain dew see Good old mountain dew
Old Nantucket whaling song: H
Old Nassau: R2
The old oak tree: F3
The old oaken bucket: B E2 F4 F5 F7 G3 W3 W7 W9
The old orange flute: I2
Old paint see I ride an old paint
Old Pee Dee: C see also On the banks of the old Pee Dee
   and Way down on the old Pee Dee
Old Rattler: L7 Old Riley: W
An old refrain (Austrian song) P2
Old Riley (crossed the water) see Old Rattler
Old Robin Gray: G3
Old Rosin the beau: I
The old rugged cross: L3
Old Santa Claus: W5
The old settler's song see Acres of clams
Old ship of Zion see Ship of Zion
Old shoes and leggings: L8
Old skiers never die: K2
Old Smokie: C10
Old Smoky see On top of Old Smoky
The old soldiers of the king: B9
The old spinning wheel: T4
The old spotted cow: C6
Old Stormy: S2 Stormy: H
Old Tar River: C
Old Tare River: C
Old Texas: B B6 L4 Going to leave old Texas: P2
Old Thompson's mule: G3
Old time religion: A3 B6 L3 R2 (Give me) that old time
   religion: E4 G3 L4 W3

The old tobacco box: C7

Old Uncle Ned see Uncle Ned

Old woman all skin and bone: D

The old woman and the devil see The devil and the
    farmer's wife

The old year now away has fled: B5 R A happy New Year:
    B9

Old Zip Coon: D E4 Zip Coon: L5 see also Turkey in
    the straw

ole see old

El ole: K(e. s.)

Oleana: B7 L6

Olive trees are standing: P2

Oliver and the fairy maid see Olafur og Alfamaer

Omie Wise: L6

Omnipotence (Die allmacht, by Schubert) S15

On a little street in Singapore: T4

On a Monday (I was arrested) S13

On a Saturday night: A E3 F4 F5 F6 G3

On a Sunday afternoon: B2

On billow rocking (from Chimes of Normandy) W3 W8

On board the Kangaroo: I2

On Christmas night all Christians sing: R Y

On freedom (Men, whose boast it is) S6

On Ilkla Moor baht hat: B6 C8

On m'appelle Manon: G4(f.)

On Meeesh-e-gan: D L7

On my journey home: L4 L6 W

On our way rejoicing: L3

On Springfield Mountain see Springfield Mountain

On that Christmas day morn: R

On that hill by the Tennessee: C

On the Atchison, Topeka and the Santa Fe: T5

On the banks of the Little Eau Peine: C

On the banks of the Ohio (I asked my love to take a walk)
    see Banks of the Ohio

On the banks of the Ohio (we'll hunt the buffalo) see We'll
    hunt the buffalo

On the banks of the old Pee Dee: C see also Old Pee Dee
    and Way down on the old Pee Dee

On the banks of the Sacramento see Sacramento
On the banks of the Wabash far away: B2 G3
On the bridge of Avignon see Sur le pont d'Avignon
On the chapel steps: R2
On the corner: S3
On the eighteenth of July see Venga jaleo
On the first Thanksgiving Day: F5
On the good ship Lollipop: E5
On the Kazanka: P2
On the line: F8
On the night see Ked som isiel
On the river see Zvenit gitara nad rekoiu
On the road to Tipperary see Idir chaiseal agus durlas
On the road to Valencia see Camino de Valencia
On the rocks by Aberdeen: G3
On the shore across the lake see Z tamtej strony jeziora
On the trail to Mexico see The trail to Mexico
On the way home from Riley's: G3
On top of Old Smoky: B4 G3 H5 L L4 L6 R2 S2 S11
    W Smoky Mountain: B6 Way up on Old Smoky: D
On wings of song (Auf flugeln des gesanges) F(e.g.) G3
    S15
Once I fell in love see Zamiloval som si dievca
Once (Wunst) I had an old gray mare: L8
Once I loved a maiden: B3
Once I saw a sweetbriar rose see Sah ein knab' ein
    roslein stehn
Once I went in swimming: B6
Once in a while: T5
Once in our lives: T
Once in royal David's city: L3 R S3 Y
Once more a-lumbering go: L
Once to every man and nation: L3 P2 S6
Once was enough for him: G3
One day I had to mow see Ked som travu kosil
One day the lovely rose complained see Es hat die rose
    sich beklagt
One dime blues: L6
The one-eyed Reilly: B8
One father: T6

One fish ball see The lone fish ball
One for the little bitty baby: B5
One happy Swede: F8
One lovely summer evening see Ol' kaunis kesailta
One man shall mow my meadow: K
One meat ball see The lone fish ball
One more day: B4 H
One more drink for the four of us see Drunk last night
One more river to cross: B4 B6 C7 Noah's ark: G3 L5
One morning in May: Z
One of his legs is longer than it really ought to be: A
The one rose (that's left in my heart) T3
One said to the other see Jedna druhej riekla
One sweetly solemn thought: F L3 W3 W7
One, two, button your shoe: J2
The one who hath created things of beauty see A tribute
One world this: S6
Only a hundred girls: G3
Only forever: J2
Only four hours see Styri hodiny
Only one girl in the world for me: A E3 F6 G3
Only trust him: A3
Only you can tell me see Povedz mi
Onward Christian soldiers: A3 E2 F L3 R2 W3 W4 W7
Oola (I'm Oola, ski-yumper from Norway) B6 K2
Oola had a cousin Sven: K2
Open, open see Hiraita, hiraita
Open the gates of the temple: F
Open thy lattice, love: S15
Or sai, chi l'onore: G4(e.i.)
Oran talaidh an eich-uisge: K(e.ga.)
The orange and the black: R2
Oranges and lemons: W5
Orchestra song (Quodlibet) P2
Original talking blues: S13
O''Rourke's revel rout see Plearaca na Ruarcach
Osaru no kagoya: W2(e.ja.)
Osterreichische bundeshymne: S4(e.g.) Austrian
    National Anthem F(g.)

Ostrov's limetrees see Od Ostrova
Ot Azoy neyt a shnayder: R5(e.y.)
Otche tchornia see Dark eyes
The other shore: L7
Ou som souroucou: L7(cr.)
Ou va la jeune indoue (Legende, from Lakme) G4(e.f.)
Ouma: W2(e.ja.)
Our baby (French lullaby) W5
Our baby died: B6
Our beautiful earth: T6
Our flag is there: F5 W7
Our God, our help see O God, our help in ages past
Our goodman: B8 N Four nights drunk: S11 Three
    nights drunk: L8 You old fool: W
Our grandfathers' days: G3
Our holy guest: T6
Our home is on the mountain's brow: J
Our land, o Lord (by Haydn) W7
Our own beloved land: F5
Our school will shine tonight: P2
Out in the cold again: J2
Out in the great Northwest: B6
Out of my soul's great sadness see Aus meinen grossen
    schmerzen
Out of work: J
The outing: W6
Outskirts of town: S13
Outward bound: H
Over field and meadow: W7
Over Jordan see Iwwer dem Jardon and Wayfaring
    stranger
Over the bannister: W3
Over the bright blue sea (from Pinafore) G3 W8
Over the hill to the poor house: E3 F4 F5 F6
Over the hills (Polish song) see Za gorami
Over the hills and far away: W5
Over the meadows: Z
Over the mountains: C8
Over the rainbow: C4

Over the river and through the woods: F5 P2
    Thanksgiving Day: W7
Over the stars there is rest: W3 W7 W8
Over the stone (Tros y gareg) C8(e.w.)
Over the summer sea (from Rigoletto) see La donna e
    mobile
Over there (Potatoes, they grow small) see The famine
    song
Overtures from Richmond: S5
Owen Coir see Eoghan Coir
The owl and the pussy cat: G3
The ox-driving song: I L8
Oxen and sheep see Entre le boeuf et l'ane gris
The oxen song: B
Oy, dortn, dortn, ibern vaserl: R5(e.y.)
Oy, khodyla divchyna: K(e.r.)
Oyama no osaru: W2(e.ja.)
Oyf dem yam veyet a vintele: R5(e.y.)
Oyfn barg, ibern barg: R5(e.y.)
Oyfn oyvn zitst a meydl: R5(e.y.)
Oysters, sir: J

P

Pa meme: K(e.a.)
Pace, pace (from La Forza del Destino) G4(i.)
Paddle your own canoe: F5 F6 G3
Paddy and the frog: G3
Paddy and the whale: I3
Paddy Doyle and his boots: H
Paddy Duffy's cart: G3
Paddy Murphy: K2 Patty Murphy: B6
Paddy works on the (Erie) railroad: B4 E4 H H5 L L5
    L7 Fillimeeooreay: S11 Pat works on the railroad:
    B9 D F8 I I3 Z see also Patsy Ory-ory-aye
Padre! a costoro (from Aida) S14(e.i.)
The painter see Pintor de cannahy
Painting the clouds with sunshine: S10

Pajarillo barranqueno: C12(s.) L9(e.s.)
Pakistani National Anthem: S4(e.u.)
Pal of my dreams: E3
Pala magla: K(e.sc.)
The Palatine's daughter <u>see</u> Inghean an Phailitnigh
The pale ring: N
El palito: C12(s.)
Palm branches: P2
The palms (Les rameaux) E2 F(e.f.) F7 G3 W3 W7
La paloma: C12(s.) E(e.s.) E2 F(e.s.) F7 L4 W3 W7
La pampa y la puna: C12(s.)
Pan ch'iao tao ch'ing: C11(e.ch.)
Panama'm tombe: L2
Panamanian National Anthem: S4(e.s.)
Paper doll: E5
Paper of pins: B3 I L4 L7 <u>I'll give you a paper of pins:</u>
    W5
Papillon: L9(e.f.)
Papir iz doch vays: B7(e.y.) R5(e.y.)
Paradise: C4
O paradise (Who doth not crave for rest, by Barnby) L3 W7
O paradiso (from L'Africaine) C9(e.f.) G4(e.f.)
Paraguayan National Anthem: S4(e.s.)
The pardon came too late: G3
Parigi, o cara: G4(e.i.) S14(e.i.)
Parla: E(e.i.)
Ye parliaments of England: B I I3
Parmi veder le lagrime: G4(i.)
The parsley vine: N
Parting friends: L7
The parting glass: C8
Parting song: W7
Partizaner lid: R5(e.y.)
Partners (Who digs a well) T6
The party at Odd Fellow's hall: G3
Pasli ovce valasi <u>see</u> Shepherds watched their flocks
    by night
Pasol Janko dva voly: D2(e.sl.)
Pass around the good old beer <u>see</u> Drink it down

Pass around your bottle: L8
Pass through this gate <u>see</u> Toryanse
Passengers will please refrain: B8
Passing by: B3 L10 P2 S15 <u>There is a lady sweet and kind</u>: G
Passing through: S11
Passing through Seville <u>see</u> Al pasar por Sevilla
The passionate shepherd to his love: L10
Past three o'clock: R Y
Oj pastiri <u>see</u> Hear, o shepherds
La pastora: C12(s.)
A pastoral (Flocks are sporting, by Carey) S15
Pat Malloy: G3
Pat Malone (forgot that he was dead) A
Pat Maloney's family: G3
Pat Murphy of the Irish Brigade: S5
Pat O'Brien: F3
Pat works on the railway <u>see</u> Paddy works on the (Erie) railroad
Pat-a-cake: W5
Patapan (French carol) B5 S3(e.f.) Z <u>Willie, take your little drum</u>: R
El patio de mi casa: L9(e.s.)
O patria mia (From Aida) G4(e.i.) S14(e.i.)
Patrick Spenser: N
Patrick works on the railroad <u>see</u> Paddy works on the railroad
Patriotic diggers: B9 I I3
Patsy Ory-ory-aye: B6 R2 <u>see also</u> Paddy works on the railroad
Patty Murphy <u>see</u> Paddy Murphy
Paul Bunyan: S2
Paul Jones: C6 D <u>An American frigate</u>: B9
Pauline (I don't love nobody but you) L8
Pauline's romance: S16(e.r.)
Pauvre petite Mamzelle Zizi: V(f.)
The paw-paw patch: L6
Pay day at Coal Creek: L6 L8 S13
Pay me my money down: L6 W

Peace of the river: B6
Peace, perfect peace: L3
Peaceful evening (Beau soir, by Debussy) S15
The peach see El durazno
Peanut song: F5 G3
The peanut stand: B9
The peanut vendor: E5(e.s.)
The pearl fishers: W3
Pearla an bhrollaigh: K(e.ir.) O(e.ir.) The snowy-
   breasted pearl: G3 I2 Z
Peas and the rice: L2
A peasant would his neighbor see see Ain boer wol noar
   zien noaber tou
Pease porridge hot: W5
The peatbog soldiers: B4 F8 H5(e.g.)
Pecos Bill: S2
The pedlar (Russian song) Z
The pedlar's caravan: W6
Peek-a-boo: A E3 F6
Peg and awl: L6
Peg o' my heart: T5
Peggy O'Neil: C4
Pennies from heaven: J2
Pennsylvania polka: T3
A penny a kiss, a penny a hug: T4
Penny serenade: T4
Pentozalis: K(e.gk.)
Ah perche non posso odiarti: G4(e.i.)
Perdikitza: K(e.gk.)
Une perdriole: K(e.f.) V(f.)
O perfect love: L3
The perfect skier: K2
La perica: C12(s.)
El pericon see Every small inch of farm land
La perla: G3(s.)
La pernette se leve: K(e.f.)
Perrine etait servante: B7(e.f.)
The Persian kitty: B6
A personal friend of mine: B6

Peruvian National Anthem: S4(e.s.)
The pesky sarpent see Springfield Mountain
Pesnia o vstrechnom: R4(e.r.)
A petal from a faded rose: T2
Peter Emery: F3
Peter Gray: B4 C C7 I L8
Petit laboureur: K(e.f.)
Le petit mari: L8(e.f.)
Le petit navire: V(f.)
Petticoat Lane: C6 The cambric shirt: F3
Phengaraki mou see Shiny little moon
Philippines National Anthem: F S4(e.s.tg.)
Piacer d'amor: E(e.i.) Plaisir d'amour: B3(e.f.)
   F(e.f.) G3
O piao: L9(e.pr.)
Picayune Butler: S12
Piccaninny mine, good-night: G3
Piccolo! piccolo (from Waltz Dream) W8
Pick a bale of cotton: B B6 L L7 S11
Picket line Priscilla: H5
A picture no artist can paint: F5 F6
The picture that is turned toward the wall: E3 F4 G3
Pie in the sky: L5 L6 The preacher and the slave: D F8
Pierlala: P2
Pieta Signore: E(e.i.)
La Pietade (from Lucia di Lammermoor) G4(e.i.)
Pietoso al par del Nume: G4(e.i.)
The pig and the inebriate: B6
Pigeons see Hato popo
Pilgrim chorus (from Tannhauser) W3 W8
A pilgrim us preceding: H4
The Pilgrims' legacy: J
Pilgrim's melody (Our Israel may say) B
Pili aoao see Dawn in Hawaii
The pinery boy: L6
The Pinta, the Nina, the Santa Marie: S6
Pintor de cannahy: L9
Pioneers, o pioneers: S6
The piper (I had a willow whistle) T6

The piper of Dundee: C8
Pipes, o so sweetly ringing see O ma tendre musette
Pippa's song: T6
The pirate crew: P2
The pirate of the isle: H
The pirate song: I I3
Piri-miri-dictum domini: N
Pity the downtrodden landlord: H5
Pkiaste kopelles, sto choro: K(e.gk.)
La Place Congo: L2
The plains of Illinois: C6
Plaisir d'amour see Piacer d'amor
Planting rice (is never fun) F8 S6 T6
Plantonio: F2
Play, fiddle, play: E5(e.f.)
Play gypsies, dance gypsies: H2
Play on the seashore: S6
Play time: W5
Playmates: F4 G3
Plearaca na Ruarcach: O(e.ir.)
Pleasant are thy courts above: L3
Please go 'way and let me sleep: B2
Please think of me: S9
Pledge me gaily, lady mine: G3
The ploughboy: H5
Ploughing (Czech song) T6
Ploughing song (French) see Petit laboureur
Ploughman's lilt see Loinneog oireamh
Plum pudding: G3
Plymouth town: B8
po' see poor
Po deszczyku, po majowem: P(e.p.)
Po doline: D2(e.sl.)
Pobre cega: L9(e.pr.)
Pobre corazon: C12(s.)
Pochvalen bud pan jezis: D2(e.sl.)
The poco's daughter: G3
Pod Belehradom: D2(e.sl.)
Pod tym nasim okieneckom: D2(e.sl.)

Podkoweczki, dajcie ognia: P(e. p.)
Podmoskovnye vechera: R4(e. r.)
Poem of night: W3
Pognala wolki: P(e. p.)
Poi waka see Canoe song
Poinciana: E5(e. s.)
Pojde do sadu: P(e. p.)
Pojedziemy na low, na low: P(e. p.)
Poker song: G3
Pokochal sie mlodzieniaszek w pannie: P(e. p.)
A Pole was journeying see Jechal jeden Polak
A policeman's lot: G3
Polish lullaby (Lulajze Jezuniu) S3(e. p.)
Polish May song: W6
Polish National Anthem: S4(e. p.)
Poliushko-pole: R4(e. r.) Meadowlands: B4 H5
Pollerita: B7(e. s.)
Polly, put the kettle on: F W5
Polly Williams: L7
Polly-wolly-doodle: B6 E2 E4 F4 F5 F7 G3 L4 L5
Pomalu ja rozbierajcie: P(e. p.)
An poni beag bui: O(e. ir.)
Le pont d'Avignon see Sur le pont d'Avignon
Poor and foreign stranger: C6 see also The wayfaring
    stranger
Ah, poor bird: H5
Poor boy: B6 D I
Poor butterfly: M T8
Poor Ch'iu Hsiang see K'o lien ti Ch'iu Hsiang
The poor countryman: C6
Poor dog Bright: W5
Poor farmer: L6 L8
Poor Howard: W
Poor Juna: C
Poor Lazarus: L L6 L7 L8
Poor little Jesus: B5 L S W
Poor little Mary: G3
Poor little turtle dove: I3
Poor lonesome cowboy: F2 S12

Poor man blues: S13
Poor Mister Morgan: H5
Poor old Joe: H
Poor old man (came riding by) H
Poor Omie: C
Poor Paddy works on the railroad see Paddy works on
  the railroad
Poor Ralpho: T
The poor sailor boy: F3
Poor wandering one (from Pirates of Penzance) F W3 W8
Poor wayfaring stranger see The wayfaring stranger
The poor working girl: E4
Pop! goes the skier: K2
Pop! goes the weasel: B C7 F F4 W5
The Pope (he leads a jolly life) B6 R2
Por un beso de tu boca: C12(s.)
Porgi amor: G4(e.i.)
Porridge time: W5
Portuguese National Anthem: S4(e.pr.)
The Portuguese washerwomen: S8
Las Posadas see Christmas in Mexico
Possente Ftha: S14(e.i.)
The potter and Robin Hood: N
Pour cette cause sainte: G4(e.f.)
Povedal si: D2(e.sl.)
Povedz mi: D2(e.sl.)
The prairie: P2
Praise and thanksgiving: T6(e.g.)
Praise for peace: A3
Praise for water: S6
Praise God from whom all blessings flow see Old
  hundred
O praise Jehovah: H4
Praise, my soul, the king of heaven: L3
O praise the Lord (ye that fear him) T
Praise the Lord, ye heavens adore him: L3
Praise to God in the highest: R
Praise to the Lord: Z
O praise ye the Lord: T6

Praised and exalted be the divine sacrament see Alabado
The praties they grow small see The famine song
Pray Papa: L5
Pray, remember: T
Prayer (from Der Freischutz) W3 W8
Prayer (from Hansel and Gretel) Z
Prayer for airmen: T6
Prayer of thanks (Alsatian song) T6
Prayer of thanksgiving (Dutch song) (Wilt heden nu treden)
    F Thanksgiving prayer: Z We gather together: A3 L3
    We're singing our praises: B(e. d.)
Prayer to the child Jesus (Gebet an den heiligen Christ)
    S3(e. g.)
Preab san ol: O(e. ir.)
The preacher and the bear: E3 F6 G3
The preacher and the slave see Pie in the sky
The precious treasure see An sealbhan seo
Prelet sokol: D2(e. sl.)
Preletel sokol: D2(e. sl.)
Prendi, l'anel ti dono: G4(e. i.)
Pres des remparts de Seville see Seguidilla
The President's proclamation: S5
O press your cheek upon my own see Lehn' deine wang'
    an meine wang'
Pretty baby: T8
Pretty boy Floyd: L6
A pretty fair miss: S7
The pretty girl milking her cow: G3 I2
Pretty girls and the shoemaker see Ninas hermosas
Pretty little miss: L4
Pretty Polly: I I3 L L8
Pretty Saro: B Z
The pretty widow see Senhora viuva
Prevez, prievoznicku: D2(e. sl.)
Pri Dunaju: D2(e. sl.)
Pri Presporku: D2(e. sl.)
Pri Skalici: D2(e. sl.)
Pride of Idaho see Little Dolly Daydream
Pridi ty, suhajko: D2(e. sl.)

The priest and the nuns: H
The Princeton cannon song: R2
Printemps qui commence: G4(e. f.)
Priosun Chluain Meala: O(e. ir.)
El prisionero: K(e. s.)
Prison bound: S13
Prison moan (If I had a-listened what my mother said) L8
Prithee, pretty maiden: B3
Prize song (from Die Meistersinger) see Morgenlicht
    leuchtend
The procession (When the snow has gone away) S6
Proface, welcome, welcome: R3
Prologue (from Pagliacci) see Si puo
O promise me: B F G3 L4
The promised land see Bound for the promised land
Proshchai radost: B7(e. r.) R4(e. r.)
Provozhane: R4(e. r.)
Przed dom przyjechali: P(e. p.)
Przelecial-ci slowiczek, slowiczek: P(e. p.)
Przy wielkiem zamku: P(e. p.)
Przylecieli tak sliczni anieli: P(e. p.)
Przywioze z miasteczka: P(e. p.)
Psalm 3: I
Psyche (by Paladilhe) S15
Ptsach bazemer: B7(e. h.)
Pua sadinia see Gardenia flower
Puff: W6
Pulse of my heart see Cuisle mo chroi
Punto guanacasteco: C12(s.)
La pupusera: C12(s.)
Pura siccome un angelo: G4(e. i.) S14(e. i.)
Purple bamboo see Tzu chu tiao
Pussy cat, pussy cat: F W5
Put it on the ground: H5
Put on a bonnet with a red cross on it: F5
Put on your old grey bonnet: T7
Put the old man to sleep: L6(e. ga.)
Putney hymn: D
Putting on the style: C6 S11

Q

The Quaker's courtship: L6
The Quaker's wife sat down to bake: W5
Quando ero paggio: G4(i.)
Quando m'en vo': G4(e.i.)
Quantrell: L7
Quartermaster Corps: B6
Qu'avez-vous, oui, belle blonde: L8(e.f.)
Que bonita bandera: S11(s.)
Que bonita eres: L9(e.s.)
Que lejos estoy: Z(e.s.)
Que ne suis-je la fougere: B3(e.f.)
Queen Eleanor's confession: N
The queen's garden: L6
Queer little cradles: S6
Quel suon, quelle preci: G4(e.i.)
Quell' uomo al fiero aspetto: G4(e.i.)
Quelle est cette odeur agreable see Whence is that goodly
    fragrance
Quest' assisa (from Aida) G4(e.i.)
Questa o quella: C9(e.i.) E(e.i.) G4(i.)
Qui sola, vergin rosa see The last rose of summer
Quid petis o fili: G2(e.l.)
Quiereme mucho: C12(s.) Yours: E5(e.s.)
The quilting party: B F4 F5 F6 W3 Aunt Dinah's
    quilting party: G3 R2 Z Seeing Nellie home: B6 E2
Quisiera: C12(s.)
Quoc thieu Viet-Nam: S4(e.an.)
Quodlibet see Orchestra song
Quoth Roger to Nelly: T

R

Rabbit-foot blues: S13
Rabbit hash: L7
Rabbits (Japanese song) see Usagi
Rabble soldier see My horses ain't hungry

The races of Ballyhooly see Raiseanna bhaile atha ula
Rachel, quand du Seigneur: G4(f.)
Ragged but right: B6
The raggle taggle gypsies: I3 S7 S12 The wraggle taggle
    gypsies: B4 C3 K
Raghupati: W(hn.)
Railroad Bill: L6 L7
The Railroad Corral: D G3 L4 L6
A railroader for me: L6
The rain sings a song: S6
The "Rainbow": C6
Raindrops falling gently in May see Po deszczyku, po
    majowem
The raindrops' song: W5
A rainy night in Rio: S9
Raise a ruckus tonight: L L2 L7
Raiseanna bhaile atha ula: O(e.ir.)
Ral la la la (from Hansel and Gretel) G4(e.g.)
Rally round the flag: F5
The ram of Darby see The Darby ram
The rambling boy: L6
Les rameaux see The palms
Ramon del alma mia: L9(e.s.)
Ramona: C4
El rancho grande see Alla en el rancho grande
The ransomed maiden see Sto s'ono cuje
The ransomed soldier see Hej! zabujaly biale labedzie
Le ranz des vaches: K(e.f.)
Raskinulos more shiroko: R4(e.r.)
Raslo drvo: K(e.sc.)
Rat in the rice sack see Zui, zui, zukorobashi
The Rattin family: B6
Rattle snake see Springfield Mountain
Rattlesnake (What makes your teeth so white) L6
Re dell' abisso affrettati: G4(e.i.)
Ready when the great day comes: B6
The reaper on the plain: J
Reason I stay on job so long: L7
Der rebe elimelech: B7(e.y.)

The rebel soldier: S5
The rebel's escape: C
Recitar (from Pagliacci) <u>see</u> Vesti la giubba
Recondita armonia (from Tosca) C9(e.i.) G4(i.)
The red and blue (Pennsylvania college song) R2
Red beans <u>see</u> Butsu, butsu mame
Red birds ski club song: K2
Red Cross store: S13
The red flag: F8
The red-haired man's wife <u>see</u> Bean an fhir ruaidh
The red herring: C7
Red iron ore: L6 L7
The red light saloon: B8
Red, red roses: I3
The Red River shore: C L6
Red River Valley: B4 B6 C D E2 F4 F5 F7 G3 I3 L
    L4 P2 R2 S2 W3 Z
The red rosebud <u>see</u> En yndig og frydefuld sommertid
The red, white and blue <u>see</u> Columbia, the gem of the
    ocean
The reek and the rambling blade: L8
Regimental polka <u>see</u> Gvardeiskaia polka
Regina celi, letare: R3
Regnava nel silenzio: G4(e.i.)
The regular army, O: L5 L6
A regular royal queen: G3
Rejoice in love we know and share: S6
Rejoice my friends (the Lord is king) S
Rejoice, rejoice, ye wedding guests <u>see</u> Ermuntert euch,
    ihr frommen
Rejoice, ye pure in heart: L3
Remember me?: C5
Remember, o thou man: G2
Remember thy creator: W7
Remember when: E5
Remon: D(e.cr.) L7(cr.)
Renaldine: F3
The repentance of John Hoare <u>see</u> Aithri Sheain de Hora
Rescue the perishing: A3

Rest sweet nymphs: G
The resurrected sweetheart: N
The resurrection: C6
Le retour du marin: V(f.)
Retrospect: F3
Reuben (When old Reuben left home) L6
Reuben and Rachel: E3 L5
Reuben James: H5 S11 The sinking of the Reuben James:
    W
Reuben Ranzo: H
Le reve (from Manon) C9(e.f.)
The revellers see Vasovalska
Reverie interrompue see Broken reverie
Revive us again: A3
The rhinossorheeagus: C7
Rhyfelgyrch gwyr Harlech see Men of Harlech
The rhyme of the chivalrous shark: B6
Rice planting see Taue
Rice pudding see Arroz con leche
Rich and rare were the gems she wore: C3 G3
Rich gal, poor gal: B6
The rich man and the poor man: F8 H5
The rich old lady: L6 L8
Richmond is a hard road to travel: S5
The riddle song: B4 B6 I L10 N R2 S2 S11 I gave my
    love a cherry: G3 L4 see also I will give my love an
    apple
Ride a cock-horse to Banbury Cross: F W5
Ride on, ride on in majesty: L3
Riding a raid: S5
Riding in a buggy: L6
Riding in the morning: Z
Riding on a donkey: H Donkey riding: P2
Riding song (Draw near, young men, and learn from me)
    F5
The riflemen's song at Bennington: I I3
Rig-a-jig: G3
Rig-jag-jig-jag: G3
Riley (Riley, where are you) L6

Ring around a rosy: W5
Ring, bells, ring: S6
The ring dang doo: B8
Ring out, wild bells: L3 R S6 Z
Ring the banjo: F4 F7 W3
Rio Grande: B4 B6 C D E4 G3 H L4 L7 Z
   Away Rio: I
The Rio Grande (is flowing, and the starry skies are
   bright) F5
Rio rio: C12(s.) Flowing river: Z(e. s.)
A ripping trip: I I3
Riqui, riqui, riquirran: L9(e. s.)
Rise and stretch: L2
Rise, arise (the dawn is here) S6
Rise, flowers, rise: S6
Rise, my soul, and stretch thy wings: L3
Rise, rise, thou merry lark (Codiad yr hedydd) C8(e. w.)
Rise up, brothers see Auf, ihr brieder
Rise up, gentlemen see Sculati-va
Rise up, o men of God: A3
Rise up, shepherd, and follow: B4 B5 L6 S S3
The rising of the moon: B7 C8
Rising star, shine over the steeple see Zeszla gwiazdka
   nad koscolkiem
The rising sun blues see House of the rising sun
Ritorna vincitor see E l'amor mio
La rivedra: G4(e. i.)
The river in the pines: L6
Ro ro relte: K(e. n.)
Road like brown ribbon: S6
The road to the isles: B6 C8
Roar, lion roar: R2
Robin: I
Robin Adair: B C8 G3 W3 W7
Robin and John: N
A robin, gentle robin: G2
Robin Hood and Arthur O'Bland: L6 S7
Robin Hood and the old maid: N
Robin Hood and the twenty pounds of gold: N

Robin Hood's dying: N
Robin loves me (Robin m'aime) B4
Robin redbreast (Robin goch) C8(e.w.)
Robin, robin (Dear little robin perched up in a tree) W6
Robinson Crusoe: W6
Rock-a-bye, baby (on the tree top) F5 F6 W5
Rock-a my soul: B4 L2
Rock about, my Saro Jane: L L6
The Rock Island Line (As I 'rived in St. Louis on April
    the tenth) C6
The Rock Island Line (it's a mighty good road) L2 W
Rock of ages (cleft for me) A3 B4 E2 F L3 W3 W4 W7
Rock of ages, let our song: S6 Hanukkah hymn: L4
Rocked in the cradle of the deep: E2 F5 G3 L4 W3 W7
Rocking see Little Jesus, sweetly sleep
Rocking song (Czech carol) see Hajej, nynej, jezisku
Roeh veroah see Shepherd and shepherdess
Le Roi d'Yvetot: V(f.)
Roisin dubh: O(e.ir.)
Roll, Alabama, roll: S5
Roll, Jordan, roll: B E2 F5 F7 G3 L4 L6 L8 W3
Roll on, buddy: L6
Roll on, Columbia: L6
Roll on, silver moon: E2 F6 G3 W3
Roll out! heave that cotton: C
Roll the cotton down: H see also Lowlands and Mobile
    Bay
Roll the union on: F8 H5
Roll your leg over: B8
Rolling down the mountain: B8
Rolling down to old Maui: H
Rolling home: H I I3
Rolling in the dew: C6
The rolling stone: C6 G3 The Wisconsin emigrant's
    song: F3
Rolly trudum see Lolly-too-dum
Romance de mi destino: C12(s.)
Romany life: G3
The Romish lady: L8

A rookie's lament: L5 L7 <u>see also</u> I don't want no more
  army
Root, hog, or die: L6
Rory O'More: E2
Rosa (let us be dancing) D(e.d.)
Rosa Lee: G3
La rosa y el clavel: C12(s.)
Rosalie: G3
Rosalie, the prairie flower: G3
The rosary: B2 F(e.f.g.) G3
The rose (Canadian song) Z
The rose (German song) Y
Rose Connelly <u>see</u> Down in the willow garden
The Rose of Alabama: C
The Rose of Tralee: B3 F7 G3 L4 W3
Rose, rose (shall I ever see thee red) Z
A rose with a broken stem: F4 F6
Roseas flores d'alvorada: C12(pr.)
Roselil: Z
The rose's age: Z
Rosie: L7
Rosin the beau <u>see</u> Old Rosin the beau
Rotation blues: S13
Round and round the picket line: H5
Round and round the village: W5
Round of the oats: T6
Round the Bay of Mexico: L8
Round the Lord in glory seated: L3
Round the mulberry bush: E2
Round the world (German song) T6
Roustabout holler: L8
The roving gambler: D L7
The roving kind: W
The roving pedlar: C6
Row, bullies, row: L6
Row de dow de dunfer: C7
Row, row, row your boat: B6 E3 R2 T
The Rowan County crew: L8
O Rowan tree: C8

The royal banners forward go: L3
Rozhinkes mit mandlen: B7(e. y.)
Ruchot hayam: R5(e. h.)
Rue (Irish song) B7
Rugged mountain slopes see Blazhena stara-planina
Rule, Britannia: G3
Rumanian National Anthem: S4(e. rm.)
Rumors are flying: J2
Rumsty-ho: G3
Run along, you little dogies: L8 see also Get along,
    little dogies
Run, nigger, run: L7
Running bear: T2
Rurey Bain: N
A Russian landscape: T6
Russian National Anthem: S4(e. r.)
Rusty Jiggs and Sandy Sam: L5
Rye whiskey: D L L5 L7 S11 Clinch Mountain: C7
    Way up on Clinch Mountain: S12 see also Jack of
    Diamonds

S

Sa huo k'ei lei: C11(e. ch.)
Sacramento: B D I L (On) the banks of the
    Sacramento: C C10 E4 H
O sacred head: A3 L3
Sad news from home: J
Sadla dole: D2(e. sl.)
Saeynu: W(h.)
Safely through another week: L3
Sag bist als schutzgeist du: C9(e. g.)
Sah ein knab' ein roslein stehn: G3(g.) Hedge rose: F7
    Once I saw a sweetbriar rose: W6
Said I to myself, said I: G3
Said Sir John to his lady: T
Sail along, silvery moon: J2
Sail on, o ship of state: S6

The sail-boat (upon our little lake) W6
Sailing in the boat: L6
Sailing on the sea: B9
Sailing, sailing (over the bounding main) B6 E2 G3 L4
    P2 R2 W7
The sailor cut down in his prime: L6
The sailor's alphabet: H
The sailor's bride: F3
The sailor's grave: I3 J
The sailor's return: I3
St. James infirmary: B6 D
St. John's River: I3
St. Jovite Ski Club song: K2
St. Louis blues: B
St. Patrick was a gentleman: G3
St. Patrick's Day in the morning: E2 G3
Saint Stephen: Y
St. Valentine's Day: T6
Sainte nuit: V(f.)
The saint's delight: D
The saints go marching in see When the saints go
    marching in
Sairy Ann see Sally Ann
Sakura sakura: W2(e.ja.)
Salamagundi: G3
Salangadou: D L7(e.cr.)
Sally Ann: C7 L6 S11
Sally Brown: H L6
Sally go round the sunshine: L8
Sally Goodin: C7 L6
Sally in our alley: B3 E2 F7 W3
Salten y ballen: K(e.f.ct.)
Salut! demeure chaste et pure: G4(e.f.) S14(e.f.)
The salutation of the angel: R3
El Salvador National Anthem: S4(e.s.)
Salvator mundi (by Tallis) G2(e.l.)
Sam Bass: L L7
Sam Hall: B6 B8 C7 L7 R2
Sambo's right to be killed: S5

The same the whole world over see It's the same the
    whole world over
Samoa: T6
Samson (Delilah was a woman fine and fair) L6 L8
San Marino National Anthem: S4(e. i.)
San min chu i: S4(e. ch.)
El San Pedro: C12(s.)
San Sereni: L9(e. s.)
Sancta Maria (by Dunstable) G2(e. l.)
O sanctissima: B4(e. l.) B5 O thou joyful day: L3(e. l.)
    S3(e. l.) W3 W8
Sanctus (by Henry IV) G2(e. l.)
The sandman (When the toys are growing weary) F5
The sandman comes: W5
Sandmannchen see The little sandman
Sandy land: L7
Sandy McNab: T
Sano duso: B7(e. j.) W(e. j.)
Sanrasoen phra barami: S4(e. Thai)
Sans souci (Columbia college song) R2
Santa Ana see Santy Anna
Santa Lucia: B4 E(e. i.) F F7(e. i.) G3 L4 R2 W3 W7
Santa Maria, my joy, my pride: G3
Santa Marta: C12(s.)
Santo San Juanito: Z(e. s.)
Santy (sea chantey) H see also Santy Anna
Santy Anna: B H I3 L L6 L8
An saol meallta: O(e. ir.)
Sap is running see Z brezoveho dreva
Saper vorreste: G4(e. i.)
Sarah Jane's tea-party: W6
Saranta pallikaria: K(e. gk.)
Satan's kingdom: L6
Saturday night (and Sunday too, pretty gals on my mind)
    L6
Sauerkraut see Sourkraut
Save your sorrow (for tomorrow) T3
Savin Rock: C7
Saviour, again to the dear name: L3

Saviour, breathe an evening blessing: L3
Saviour, like a shepherd lead us: A3 L3
Saviour, teach me, day by day: W4
Saviour, when in dust to thee: L3
The saviour's work: S3
The sawyer see Chanson des scieurs de long
Say "au revoir" but not "good-bye": A B3 E3 F5 F6
    F7 G3 W3
Say "si si": E5(e.s.)
Say, what shall my song be tonight: F5
The scabs crawl in: F8 H5
Scanlan's rose song: F5 F6
Scarborough fair: B4
The scare-crow: W6
The scarlet sarafan: C3 W7
Scenes of Wusih see Vu Si Ching
Scenes that are brightest: W8
Schlaf, kindchen, schlaf: G3(g.) see also Schlof,
    bobbeli, schlof
Schlof, bobbeli, schlof: D(e.pd.) H4(e.pd.)
Die schnitzelbank: B6(g.) H4(e.pd.)
Schoon lief, hoe ligt gij hier: K(e.fl.)
Schpinn, schpinn see Spinn, spinn
Schussing through the night: K2
Schuylkill rowing song: C
Schwab, Schwab: H5
Schy-heil: K2(e.ss.)
Scintille, diamant: C9(e.f.) G4(f.)
Scotch lullaby: W5
Scotland's burning: B6 R2
Scots wha hae with Wallace bled: B7 C8 G3
Sculati-va: K(e.rm.)
S'dremlen feygl oyf di tsvaygn: R5(e.y.)
Se (Italian song) E(e.i.)
Se acaso madama la notte ti chiama: G4(e.i.)
Se nao me amas, o mulher: G3(pr.)
Se tu m'ami see If thou love me
Se ug'di: R5(e.h.)
Se vuol ballare: G4(e.i.)

The sea (by MacDowell) S15
An sealbhan seo: O(e. ir.)
Sean o Duir a' ghleanna: O(e. ir.) John O'Dwyer of the
  glen: C8
An seanduine: O(e. ir.)
Seanduine Chill Chocain: O(e. ir.)
Searching for lambs: K
Secret love: S8
See, amid the winter's snow: R Y
See my wagon, it's full-laden: B(e. d.)
See-saw (Now we're up or down) W7
See-saw Margery Daw: F7 W5
See, the conqueror mounts in triumph: L3
See the Mazur, hey the Mazur see Hop! hop! dzis, dzis
  za kominem
Seed I planted see Zasadil som fialenku
Seeds we bring: T6
Seeing Nellie home see The quilting party
Seguidilla (from Carmen: S14(e. f.) Pres des remparts
  de Seville: G4(e. f.)
Seguir vegg' io: G4(e. i.)
Sel bych rad k Betlemu see To Bethlehem I would go
The self-banished: B3
Sempre libera (from La Traviata) E(e. i.) G4(e. i.)
  S14(e. i.)
Senhora of San Benito: L2
Senhora viuva: L9(e. pr.)
Sept ans sur mer: L8(e. f.)
September in the rain: C5
Serdtse see Kak mnogo devushek khoroshikh
Serenade (by Drigo) E2 F7 W3
Serenade (from Faust) C9(e. f.) Sing, smile, slumber:
  S15
Serenade (by Schubert) E2 F(e. g.) F7 W3
Serenade (from Die Fledermaus) G3
Serenade of the roses: E(e. i.) W3
The serenaders (Bright the moon) P2
Serenata (En medio de esta noche) C12(s.)
La serenata (by Braga) E(e. i.)

Serenata d' 'e rose see Serenade of the roses
Serenata Napolitana: E(e. i.) G3(i.)
The sergeant: B8
Sergeant McGee of the N. Y. M. P. : G3
Ye servants of God, your master proclaim: L3
Set down, servant: L L7 S2
The seven blessings of Mary see The seven joys of Mary
The seven daughters: L2
Seven great towns of Greece: T
The seven joys of Christmas: S3
The seven joys of Mary: B4 I R S3 Y The joys of Mary:
    F3 The (seven) blessings of Mary: L6 S W
Seven lonely days: E5
Seven years at sea see Sept ans sur mer
Seventeen come Sunday see I'm seventeen come Sunday
77 Sunset Strip: S8
Sevivon, ssov, ssov, ssov: B5
Sextette (from Lucia di Lammermoor) see Chi mi frena
Sha! shtil: B7(e. y.) R5(e. y.)
Shabbat hamalka: R5(e. h.)
Shabes beyn Hashmoshes: R5(e. y.)
Shabes licht un Shabes lompn: R5(e. y.)
Shack bully holler: L7
Shadow waltz: C5
Shadows: W3
The shadows of the evening hours: L3
Shady grove: L6
The shady old camp: I I3
Shaker funeral hymn: L6
Shall we gather at the river: A3 B4 L3
Shallow Brown: H
Shalom havayreem: S6(h.) Shalom chaverim: W(e. h.)
Shamrock, thistle and rose: G3
Shan van Voght: I2
Shanadar: K
Shannon and Chesapeake: H
The shanty-boy and the farmer's son: L7
A shantyman's life: C C6 C10 D E4
Shawl weaver's song: T6

Shawnee town: C10
She drove her oxen see Pognala wolki
She is more to be pitied than censured: A B2 B6 E3 F4
    F6 G3 R2
She may be somebody's mother: G3
She may have seen better days: E3 F4 F6 G3
She moved through the fair: B7 C8
She never told her love (by Haydn) S15
She perished in the snow: C6
She promised to meet me: B6
She was bred in old Kentucky: B
She was happy till she met you: A E3 F5 F6 G3
She wore a yellow ribbon see Around her neck
The sheep and the boy: W6
She'll be coming round the mountain: B4 E2 F F4 F5
    F6 F7 G3 L4 L6 M P2 R2 W3
She'll be skiing down the mountain: K2
She'll do it: B8
Shenandoah: B4 B6 D F4 H I I3 L L4 L6 L7 R2
    S11 Z (Across) the wide Missouri: C G3
Shepherd and shepherdess (Roeh veroah) B3(e.h.)
Shepherd, shepherd (where'd you leave your lambs) S
Shepherd, whence comest thou see D'ou viens-tu, bergere
The shepherdess (Mexican song) L2
The shepherd's daughter and the king: N
Shepherds expecting the break of day see Tuszac
    pasterze ze dzien blisko
Shepherds, hark see Weihnachtslied
Shepherds in Judea: S
Shepherds, rejoice, lift up your eyes: S
Shepherds watched their flocks by night (Pasli ovce
    valasi) S3(e.c.)
She's going to be my wife see Vassar hygiene song
She's gone, let her go see Let her go
She's my sweetheart: P2
Shifting, whispering sands: T2
Shine like a star in the morning: S
Shine on: D
"Shinning" on the street: J

Shiny little moon (Phengaraki mou) T6(e.gk.)
A ship a-sailing: C10
The ship Lord Wolseley: H
The ship of Zion: B C6
The ship on fire: J
The ship Titanic see Titanic
The ship's carpenter: C6
Shir eres: R5(e.h.)
Shir ha-emek: R5(e.h.)
Shir ha-palmach: R5(e.h.)
Shir hag'ula see Yom l'yabasha
Shir hakvish: R5(e.h.)
Shir la-negev: R5(e.h.)
The shirt of lace: N
Shlof mayn kind, shlof keseyder: R5(e.y.)
Shlof mayn zun: R5(e.y.)
The shoemaker: D W7
Shoes squeak see Kutsu ga naru
Shoo fly, don't bother me: B F4 F5 F6 L5 R2
Shoo, shoo, barata: L2
Shoo, shoo, shoo-lye: L7
Shool: G3 L5
Shoot the buffalo: D L L7 see also We'll hunt the buffalo
Shortening bread: B6 F4 G3 L2 L5 L6 L7 R2
Shorty George: L L7 S13
S'hot gelebt mit undz a chaver: R5(e.y.)
Shot my pistol in the heart of town: L7
Should the Volga's banks be flooded see Esli Volga
    razoletsia
Shout the glad tidings: L3 S3
Shpilt-zhe mir dem nayem sher: R5(e.y.)
Shto ne byelaya: K(e.r.)
Shu-alim m'yal'lim: R5(e.h.)
The shucking of the corn: B B9 Z
Shucking sugar blues: S13
Shule agra: B
Shule aroon: C8(e.ga.)
Si algun cadete: L9(e.s.)
Si and I: C7

Ah si, ben mio (from Il Trovatore) G4(e. i.)
Si, fugiam da questa mura: G4(e. i.)
Si me quieres escribir: W(e. s.)
Si, pel ciel (from Otello) G4(e. i.)
Si puo (from Pagliacci) G4(e. i.) S14(e. i.)
Oj siadaj, siadaj, moje kochanie: P(e. p.)
Sichelein rauschen: K(e. g.)
Siciliana (from Cavalleria Rusticana) W3
The sidewalks of New York: F F7 G3 P2
Siedze ja w oknie: P(e. p.)
The siege of Plattsburg: L7
Siegmund's love song (from Die Walkure) C9(e. g.)
Sierra Sue: T3
Signor MacStinger, the baritone singer: G3
Sigurd and Hamling see Kong Diderik og Hans Kaemper
Sigurd and the dragon see Sjurdar kavedi i
Sihote, zelene sihote: D2(e. sl.)
Silent night: A3 B4 B5 C2(e. g.) E2 F G3 L3(e. g.)
    L4 P2 R R2 S3(e. g.) S6 W3 Y
The silent rose: G3
Silently see Tishina
Silently falling snow: W6
Silicosis blues: S13
Silly boy, tis full moon: G
A silver dollar: B6 R2
Silver Jack: L6
The silver sea: P2
The silver Shenandoah: T3
The silver swan: S15 T
Silver threads among the gold: B E2 F F5 F6 F7 G3
    L4 M W3
The silvery Rio Grande: C
Simchu na: R5(e. h.)
Simon the cellarer: G3
Simple little Nancy Brown: C6 C7
Simple Simon: E2 F W5
Since first I saw your face: G
Since McManus goes down to the track: G3
Since others do so much for me: S6

Since time so kind: T

Since without thee we do no good: L3

The sinful maiden: N

Sing-a-lamb: S

Sing-a-ling-a-ling: P2

Sing a song of cities: B6

Sing a song of sixpence: F W5

Sing a song of sunbeams: J2

Sing again that sweet refrain: E3 F4 F5 F6

Sing, baby, sing: E5

Sing, gaily sing: W7

O sing God's praises in winter too: W7

Sing hallelu (Down in a valley) S

O sing of the love of John see Chantons les amours de
    Jean

Sing! sing! sing! (Brazilian children's song) L2

Sing, smile, slumber see Serenade (from Faust)

Sing this grave and simple strain: T

Sing to the Lord of harvest: L3

Sing we now merrily: G

Sing we now the life within us: Z

Sing with thy mouth: T

Sing you now after me: T

Sing your song see Spievajze si

Sing your way home: P2

Het singelshuis: K(e. fl.)

Singing a vagabond song: J2

Singing at the hallway door: G3

Singing for Jesus: W7

The singing hills: J2

Singing in the land: S

Singing in the rain (children's song) W6

The single girl see I wish I was a single girl

Sink the Bismarck: T2

The sinking of the Reuben James see Reuben James

The sinking of the Titanic see Titanic

Sinner man: W

Sinner, please don't let this harvest pass: S12

Sin's reward: N

Sioux Indians: I I3
Sir Gaunie and the witch: N
Sir Lionel: N
Sir Patrick Spens: N
Sir Peter Parker: I I3
Sis Joe: L8
Sister May: W6
Sister Ruth: W6
Sister, thou wast mild and lovely: S12
Sistern and brethren: D
Sit down, servant see Set down, servant
Sit down, sister: B4
Sitting by the window: T4
Sitting on a rail: G3
Six little snails: W5
Sixteen tons: F8 L6
Sixty-six highway blues: S13
Sjurdar kvaedi i: K(e. dn.)
Skalicka veza: D2(e. sl.)
Skating on the ice: G3
Skating song: J
Ski heil see Schy-heil
Ski-patrol toboggan: B6
Ski, ski, ski: B6 Skier's whiffenpoof: K2
Ski slow, o ski patrol: K2
Ski-time in Sun Valley see When it's ski-time
Skier Jake: K2
A skier one day: B6
Skier's requiem: B6 K2
Skier's whiffenpoof see Ski, ski, ski
Skillet good and greasy: S13
Skip to my Lou: B3 C7 D E4 H4 I I3 L L4 L7 S11
Skirts: S9
Skladej, andulko, cepeni: K(e. c.)
Skoda ta: D2(e. sl.)
Skye boat song: B4 B6 C8 L4
Slan chun Carraig an Eide: O(e. ir.)
Slan le Maigh: O(e. ir.)
Slapander-gosheka: H

The slave (L'esclave, by Lalo) S15
Slavery chain: D H5 S5
Sledgehammer see Dubinushka
Sleep, baby, sleep: E3 F7 G3 L3
Sleep, my little Jesus: L3 S3
Sleep, my saviour, sleep: S3
Sleep, my sweet baby (from Il Trovatore) W5
Sleep, o holy child of mine (Dormi, dormi, o bel bambin)
    S3(e. i.)
Sleep, o sleep: W5
Sleep of the infant Jesus (Le sommeil de l'enfant Jesus)
    Z(e. f.)
Sleep, sleep, my darling (French lullaby) W5
Sleepers wake: A3 Y
Sleepy time gal: C4
The sleigh song: W5
The slender mountain ash see Tonkaia riabina
Sliczne gwozdziki: P(e. p.)
Slide, Kelly, slide: F4
Sloma krytej, w niskiej chatce: P(e. p.)
Sluchaj chlopcze, masz mnie kochac: P(e. p.)
Slumber song (by Kucken) W5
Slumber song (by Gretchaninoff) S15
The small black rose see Roisin dubh
The smart schoolboy: N
Smile praises, o sky: S6
Smiles (There are smiles that make us happy) M T8
Smiling through: T8
Smoke! smoke! smoke! (that cigarette) T2
Smoky Mountain see On top of Old Smoky
Snagtooth Sal: L7
Snaidhm an ghra: O(e. ir.)
The snail see Dendenmushi
Snow flurries see Vdol po ulitse metelitsa metet
The snow man: W6
The snow storm: J
The snow white bird see Daar was een sneeuwwit
    vogeltje
Snowflakes are falling: S6

The snowy-breasted pearl see Pearla an bhrollaigh
Snyezhnaya kolibellnaya: B7(e. r.)
So anch' io la virtu magica: G4(e. i.)
So beauty on the waters stood: G
So ben che difforme: G4(e.i.)
So handy, my boys, so handy: H
So leb denn wohl, du stilles haus: G3(g.)
So long: T4
So long, it's been good to know you: B7 F8 H5 S11 W
So many white dresses see Tanto vestido blanco
Ah! so pure (from Martha) see M'appari tutt' amor
So quick, so hot, so mad: G
So, so, leave off this last lamenting kiss: G
So statt' a l'ortu: K(e.i.)
Soaking hemp see Maca dievca konope
The society upon the Stanislow: B6
The soft deal board see An clar bog deil
Soft music is stealing: W7
Softly and tenderly: A3
Softly now the light of day: F F7 L3
El sol y la luna: K(e. s.)
Sola perduta: G4(e.i.)
The soldier and his lady: N
Soldier boy (children's song) W5
Soldier boy (one kiss before you go) F5
Soldier, soldier, will you marry me: B L10 R2 S2 W5
Soldier song (A dapple grey horse and a bright shiny gun)
    W6
Soldiers' chorus (from Faust) see Gloire immortelle
Soldiers' chorus (from Il Trovatore) see Concerto
    militare
The soldier's farewell: G3
Soldiers field (Harvard college song) R2
The soldier's life: B9
Soldiers of Christ, arise: L3
The soldiers of the queen: G3
A soldier's song see Amhran na bhfiann
O sole mio: E(e.i.) E2 F(e.i.) F7 W3 W7
Soleares: B7(e.s.)

Solenne in quest' ora: G4(i.)
Solidarity forever: F8 H5 S11
Solo profugo: G4(e.i.)
Solomon Levi: E2 L5
Solovey <u>see</u> Visota li, visota podnebesnaya
Some day (I know not when the day shall be) W3
Some day I'll wander back again: E3
Some folks: F4 P2
Some say that true love is a pleasure: G3
Some Sunday morning: H3 S9
Somebody (Somebody's tall and handsome) S12
Somebody else is taking my place: T3
Somebody loves me (How do I know) G3
Somebody's darling: S5
Somebody's knocking at your door: E2 G3 L2 L4
Somebody's waiting for me: F6
Something to remember you by: C5 H2
Sometime (to every lonely one) S8
Sometimes I feel like a motherless child: C12 F L L4
    S6 S11
Sometimes I'm happy: H2
Le sommeil de l'enfant Jesus <u>see</u> Sleep of the infant Jesus
Son, come tell to me <u>see</u> Svend i rosensgaard
Son of a gambolier: G3 R2
The Son of God goes forth to war: A3 L3
Son pochi fiori: G4(e.i.)
Sonata (my sonata, I hear your haunting theme) J2
Song for a little house: S6
Song of a thousand years: F5
The song of all songs: J
A song of India (by Rimsky Korsakoff) E2 F7 W3
    Chant hindou: C9(e.f.)
A song of Jefferson and the common man: S6
The song of lies <u>see</u> Amhran na mbreag
Song of the bells: P2 W5
Song of the carbine: G3
Song of the fishes <u>see</u> The Boston come-all-ye
Song of the French partisan: H5(e.f.)
Song of the golden corn: L9 S6

Song of the great wall: B4
Song of the guaranteed wage: F8
Song of the hoe see Ch'u t'ou ko
Song of the islands (Na lei o Hawaii) E5(e. hw.) P2
Song of the Kansas emigrants: C
Song of the moon: W6
Song of the pearl fishers: W3
Song of the pennies: H5
Song of the plumber: G3
Song of the soldiers (from Il Trovatore) see Concerto
   militare
Song of the South: J2
The song of the Vermonters: F3
Song of the Volga boatmen: E2 R4(e. r.) W3 Volga boat
   song: F7
A song to sing (I have good right) R3(e. l.)
Song to the flag (wave, wave, wave) F5
Songs I sing see Spievanky
Songs my mother taught me (Als die alte mutter) E2
   F7(e. g.) G3 S15 W3 W8
O sons and daughters, let us sing: L3
Soon I will be done: L6
Soon one morning death come creeping: L L8
Sooner or later: J2
Sophie was craving berries ripe see Chcialo sie zosi
   jagodek
Sorghum syrup: L6
Sorry am I see Skoda ta
Sospan vach see The little saucepan
Soumis au silence: G4(f.)
Sound off: L6
Sound the battle cry: L3
Sound the fire alarm: A2
Sounds of the singing school: T
Sounds that make us glad: T6
Soup song (All you little rookies) F5 F8 H5
Sourkraut: L5
Sourwood Mountain: D I I3 L L4 L5 L7 S2 W9 Z
   Hey dum diddle um day: C7

Sous le dome epais: C9(e.f.)
South America, take it away: S9
South American way: H3
South Australia (is my native land) H
South sea island magic: J2
South wind see A ghaoth andeas
A southerly wind: T
Southern memories see In the evening by the moonlight
The Southern soldier: S5
The Southern soldier boy: J S5
Souvenir (The world has gone to rest) E2
The sow took the measles: I L6
The spacious firmament on high: F L3 S6
La spagnola: E(e.i.)
The Spanish cavalier: E2 F4 F5 F6 F7 G3 W3
The Spanish girl see La spagnola
The Spanish guitar: G3
Spanish is the loving tongue: B6
Spanish Johnny: L7
The Spanish ladies: B B9 L4
Spanish proverb: G3
Spargi d'amaro pianto: G4(e.i.)
The sparrow on the tree: W6
Sparrows' music school see Suzume no gakko
An spealadoir: O(e.ir.)
The spider and the fly: A F6 W6
Spievaj si, slavicku: D2(e.sl.)
Spievajze si: D2(e.sl.)
Spievanky: D2(e.sl.)
Spiewam wesol juz od rana: P(e.p.)
Spin, sevivon see Sevivon, ssov, ssov, ssov
Spinn, spinn: K(e.g.) Schpinn, schpinn: H4(e.pd.)
The spinner see La filadora
Spinning sisters hymn: H4
Spirit divine, attend our prayers: L3
Spirit of God, descend upon my heart: L3
Spirit of man, ascend thy throne: S6
O spirit sweet of summer time: Z
Spirito gentil: G4(e.i.)

The spiritual railway: F3
Splendid are the heavens: T6
Splendor of the morning sunlight: S6
The sporting bachelors: L
The sporting cowboy: L8
Sporting life blues: S13
La sposa di Beltramo: K(e. i.)
A spotless rose: R
Spring (Swedish song) Z
Spring carol: B9
Spring! gentle spring: W6
Spring has now unwrapped the flowers: S6
Spring song (Japanese) see Haru ga kita
Spring tidings see Ch'un hsin
Springfield Mountain: D F3 L L6 On Springfield
    Mountain: B6 I I3 The pesky sarpent: B Rattle
    snake: L7
Spring's message: W6
The springtime: W6
Squaws along the Yukon: T2
Squilli echeggi la tromba see Concerto militare
The squire of great renown: B8
The squirrel loves a pleasant chase: W6
Sredi doliny rovnyia: R4(e. r.)
Stagolee: L6 L7 S11
Stand by your glasses: G3 L6
Stand Columbia: R2
Stand to your glasses see Stand by your glasses
Stand up, stand up for Jesus: A3 B4 F L3
Standing in the need of prayer see It's a me, o Lord
Stands a duck see Kacer na doline
Star festival see Tanabata
Star in the East see Brightest and best of the sons of
    morning
Star light, star bright (from Wizard of the Nile) G3
The star of Bethlehem: W3
Star of Columbia: D
O star of eve see Evening star
Star of the East: G3 Y

The star-spangled banner: A3 B B4 B9 E2 F F4 F5
  G3 H5 L3 P2 S4 W3 W7 W9 Z
Starlight and sunshine see Andantino
The starlight in your eyes: W3
The stars and stripes forever: B2 T3
Stars in the heaven: S
Stars of ice: C2
Stars of the summer night: F5 F7 G3 P2 W3 W6 W9
Starving to death on a government claim: L
State of Arkansas: D L L6 W
The statue at Czarskoe-Selo: S16(e. r.)
Stavin' Chain: L8
Steal away (to Jesus) B4 B6 F G3 L4 S5 W3 W9
Steal, Miss Liza: L6 see also Liza Jane
Steel laying holler: L7
Steel-linin' chant: S2
A stein song (It's always fair weather when good fellows
  get together) B2 R2
Stein song (Maine stein song) B6
Die stem van Suid-Afrika: S4(e. af.)
Stenka Razin: B6 B7 R4(e. r.)
Step it up and go: S13
Step together: I2
Steuermann! lass die wacht: G4(e. g.)
Stewball: L7
Stick to your mother, Tom: A
Still and dark the night see Christmas cradle song
Still as the night: E2 F7 S15 W3 Still wie die nacht:
  B3(e. g.) F(e. g.)
Still, still with thee: L3
Still wie die nacht see Still as the night
Still you've not come see Co si k nam neprisiel
Stille nacht see Silent night
Sto s'ono cuje: K(e. sc.)
Stodole, pumpa see Walking at night
Stole mi se ozeni: K(e. m.)
The stolen bride see La sposa di Beltramo
Stone River: C
Stonewall Jackson's requiem: C

Stonewall Jackson's way: C S5
Stop that knocking at the door: G3
Stor Ola, lill' Ola: K(e.sw.)
Stories of Jesus: T6
Storm along John see Stormalong
Storm warning: A2
Stormalong: C10 H I3
Stormy see Old Stormy
The story of the coachman see Kogda ia na pochte
The story of the rose: G3
The story of twelve: S2
Stoyan's wife see Stole mi se ozeni
Strains of guitar see Zvenit gitara nad rekoiu
Strange fruit: H5
Strangest dream see Last night I had the strangest dream
Strawberry Lane: L6
Strawberry roan: B6
Streets of Cairo: B2
The streets of Laredo: B B6 L R2 S11 The cowboy's
    lament: F3 I I3 L4 The dying cowboy: L6
The streets of New York: T7
The strength of the lion: L2
Stride la vampa: G4(e.i.)
Stridono lassu: G4(e.i.) S14(e.i.) Ballatella: C9(e.i.)
The strife is o'er, the battle done: L3
Strike the harp gently: G3
Strolling home see Provozhane
Strolling over the Brooklyn Bridge: C
Strolling slowly, a trim maiden see Wedrowala,
    wedrowala
Strong is the oar see C'est l'aviron
Strong Son of God, immortal love: L3
The student in a tunnel: B6
Study war no more see Down by the riverside
Stumbling: C4
Style all the while: P2
Styri hodiny: D2(e.sl.)
Su! del Nilo: G4(e.i.) S14(e.i.)
Such a getting upstairs: C

Such a really lovely sweetheart see Taku som si
  frajerocku
Such chiming melodious (from The Magic Flute) Z
Such lovely things to hear and see: S6
Sucking cider through a straw: B6 R2
Sudanese National Anthem: S4(e.ar.)
The Suffolk miracle: F3 N
Sugar babe: L L2 L7 S13
Suhajko biju mna: D2(e.sl.)
Suhajko Luteran: D2(e.sl.)
Suicidio (from La Gioconda) G4(e.i.)
Suliram: W(e.in)
Sulla lulla: K(e.n.)
Sumer is icumen in: B9 C3 G2 T Z
Summ' und brumm' du gutes radchen: G4(e.g.)
Summer is a-coming in: B9 C3 G2 T Z
Summer is coming: W6
Summer is gone and the fall is here: S6
The summer wind blows off the shore see Neapolitan
  song
The sun and the moon see El sol y la luna
Sun down below: H
Sun going to shine in my door some day: L8
Sun of my soul: A3 L3 W3 W7
The sun shines in splendor see Hymn of praise
Sunday (that one day when I'm with you) T5
Sunday song: W7
Sung at harvest time (Peruvian song) L9 S6 T6
Sunrise on the Ganges (Gia il sole dal Gange) S15
Sunset (Chinese song) see Wan ching
Sunset song: W6
The sunshine of Paradise Alley: A E3 F6 F7 G3 W3
The sunshine of your smile: H2
Sur la route: B7(e.f.)
Sur le gazon: K(e.wa.)
Sur le pont d'Avignon: F4(f.) V(f.) On the bridge of
  Avignon: W5 Le pont d'Avignon: F(f.)
Surabaya to Pasoeroean: H
Surinamese National Anthem: S4(e.d.)

Surrender: J2
Sus in poarta raiului: K(e. rm.)
Susan Jane: G3 W3
Susani (German cradle song) B5
O Susanna: B4 B6 D E2 F F4 F5 F7 G3 L4 L5
    R2 S11 W3 W9
Susanna fair sometime assaulted was: G2
Susie Q: C7
Suzanne (Creole song) P2 see also Ah, Suzette
Ah, Suzette (Creole song) P2 see also Suzanne
Suzume no gakko: W2(e. ja.)
Sven: B6
Svend i rosensgaard: K(e. dn.)
The swallow see La golondrina
Swallow's castle see Au chateau d' hirondelle
Swanee River see The old folks at home
The swapping song: C7 I3
Swedish National Anthem see Du gamla, du fria
Sweet acacia see Raslo drvo
Sweet Adeline: T7 You're the flower of my heart: B2
Sweet Alice, Ben Bolt see Ben Bolt
Sweet and lovely: T5
Sweet and low: B6 E2 F4 F7 G3 L4 R2 W5
Sweet Betsy from Pike: B4 D I L L4 L6 L7 L10 S2
Sweet bunch of daisies: G3
Sweet by-and-by see In the sweet by-and-by
Sweet Chacoun: A2
Sweet dreamland faces: W7
Sweet dreams, sweetheart: S9
Sweet Eloise: T4
Sweet enslaver: T
Sweet Evelina: F4
Sweet Eveline: B6
Sweet Genevieve: B3 E2 F F5 G3 L4 M W3
Sweet Georgia Brown: S10
Sweet Gramachree: F3
Sweet hour of prayer: A3 L3 W7
Sweet if you like and love me still: G
Sweet Kate: G

Sweet Kitty Klover: I3

Sweet Lei Mamo: G3

Sweet Leilani: J2

Sweet Maisry: N

Sweet Marie: A E3 F6 F7 G3 W3

Sweet oranges: L2

Sweet patate: L2

Sweet Rosie O'Grady: B2 F G3

Sweet song-bird: W6

Sweet the evening air of May: B6

Sweet thing: L L8

The Sweet Trinity see The Golden Vanity

Sweet turtle doves see Mae'r durtur ber

Sweet violet (Hawaiian song) G3

Sweet violets: A B8 S12

Sweet was the song the virgin sang: G R

Sweet William: L8

O sweet woods: G

The sweetest story ever told: F F4 F7 G3

Sweetheart of all my dreams: T3

Sweetheart out a-hunting: Z

Sweetly does my baby sleep see Koimatai to
    moroutzko mou

Sweetly sings the donkey: B6 P2

Swing low, sweet chariot: B4 B6 E2 F F4 F5 F7 G3
    L4 L7 P2 R2 S11 W3 W7 W9

Swing on the corner: D

Swiss National Anthem: S4(e.f.g.i.)

Swiss palm: S4(e.f.g.i.ro.)

Sylvie see Bring me little water, Sylvie

Szanyvarosba: K(e.hu.)

Szeroki mosteczek ugina sie: P(e.p.)

Szla dziewczyna kolo mlyna: P(e.p.)

Szlo sobie dwoch dziadow: P(e.p.)

Szolohegyen korosztul: K(e.hu.)

T

T. B. blues: S13
The T. V. A.: D
Ta 'n-a la: O(e. ir.)
Ta-ra-ra-boom-der-e: B F4 F6 G3 M
Tacea la notte: G4(e. i.)
Tachanka: B4
Taffy was a Welshman: W5
An tailliuir aerach: O(e. ir.)
The tailor and the mouse: I I3
Taim sinte ar do thuama: O(e. ir.)
Take a car: F4
Take a whiff on me: L L7
Take back the engagement ring: A
Take back the heart that thou gavest: B3 G3
Take back your gold: B
Take casy: D2(e. sl.)
Take it easy: J2
Take me a ride in the car, car: B7
Take me home see Margarita
Take my life, and let it be: L3
Take this hammer: B B6 F8 H5 L L8
Take time to be holy: L3
Taku som si frajerocku: D2(e. sl.)
Un tal gioco: G4(e. i.) S14(e. i.)
Tale of a little pig: L7
Talking atomic blues: H5
Talking blues: L6 W
Talking Columbia: L6
Talking dustbowl blues: L6
Talking union: F8 H5
Tally ho: G3
Tam na bloniu blyszczy kwiecie: P(e. p.)
Tam na cmentarzu: P(e. p.)
Tam poza gory: P(e. p.)
Tam za Krakowem na bloniu: P(e. p.)
The tambourine see Baile de pandero
Tammany: T7

T'an ch'in chia: C11(e. ch.)

Tan ta ra ran tan tant: G2

Tanabata: W2(e. ja.)

Tancuj: D2(e. sl.)

Tanglefoot Sue: C7

O tannenbaum: B(e. g.) B5 F O Christmas tree: F4
    S3(e. g.) W3 W8

Tanto vestido blanco: L9(e. s.)

Una tarde fresquita de mayo: L9(e. s.)

Tarpaulin jacket see Wrap me up in my tarpaulin jacket

Tarrier's song see Drill, ye tarriers, drill

The tar's farewell: G3

The tattletale birdy: N

The tattooed lady: F6

The tattooed man (from The Idol's Eye) G3

Taue: W2(e. ja.)

Tea for two cha cha: S8

The tea party: I I3

The tea tax see The Boston tea tax

Teach me how to kiss, dear: G3

Teacher's blues: S13

The teacher's lament: F8

Teaching McFadden to waltz: A

Teamster's song: D

Tearing out-a wilderness: L7

Tears (for souvenirs) T3

Tears on my pillow: T2

Tech'zakna see Birkat am

Tecie potok od krivana: K(e. sl.)

Tecie voda: D2(e. sl.)

Tecolote: B9

Tee roo (Got up one morning) L8

Telephone book: S12

Tell-a-me true: C7

Tell Irene hello: S12

Tell me the story of Jesus: A3

Tell me why (the stars do shine) B6 L4 R2

O tell me, wind: S6

Temnaia noch: R4(e. r.)

Temper my spirit, o Lord: P2
Le temps des lilas: S16(e.f.)
Ten little Indians: W5 Ten little kiddies: G3
Ten thousand men of Harvard: R2
Ten thousand miles see Who's going to shoe your pretty
   little foot
Ten thousand miles away: G3 H L4
Ten thousand miles from home: L7
Ten thousand times ten thousand: L3
The tennis balls: N
Tenting on the old camp ground see Tenting tonight
Tenting tonight: B D E2 F5 G3 P2 S5 W3
Teresita mia: G3
O terra addio (from Aida) G4(e.i.) S14(e.i.)
Teru, terubozu: W2(e.ja.)
The Teuton's tribulation: J L5
Texas cowboy: F2
The Texas rangers: C10 F3 L6 L8
The Texian boys: L
Thai National Anthem: S4(e. Thai)
Thais (One time in Alexandria, in wicked Alexandria) B6
Thank thee, God (for soft, green grass) T6
Thankful every time: G3
A thankful song (Alsatian song) T6
Thanks to God (In the morning when I waken) T6
A thanksgiving (for summer rain and winter's sun) T6
Thanksgiving Day see Over the river and through the
   woods
Thanksgiving prayer (Dutch song) see Prayer of
   thanksgiving
That big rock candy monntain see Big rock candy
   mountain
That great getting-up morning: B9 Great getting-up
   morning: L
That little old red shawl see The little old red shawl
   my mother wore
That lonesome stream: L7
That old feeling: C4
That old time religion see Old time religion

That suits me: L2

That Viennese waltz (from Waltz Dream) G3

That wonderful mother of mine: T8

That's all right, baby: L7

That's an Irish lullaby: T8   Too-ra-loo-ra-loo-ral: M

That's where my money goes: B6 F4 R2

the (article) see next word of title

Them bones: L8

O! them golden slippers: B E2 F F4 F5 G3 L2 L5
    W3 Golden slippers: B6 Those golden slippers: P2

Then I'd be satisfied with life: A E3

Then you'll remember me: B3 E2 F7 W3

There are loyal hearts: S6

There are moments when one wants to be alone: G3

There are three brothers: H5

There are twelve green leaflets see Dwanascie listeczek

There goes McManus: G3

There is a fountain filled with blood: A3 L3

There is a green hill far away: L3

There is a happy land: A3 L3 W7

There is a lady sweet and kind see Passing by

There is a tavern in the town: A B3 B6 E3 F6 G3 R2
    W3

There is a tree see Dar star ett trad

There is joy in every day: W7

There, I've said it again: E5

There, little girl, don't cry: W3

There lived a king (from The Gondoliers) G3

There was a crooked man: W5

There was a little girl, and she had a little curl: W6

There was a man in our town: W5

There was a wily lad: G

There was an old lady: B9

There was an old soldier: D S5

There was an old woman and what do you think: W5

There was an old woman tossed up in a basket: W5

There we will walk the golden streets see Datt wandlen
    wir die goldne schtrose

There were three crows: G3

There'll be a hot time: B B2 G3
There'll be some changes made: E5
There'll come a time: F4 G3
There's a big cry baby in the moon: F5 F6
There's a home in Wyoming: T4
There's a little wheel: W3
There's a long, long trail: M T8
There's a wideness in God's mercy: L3
There's music in the air: F5 G3 W7 W9
There's the day see Ta 'n-a la
There's yes, yes in your eyes: M S10
Therezinha: L9(e. pr.)
These bones going to rise again: B6 L6 L7
These things shall be: F8 S6
They call me the belle of New York: G3
They would if they could, but they can't: G3
They're either too young or too old: S9
They're laying eggs now: B6
The thievish mouse: W6
Thine eyes so blue and tender: G3 W3 W7
Things about coming my way: S13
The things I've neglected to do: G3
Think truly: S6
The thinker: S6
Thinking of you: H2 S8 S10
Think'st thou to seduce me then: G
This is a sin-tryin' world: D
This is my father's world: T6
This is the day: A3
This is the truth sent from above: R
This is worth fighting for: S9
This land is your land: B6 S11 W
This lesson all around we see: S6
This new Christmas carol: Y
This old hammer: Z
This perverse world see An saol meallta
This train: L6 L7
Thomas and Ellen: N
O those golden slippers see O! them golden slippers

Those songs my mother used to sing: T7
Thou, earth, art ours: S6
O thou joyful day see O sanctissima
Thou must leave thy lowly dwelling: R
Thou only see Nur du
Though I should travel all day and all night see Chocbym
    ja jezdzil we dnie
Though there's time: L9
Though your strangeness frets my heart: G
A thousand leagues away: G3
Three blind mice: B6 F W5
Three boasting girls see Trihs meitinas leelijas
The three butchers: F3
Three children sliding on the ice: W5
Three craw: C7
The three crows: W6
Three fishermen: B6 R2
Three fishers: W3
The three flies: G3
Three jolly hunters: B9 F3 I3 The jolly hunters: W6
The three kings (by Cornelius) R Z
The three kings (French song) P2
The three kings of Orient see We three kings of Orient
    are
Three little babies: N
Three little kittens: W6
Three little maids (from The Mikado) W8
Three little mice: W6
The three little pigs: G3 L7 W6
Three little words: H2
Three nights drunk see Our goodman
Three pigs see The three little pigs
The three ravens: B4 C8 N
The three ships: L3 S3 see also I saw three ships
The three sisters: C7
Three times over: C7
Three young ladies: L6
Thrice toss these oaken ashes: G
Through all the world: D

Through every land: T6
Through the dark wood's evening shadows see Ciemnem
    borem nad wieczorem
Through the fields I wander see Chodzilem po polu
Through the vale see Veje vetor
Through the village see Vdol derevni
Through the windowpane see Siedze ja w oknie
Throw another log on the fire: C4
Throw him down, McCloskey: E3 E4 F6 G3
Throw it out the window: B6
Throw out the lifeline: L3
Thus saith my Cloris bright: G2
Thy beaming eyes: B3
Thy brother: S6
Thy friend: W3
Thy little ones, dear Lord, are we (Her kommer dine
    arme smaa) C2(e. dn.)
Thy lovely bright eyes: W3
Tico Tico: L2
Tideo: L6
Tidings true: R3
Tie Nitrianske hodiny: D2(e. sl.)
Tie-shuffling chant: L7
Tie-tamping chant: L7
Tif in veldele: R5(e. y.)
Til kona kom der en ung student: B6(e. n.)
Till osterland see My homeland
Till the end of time: J2
Till the sands of the desert grow cold: T8
Till we meet again: M T8
Till we two are one: T4
Tim Flaherty: J
Time cruel time: G
O the time is long, mavourneen see An Irish love song
The time is never weary: P2
The time I've lost in wooing: C8
Time waits for no one: S9
Time was (when we were young) F5
Time will come: G3

Times a getting hard: W
Times is mighty hard: F8
Timmy Tyes: C7
Tingalayo: L2
Tinkerman true see Ked sa drotar
A tiny little man (from Hansel and Gretel) W8
Ti-pi-tin: C4
The tip-toe song: W5
Tip-toe through the tulips with me: M S10
Tiranti, my love: N
Tiritomba: B G3(i.)
tis see also it is
Ah! tis a dream: W3 It was a dream: S15
Tis autumn: S9
Tis but a little faded flower: F5
Tis not true see Non e ver
This pretty to be in Ballinderry: C8
Tis sad to leave our fatherland: G4
Tis the last rose of summer see The last rose of summer
Tis winter now: S6
Tis women: I T
Tishina: R4(e.r.)
Tiskit, itasket see Itiskit, itasket
Tit willow: G3 W3 W8 Willow, tit willow: F
Titanic (fare thee well) S13 The ship Titanic: B6
Titled widows all are we: G3
Ay tituy: C12(s.)
To Atocha goes a girl see A Atocha va una nina
To babyland: W5
To be sure, it's no business of mine: G3
To Bethlehem I would go (Sel bych rad k Betlemu) S3(e.c.)
To Bethlehem, singing (A Belen cantando) Z(e.s.)
To his sweet lute: G
To market, to market: W5
To my little flower: W6
To Portsmouth: G
To see Swainson (Hefo deio i dywyn) C8(e.w.)
To the aisle: E5
To the begging I will go: C8

To the graveyard see Isla marina
To the well a maiden went see Islo dievca pre vodu
To the West: C J
To the work: A3
To welcome Christmas in: S6
To you, sweetheart. aloha: J2
A toast (The king will take the queen, and the queen will
    take the jack) G3
Toast to the winners: K2(e.n.)
Tobacco is like love: G
Tobacco's but an Indian weed: I
Today is Monday: E2
Today the sky is very far away: S6
Tog azoy vi nacht: R5(e.y.)
Told my captain (my hands were cold) S13
Toll-a-winker: L8
Toll the bell easy see Tone the bell easy
Tom-big-bee River: C
Tom Bolyn: D L8
Tom Dooley: B6 I3 L L6
Tom Joad: D
Tom Queer: C7
Tom Tackle: L5
Tom, Tom, the piper's son: F W5
Tommy and Maizie: W6
Tommy make room for your uncle: G3
Tommy's gone to Hilo: H
Tomorrow (Spanish song) G3
Tomorrow (Morgen, by Strauss) S15
Tomorrow shall be my dancing day: Y
Ein ton see Monotone
Tonari no obasan: W2(e.ja.)
Tone the bell easy: L7
Tongo Island: L5
Tonkaia riabina: R4(e.r.)
Too late to worry - too blue to cry: T2
Too marvelous for words: H2
Too old to work: F8
Too-ra-loo-ra-loo-ral see That's an Irish lullaby

Too young: E5

Toorali (The enlisted men ride in a motor launch) B8

Toot, Toot, Tootsie, good-bye: T5

Toreador song (from Carmen) C9(e.f.) E2 F7(e.f.) W8
    Votre toast: G4(e.f.) S14(e.f.)

El torito (Echame ese toro pinto) C12(s.)

El torito (quien fuera como el zompopo) C12(s.)

Torna a Surriento: E(e.i.) Come back to Sorrento:
    F7(e.i.) W3

The torpedo and the whale: G3 W8

Torpedo Jim: F5

El tortillero: G3(s.)

Toryanse: W2(e.ja.)

Toss not my soul: G2

Totenlied: K(e.g.)

The touch of your lips: J2

Tourelay: G3

Toy duet (from The Geisha) G3

Toyland: B2 T7

Tra la la (Italian folk song) G3(i.)

Trade winds: S9

Traft ihr das schiff im meere an: G4(e.g.)

Tragedia de Heraclio Bernal: L7(e.s.)

Trail of dreams: F7

The trail of the lonesome pine: T4

The trail to Mexico: L6 S2

The train (Japanese song) see Kisha

Tramp! tramp! tramp: B E2 F5 G3 S5 W3

Tramping (Hebrew song) T6

Tramping (Trying to make heaven my home) L4

Traume see Dreaming

Traveling blues: S13

Traveling man: T2

The tree (The tree's early leafbuds) W6

The tree in the forest see Langt udi skoven

A tree in the meadow: T3

The tree in the wood: B9

Tree song (The trees are waving to and fro) W5

The trees are getting high: C8

The trees they do grow high: K
Trench blues: L8
Treti, treti, treti: R5(e.y.)
Treulich gefuhrt see Bridal chorus
A tribute (The one who hath created things of beauty) Z
Trihs meitinas leelijas: K(e.lv.)
Les tringles des sistres tintaient: G4(e.f.)
Trio (from Die Fledermaus) G3
Tripolitza see Saranta pallikaria
Troika mchitsia: R4(e.r.)
Trooper and maid: N
The trooper and the tailor: C6
Tros y gareg see Over the stone
Troubadour song: B6
Trouble, trouble (I had them all my day) L8
Troubled in mind: L6 S13
True-hearted, whole-hearted: L3
The true lovers' knot see Snaidhm an ghra
The true Paddy's song: L8
The truffle song: W8
Truthful James see The society upon the Stanislow
Try, try again: W7
Tshiribim: B7(e.y.)
Tsing tien kao see High is the blue sky
Tsobanakos imoona see The young shepherd
Tsutsul see Cucul
Tsvey taybelech: R5(e.y.)
Tu (En Cuba) C12(s.) G3(s.) Cuba: Z(e.s.) You: W3
Tu alfagra land mitt: S4(e.dn.)
O tu che in seno agl' angeli: G4(i.)
Tu l'as dit (from Les Huguenots) G4(e.f.)
Tu ne peux eprouver: G4(e.f.)
Tu n'est pas maitre dans ta maison: B6(f.)
Tu-ru-ru-ru: G3(s.)
Tuchi nad gorodom vstali: R4(e.r.)
Tum-balalayka: B3(e.y.) B7(e.y.) R5(e.y.)
Tunisian National Anthem: S4(e.ar.)
Tuoll' on mun kultani: K(e.fi.) Far is my love:
    B3(e.fi.)

Turkey in the straw: B4 B6 D F4 F5 F7 I I3 L4 L5
   L6 W3 W9 see also Old Zip Coon
The Turkish lady: S2
Turkish National Anthem see Istiklal marsi
Turkish Revery: I3 see also The Golden Vanity
Turn back, o man: S6
Turn back you wanton flyer: G
Turn ye to me: P2
The turnpike gate: J
Turtle dove: B3 B7 I Z
The turtle dove's nest: W6
Tuszac pasterze ze dzien blisko: P(e.p.)
Tutte le feste al tempio: G4(i.)
Tutu maramba: C12(pr.) Z(e.pr.)
Tva jungfrur: K(e.sw.)
twas see also it was
Twas a wonder in heaven: S
Twas May Day in the morning: B9
Twas on a bright morning: T
Twas once upon a midnight clear see Dnia jednego o
   polnocy
The twelve apostles: S
The twelve days of Christmas: B4 B5 B6 L4 L6 L10
   R R2 S S3 Y Z
Twelve gates to the city: S11 W
Twelve lads see Fantje vasujejo
Twenty years ago: S12
Twickenham ferry: F7
Twilight time: E5
Twinkle, twinkle, little star: E2 F F7 W5
Twistification: L6
Two boards upon cold powder snow (Der feinste sport)
   B6 K2(e.g.)
Two brothers: N S5 W
Two guitars see Dve gitari
Two hearts in 3/4 time: H2
Two little girls in blue: B2 F4 G3
Two lovers sat lamenting: G
The two maidens (Swedish song) see Tva jungfrur

Two maidens went milking: C8 I3
Two old beggars staggered <u>see</u> Szlo sobie dwoch dziadow
The two old crows: N
The two roses: G7
The two sisters: F3 L6 L10 N S7
Two wings: L4 S2
Ty ze mnie szydzisz, dziewucho: P(e.p.)
Tying a knot in the devil's tail: L6
Tylez-ty, tyle ty: P(e.p.)
Tzena, tzena, tzena, tzena: W(h.)
Tzu chu tiao: C11(e.ch.)

U

U.A.W.-C.I.O.: F8
U studienky stala: D2(e.sl.)
Uchi ma, maycho, nayuchi: K(e.bu.)
Uh-uh, no: L6
Umarl maciek, umarl: P(e.p.)
Umocil ma dazdik na dvore: D2(e.sl.)
Umrem: D2(e.sl.)
un (article) <u>see next word of title</u>
Un, deux, trois: L7(e.cr.)
Un du akerst: B7(e.y.) R5(e.y.)
una (article) <u>see next word of title</u>
Uncle Charlie: C7
Uncle Joe: L6
Uncle John is very sick: W5
Uncle Ned: C G3 W3 <u>Old Uncle Ned</u>: F4 Z
Uncle Sam's farm: B9 <u>J</u>
Uncle Tom's religion: J
The unconstant lover: C D
Und ob die wolke sie verhulle: G4(e.g.)
Under the bamboo tree: B
Under the willows she's weeping: W3
Underneath our cottage window <u>see</u> Pod tym nasim
    okieneckom
Underneath the takeoff: B6 K2

une (article) see next word of title
Unfortunate Miss Bailey: C6 C7
Union maid: F8 H5
The union man: F8 H5
Union of South Africa National Anthem: S4(e. af.)
Union train: F8 H5
The union way: H5
United front: H5
United Nations (make a chain) H5
United steelworkers are we: F8
The unquiet grave: N
Unrest: S6
Unter a kleyn beymele: B7(e. y.)
Unter dem kind's vigele: R5(e. y.)
Unto us a boy is born: R S3
Unto us is born a son: B5
The unwilling bride: N
Up in a balloon: E4 J
Upidee: B6 E2 G3 K2 W3
Upon a lowly manger: W8
Upon the mountain: D
Ur-chnoc chein mhic cainte: O(e. ir.)
Uruguayan National Anthem: S4(e. s.)
Usagi: W2(e. ja.)
Ushag veg ruy: K(e. mx.)
The Utah iron horse: I I3
Utes: R4(e. r.)
Uxor mea, uxor polla: T(l.)
Uy! tara la la: Z(e. s.)

V

The vacant chair: E3 G3 S5
Vacation days: W7
Vagabond's song: Z
The vale of our own Genesee: C
Valenciana: K(e. s.)
The valiant conscript: S5

Valley see Dolina
Vallkulla: K(e. sw.)
Vamos a la mer: C12(s.)
Vamos, Maninha: L9(e. pr.)
Van Diemen's Land: I2
The Vance song: C L8
Vasovalska: K(e. sl.)
Vassar hygiene song: B6 She's going to be my wife: K2
Vdol derevni: R4(e. r.)
Vdol po Piterskoi: R4(e. r.)
Vdol po ulitse metelitsa metet: R4(e. r.)
Le veau d'or: G4(e. f.)
Vecchia zimarra: G4(e. i.)
Vedi, vedi (son io che piango) G4(e. i.)
Vedrai carino: B3(e. i.) G4(e. i.) S14(e. i.)
Veinticinco de diciembre see Foom, foom, foom
Veje vetor: D2(e. sl.)
Velvet moon: S9
Ven, dulce amado mio: C12(s.)
El venadito: L9(e. s.)
La vendetta (from Le Nozze di Figaro) G4(e. i.)
Venezuela: B6
Venezuelan National Anthem: S4(e. s.)
Venga jaleo: W(e. s.)
Veni, Emmanuel see O come, o come, Emmanuel
Venid, pastorcillos: C12(s.)
Venus au fond de notre ame: G4(f.)
Venus, my shining love: G3
La vera Sorrentina: G3(i.)
Vermont: F3
The Vermont boys in Gardner: F3
The Vermont farmer's song: F3
Vermonters, Song of the: F3
Verrano a te (from Lucia di Lammermoor) C9(e. i.)
    G4(e. i.)
A very precious love: S8
The very thought of you: C5
Vesti la giubba: C9(e. i.) E(e. i.) G4(e. i.) Arioso: E2
    Recitar: S14(e. i.)

Vi azoy kon ich lustig zayn: R5(e. y.)
Vi zenen mayne yinge yoren: B7(e. y.)
Vicar of Bray: B6
Vicksburg blues: S13
Victorious my heart see Vittoria mio core
La vidalita: B4 C12(s.) Z(e. s.)
Videirinha: K(e. pr.)
La vie en rose: S8
Vieni, che poi sereno: S16(e. i.)
Vieni sul mar: E(e. i.) G3(i.) Come to the sea: F7(e. i.)
Vienna my city of dreams: H2
Viennese refrain: F7
Viet-Namese National Anthem: S4(e. an.)
Vigndig a fremd kind: R5(e. y.)
Vilia song: F7 W3 W8
Village festival see Mura matsuri
The village on the road see Vot na puti selo bolshoe
Villancico: L9(e. s.)
Villanelle: G3
Vin ou biere (from Faust) S14(e. f.)
Vines and girls see Videirinha
Vineyards on the hill-top see Szolohegyen korosztul
Vinko cervene: D2(e. sl.)
Violet in the leafy woodland see Cantec vechi
Viragos kenderem: K(e. hu.)
A virgin most pure: R S Y
Virginia's bloody soil: L6 S5
The Virgin's cradle hymn: R
The vision (Dutch song) Z
Visota li, visota podnebesnaya: K(e. r.)
Vissi d'arte: C9(e. i.) G4(i.)
Vittoria mio core: E(e. i.)
Vitu: L9(e. pr.)
La viudita: L9(e. s.)
La viudita del Conde Laurel: L9(e. s.)
Viva il vino spumeggiante: G4(e. i.) Brindisi: E(e. i.)
    Drinking song (from Cavalleria Rusticana) F7
Viva Jujuy: B7(e. s.)
Viva la Quince Brigada: H5(s.)

Viva L'America, home of the free: J
Viva Panama: L2
Vive la canadienne: V(f.)
Vive la compagnie: P2 R2 Vive l'amour: B6 G3
Vive l'amour see Vive la compagnie
Vniz po matushke po vol, po Volge: R4(e.r.)
Vniz po Volge reke: R4(e.r.)
Vo Luzarn: K2(e.ss.) Walking song: Z Weggiser lied:
   B6(e.g.)
Vo mine berge: K2(e.ss.)
Vo pole berezynka stoiala: R4(e.r.)
Voce di donna (from La Gioconda) C9(e.i.)
Una voce poco fa: G4(e.i.)
Der vogelfanger bin ich ja: G4(g.)
Voi che sapete (from Le Nozze di Figaro) B3(e.i.)
   C9(e.i.) G4(e.i.)
Voi lo sapete (from Cavalleria Rusticana) C9(e.i.)
   G4(e.i.)
Volga boat song see Song of the Volga boatmen
Volksliedchen (Wenn ich fruh in den garten geh') B3(e.g.)
Volta la terrea: G4(e.i.)
Vom himmel hoch: B5 H4(e.g.) From heaven above (high)
   C2(e.g.) S3(e.g.) T6 Y
Vorrei: E(e.i.)
Vot na puti selo bolshoe: R4(e.r.)
Votre toast see Toreador song
Ah, vous dirai-je, maman see Mother, shall I now relate
Vous qui faites l'endormie: G4(e.f.) S14(e.f.)
Voyageur's song: C
Vrat mi, mila: D2(e.sl.)
Vrt sa dievca: D2(e.sl.)
Vsiuto ia vselennuiu proekhal: R4(e.r.)
Vu Si ching: C11(e.ch.)
Vuela, suspiro: L9(e.s.)
Vyletel vtak: K(e.sl.)
Vysoko zornicka: D2(e.sl.)
Vyssa lulla: K(e.sw.)

W

W murowanej piwnicy: P(e. p.)
W pogodny wieczor: P(e. p.)
W tej koledzie kto dzis bedzie: P(e. p.)
The Wabash Cannon Ball: B I3 L6 S11
Wachet auf see Wake, awake, for night is flying
Wade in the water: L6
wae see woe
The wagon trains: P2
Wagon wheels: T4
The wagoner boy: L10
The wagoner's lad: C6 L6
Wagons come rolling by see Jedzie woz po pod woz
Wait for me (Russian song) see Zhdi menia
Wait for me Mary: S9
Wait for me, my dear girl see Czekaj tu dziewczyno
Wait for the turn of the tide: G3
Wait for the wagon: F5 F6 F7 G3 L10 S5 W3 W7
Wait for your soldier see Zhdi soldata
Wait till the clouds roll by: F5 F6 F7 W3
Wake, awake, for night is flying (Wachet auf) L3 S3(e. g.)
Wake Nicodemus see Nicodemus
Wake the town and tell the people: J2
Wake up, Jacob see Cowboy's getting-up holler
Wake viol and flute: S6
Waleczna krolewna: K(e. p.)
Walk in peace: H5
Walk, jaw-bone: D
Walk on by: T2
Walking at night (Stodole, pumpa) Czech song) B6 L4 Z
Walking down Broadway: F6
Walking song see Vo Luzarn
Walking the floor over you: T2
The Walloping Window Blind see A capital ship
Waltz (from Faust) see Ainsi que la brise legere
Waltz song (from The Merry Widow) see Merry Widow
    waltz
Waltz song (from Waltz Dream) W3

The waltz you saved for me: C4
Waltzing Matilda: B4 B6
Waltzing, wine, and merry song: G3
O waly, waly: C8 I3
Wan ching: C11(e. ch.)
Wandering (and it looks like I'm never gonna cease my
    wandering) F4 H5 I3 L4 L6 S12 S13
Wandering in this place: G
A wandering minstrel (from The Mikado) G3 W8
Wann ich heiraten du: H4(e. pd.)
Wanted: S8
War begets poverty: T
A war bird's burlesque: S12
O war ich schon (from Fidelio) G4(e. g.)
War song (come all you jolly soldiers) L7
The warmest baby in the bunch: G3
The warrior princess see Waleczna krolewna
The wars of America: L6
Wartime blues: S13
Was ist Sylvia see Who is Sylvia
Was it rain: J2
The washing day: J
Washington's grave see Grave of Washington
Waska Wee: G3
Wasn't that a mighty day: S
Wasn't that a time: W
A wasp and a bee: W6
A wasp bite Nobi on her conch-eye: L8
Wassail song: B4 B5 B9 R2 S3 Here we come a-
    wassailing: Y
Wassail, wassail, all over the town see Gloucestershire
    wassail
Wassermann's braut: K(e. g.)
Watashi no ningyo see My doll
O watch the stars: S
The watcher: J
Ye watchers and ye holy ones: L3
Watchman, tell us of the night: A3 L3 S3
Water come a me eye: A2 L2

The water horse's lullaby see Oran talaidh an eich-uisge
Water in me rum: A2
The water is wide: C8 S11
The waterfall (yodel) W3
Watering the roses: W6
way see also away
Way beyond Krakow see Tam za Krakowem na bloniu
Way down in Cairo: C
Way down in May: G3
Way down in the paw-paw patch: C C10
Way down on the old Pee Dee: C see also Old Pee Dee
     and On the banks of the old Pee Dee
Way down the Ohio: D
Way down yonder in the cornfield: A E3
Way down yonder in the maple swamp see Twistification
Way out in Idaho: L8
Way over in the blooming garden: L7
Way over in the heavens: L6
Way sing Sally: H
Way up on Clinch Mountain see Rye whiskey
Way up on Old Smoky see On top of Old Smoky
The wayfaring stranger: B9 I L L4 S11 Z (I am just a)
     poor wayfaring stranger: B4 D G3 P2 S2 S12 Over
     Jordan: L8
We all went home in a cab: G3
We are building a strong union: F8
We are climbing Jacob's ladder see Jacob's ladder
We are coming, Father Abraham: S5
We are marching on to victory: F8
We be three poor mariners: G2
We believe in Christmas: S6
We come from the mountains: L2
We conquer or die: S5
We did it before: S9
We don't get no justice here in Atlanta: L8
We gather together to ask the Lord's blessing see Prayer
     of thanksgiving
We give thee but thine own: L3
We got a lot for Christmas: S3

We got to all get together: H5
We have lived and loved together: F5
We march, we march to victory: L3
We meet again tonight: G3
We never speak as we pass by: E3 F4 F6
We parted by the river side: F5
We plow the fields: L3 Z
We sail the ocean blue: G3
We sat by the river, you and I see You and I
We shall go a-hunting, hunting see Pojedziemy na low,
    na low
We shall not be moved: F8 H5 S11
We sing of golden mornings: S6
We sing to thee, Immanuel: H4(e. pd.)
We three kings of Orient are: A3 B B5 G3 L3 P2 R
    R2 S3 Y
We wait beneath the blast furnace: S5
We wandered see Wir wandelten
We will overcome (some day) F8
We will speak out: S6
We wish you a merry Christmas: B5 B9 S3 W
We won't go home until morning see For he's a jolly good
    fellow
We would be building: L3
We would see Jesus: L3
The wearing of the green: B C8 E2 G3 I2 L4 R2 W3
Wearying (by Dvorak) W3
Weaving lilt: C8
We'd better bide a wee: G3
The wedding garland see Skladej, andulko, cepeni
Wedding march (by Mendelssohn) E2
Wedle Oswiecima miasteczka: P(e. p.)
Wedlock: L7
Wedrowala, wedrowala: P(e. p.)
Wee cooper of Fife: B6 I Z
weel see well
Weep all ye little rains see The Colorado Trail
Weep forth your tears, and do lament: G2
The weep-willow tree: N

Weep you no more: G
Weeping Mary: L6
Weeping sad and lonely: D J S5
The weeping willow: C
Weevily wheat: D L7
Weggiser lied see Vo Luzarn
Weigh up Susianna see Fisherman's song (Jamaican)
Weihnachtslied (Shepherds, hark) K(e.g.)
Weisst du, wie viel sternlein stehen: F(g.)
Welch' ein augenblick: G4(e.g.)
Welche wonne, welche lust: G4(g.)
Welcome (again, ye angels fair) C2
Welcome every guest: D
Welcome, Sir Christmas: R3
Welcome, sweet pleasure: Z
Welcome, sweet springtime: W6 Melody in F: E2
Welcome to Scotland: B7
Welcome to spring: W6
Welcome yule: F7 Y
We'll all go a-singing: W5
We'll all work together: B9
Well fare the nightingale: T
We'll fight for Uncle Abe: J S5
We'll hunt the buffalo: C J O-HI-O: H4 The lovely Ohio:
    L6 On the banks of the Ohio: S2 see also Shoot the
    buffalo
Well may the keel row: B3 C8
Well rung, Tom: T
We'll swim across the Schuylkill: H4(e.pd.)
Welsh lullaby see All through the night
Welsh National Anthem see Hen wlad fy nhadau
Wenn ich ein voglein war: G3(g.) K(e.g.) Were I a little
    bird: B3(e.g.) W6
Wenn ich fruh in den garten geh see Volksliedchen
Wer hat dich, du schoner wald: G3(g.)
We're all surrounded: H
We're coming, Arkansas: L6
Were I a little bird see Wenn ich ein voglein war
We're marching to Zion: A3

We're off on the morrow to ski: K2
We're singing our praises see Prayer of thanksgiving
We're tenting tonight see Tenting tonight
Were you there (when they crucified my Lord) B E4 W3
Wesprzyj-ze mnie boze: P(e.p.)
The West, a nest and you: T5
The West Virginia boys: C6
West Virginia hills: F8
We've a story to tell to the nations: L3
We've been awhile a-wandering: C2 Z
Whack fol the diddle: C8
The whale see The Greenland whale fishery
The whalemen's wives: H
What a court hath old England: D I L5 Derry down: B9
What a difference a day made: E5(e.s.)
O what a difference in the morning: A
What a friend we have in Jesus: A3 F L3 W7
What are little boys made of see What folks are made of
What are you going to do with a drunken sailor see The
  drunken sailor
What can the matter be see O dear, what can the matter
  be
What cher see Knocked them dead in the old Kent Road
What child is this: B4 B5 C2 L3 P2 S3 Y
What do we plant: T6
What do you think: E3
What does the ski runner need: K2
What flower blooms see Sa huo k'ei lei
What folks are made of: L7
What hap had I to marry a shrew: T
What harvest half so sweet is: G
What if I never speed: G G2
What is beauty but a breath: G
What is home without a mother: F4 F5 G3 W7
O what it seemed to be: J2
What mean tears to the heartless see Ite caldi sospiri
What shall I part thus: G2
What shall we do with a drunken sailor see The drunken
  sailor

What shall we give to the babe (Catalan carol) B5
What sweeter music: S3
O what their joy and their glory must be: L3
What then is love: G
What thou shalt today provide: H4
What tidings bringest thou, messenger: R3
What time is it see Hoe laat is 't
O what times see Take casy
What was your name in the states: B I
What won't we do for love: G3
What would you take for me, Papa: E3
What's icumen in: T
What's in a name: G3
What's new: C5
What's the matter with Father: T7
What's the matter with your feet: G3
What's the tapping that I hear see A co to tam stuknelo
What's wrong, little blonde see Qu'avez-vous, oui, belle
    blonde
Wheel of fortune: B7
When a deed is done for freedom: S6
When a man's in love: L6
When a woman that's buxom: T
When Adam was created: D
When boys go a-courting: D
When Christ was born of Mary free: R
When Christmas morn is dawning (Nar juldagsmorgon
    glimmar) C2(e.sw.)
When cockleshells turn silverbells: C8
When courage fails: S6
When day is done: H3 S10
When Enoch he knocked, she knocked Enoch: G3
When first by force of fatal destiny: G2
Then first to this country a stranger I came: L8
When Freedom from her mountain height see The
    American flag
When good fellows get together: G3
When he cometh: A3
When he who adores thee: I2

When Hogan paid his rent: G3
When I first came to this land: B9 S11
When I get you alone tonight: T5
When I journeyed from America see Jak jechalem z
   Ameryki
When I lay down: S13
When I marry do see Wann ich heiraten du
When I saw a little fish: S6
When I survey the wondrous cross: A3 L3
When I teach singing see A cantar a una nina
When I was a cowboy: L6 L7
When I was a lad (from H. M. S. Pinafore) F G3
When I was a lady: W5
When I was single see I wish I was single again and
   I wish I was a single girl again
When I'm gone: L6
When Irish eyes are smiling: M T8
When it's darkness on the delta: J2
When it's lamp-lighting time in the valley: T3
When it's ski-time (in Sun Valley) K2
When Jesus walked upon the earth: S6
When Jesus wept: D
When Johnny comes marching home: B4 B9 D E2 E4
   F4 F5 I3 L6 S5 W3
When Laura smiles: B3 G3
When love is kind: G3
When Love on time and measure makes his ground: G
When morning gilds the skies: L3
When mother nature sings her lullaby: J2
When my blood runs chilly and cold: L L7
O when, o when see El cuando
When other lips: G4
When Pa: B6
When Pat came over the hill: C8
When Sherman marched down to the sea: S5
When Susan Thompson tries to reach high C: G3
When the blue sky turns to gold: A
When the cock crows (Al chante il gial) B3(e. i.)
When the corn is waving, Annie dear: B3 F5 G3

When the curtains of night are pinned back: S12
When the doctor sees you: G3
When the fair land of Poland: G4
When the gladsome day declineth: S6
When the golden sun is sinking: S6
When the good Lord sets you free: L7
When the lights are low: F7
When the lights go on again: E5
When the moon comes over the mountain: F7
When the moon is shining see Humoresque
When the organ played at twilight: J2
When the robins nest again: E3 F5 F6 F7 W3
When the saints go marching in: L2 L6 W The saints
    go marching in: B6
When the snow has gone away see The procession
When the snow is on the ground: W6
When the stars begin to fall see My Lord, what a
    morning
When the sun rises: S6
When the swallows come back to Capistrano: S9
When the swallows homeward fly: E3 F7 G3 W7
When the whale get strike see The Greenland whale
    fishery
When the white lilacs bloom again: S8
When the work's all done this fall: B9 E2 F5 G3 L4
When thou must home: G
When to her lute Corinna sings: S15
When we all get to heaven: A3
When we are married: G3
When we get to church today see Jak pojdziemy do
    kosciola
When wilt thou save the people: F8
When you and I were young, Maggie: B E2 F7 G3 R2 W3
When you go a-courting: L
When you were sweet sixteen: B2 T3
When you wore a tulip: C4 F5
When your lover has gone: C5
Whence comes this rush of wings: S3
Whence is that goodly fragrance (Quelle est cette odeur
    agreable) R(e. f.)

Whence, o shepherd maiden: S6
Whenever I marry, I'll marry a maid: T
Where are you going to, my pretty maid: W5
Where are you, my beloved see Nun zirade
Where did you get that hat: B2 E2 E3 F6 G3 W3
Where do we go from here: F5
Where do you go, Alphonso see Donde vas, Alfonso Doce
Where does it lead: B7
Where has my little dog gone see Where is my little dog
gone
Where have you been, my good old man see My good old
man
Where Hudson's wave: C
Where is my little dog gone: E2 F F4 F7 W5
Where is my wandering boy tonight: A B E3 F6
Where is our holy church: S6
Where is our young groom see Mlody panie nasz
Where shall I be: S12
Where the chicken got the axe: G3
Where the morning glories twine around the door: F6
Where the river Shannon flows: T7
Where there's a will there's a way: G3
Where was Moses when the light went out: G3
O where were you see Kde si bola
Wherever you walk: B3
Which side are you on: F8 H5 S11
Which way does the wind blow: W5
While angels sing: C2
While by my sheep I watched at night (Als ich bei meinen
schafen wacht) S3(e.g.)
While Jesus sleeps (L'enfant Jesus s'endort) S3(e.f.)
While Johnny fed his horse see Jas konika poil
While shepherds watched their flocks by night: L3 R S3
W3 W8 Y
While strolling through the park one day: A B3 E3 E4
F4 F5 F6 F7 G3 W3
While the breeze see Po doline
Whirl around me see Vrt sa dievca
Whirling around see O piao
Whirling gusts of starry flakes: S6

Whirling maiden: L4
Whirlwinds raging in the valley see Na dolinie
  zawierucha
Whiskey in the jar: L6
Whiskey Johnny: B H L5 L7
Whiskey-still: G3
Whispering hope: E2 F4 F5 F7 G3 L4 W3
Whistle, daughter, whistle: L6
White as snow see Blanche comme la neige
The white captive: C F3
The white chestnut tree see Na haste do castanheiro
White coral bells: B6 P2
White-feathered geese see Lecela husicka
The white hen: T
The white house blues: L8
White llamas: L9
The white pilgrim: F3
White sand and grey sand: T
The white sheep see Ak koyun
White wings: B E3
Whither runeth my sweetheart: G
Who can retell: B4
Who did (swallow Jonah) B6
Who ever thinks or hopes: G
Who is on the Lord's side: L3
Who is Sylvia: B3(e.g.) E2 F7 G3 W3
Who is the man: B4 D L3
Who knows why see I kto evo znaet
Who passes by see Horch was kommt
Who thou art I know not: S6
Who threw the overalls in Mrs. Murphy's chowder: A B6
  E3 F6 G3 see also Mrs. Murphy's chowder
Who will care for Mother now: S5
Who will go with me to Wieringen see Wie wil er mee naar
  Wieringen varen
Who will help see Co budeme robit
Who will shoe your pretty little foot see Who's going to
  shoe your pretty little foot
Who would true valor see: S6

Whoa back, Buck: L L6
Whoa, Emma: G3
Whoa! Ha! Buck and Jerry boy: L6
The whole wide world around: H5
The whole world in his hands: L4
Who'll own New York: R2
Who'll you give me to sail away see Aeire cinn bo ruin
Whoo-pee ti yi yo see Get along, little dogies
Who's going to shoe your pretty little foot: B3 L6 N
    S11 He's gone away: D S12 Ten thousand miles: L2
    L10
Whose are those horses see Cie su to kone
Whose geese are those see Cie su to husky
Whose may be that field see Ciaze je to rolicka
The why and the wherefore: S5
Why are you weeping see Czemu ty placzesz
Why don't they do so now: G3
Why don't you fall in love with me: S9
Why, liquor of life, do I love you so see A fhuisgi, croi
    na n-anamann
Why shouldn't my goose: B6
Why, soldiers, why: I
Wicked Polly: L6 L7
The wicked rebels: B9
Widdecombe Fair: B4
The wide Missouri see Shenandoah
Widmung: B3(e. g.) Dedication: P2 S15
Widow Malone: G3
The widow's daughter: F3
Widzialem Marysie raz we mlynie: P(e.p.)
O wie lieblich ist das madchen: B3(e. g.)
Wie nahte mir der schlummer: G4(e.g.)
Wie schon leuchtet der morgenstern see How brightly
    shines the morning star
Wie soll ich dich empfangen see How shall I fitly meet
    thee
Wie todesahnung: G4(e. g.)
Wie wil er mee naar Wieringen varen: K(e. d.)
O wie wohl ist's mir am abend see O how lovely is the
    evening

Wiegenlied (by Brahms) F(e.g.) F7(e.g.) Cradle song:
    E2 W3 W5
Wiegenlied (by Mozart) see Lullaby (by Mozart)
The wife of the free: N
The wife of Usher's well: N
The wife who was dumb: C6
The wife wrapt in wether's skin: N S7
Wild Americay: C6
Wild Bill Jones: L6
The wild colonial boy: L8
Wild geese see Kari
The wild goose grasses (Tarrytown) W
The wild rippling water: L6
The wild rose: W6 W8
Wilhelmus van Nassouwe see Netherlands National
    Anthem
Wilkes Lovell: F3
Will I get a Christmas present: S3
Will said to his mammy: G
Will ye not come back again: C8
Will you come to the bower: C
Will you go out west: C6
Will you love me in December: T7
Will you love me then as now: F7 W3
Will you walk a little faster: G3 W6
William and Ellen: N
Willie McGee McGaw: N
Willie of Hazel Green: S7
Willie Reilly: L8
Willie, take your little drum see Patapan
Willie the weaver: C6
Willie the weeper: B4 B6 D L6 L7 see also Cocaine
    Bill
Willow, tit-willow see Tit willow
Willow tree: B6
Willy see Willie
Wilt heden nu treden see Prayer of thanksgiving
Wimoweh: W(z.)
The wind blew up, the wind blew down: N

The wind blow east: L8
Windsor: B
Windy Bill: F2
Wine so ruby-red see Vinko cervene
Wings of a dove: T2
Winin' boy blues: S13
Winkum, winkum: W5
The Winnipeg whore: B8
The Winnsboro cotton mill blues: F8 S13
Winter, goodbye: W6
Winter has come: B9
The winter season: B9 Burgundian carol: W
Winter's night: L6
Wintersturme wichen dem wonnemond see Siegmund's
    love song
Wir singen dir, Immanuel: H4(e.pd.)
Wir wandelten: B3(e.g.)
The Wisconsin emigrant's song see The rolling stone
The wise may bring their learning: L3
A wish is quite a tiny thing: S6
Wishing dolls see Teru, terubozu
Wisla: K(e.p.)
Witchcraft: B6
With a song in my heart: H3 S10
With all her faults I love her still: B2
With cracking of whip: G3
With lance in rest: G3
With needle and thread: T6
With songs and honors sounding loud: L3
Within a mile of Edinburgh town: G3
Within my garden see Pojde do sadu
Within this temple shrine of ours: S6
Without discord: G2
Wo chia yu ke p'ang wa see Fat baby sister
Woad: B6
Woe be unto you: L7
Woe is me: P2
The woeful heart: G3
Woeful is the hired man's fortune see Nedzne zycie
    czeladnika

Woe's me for Prince Charlie: C8
Wohin seid ihr entschwunden: C9(e.g.)
Woman blue: L7
Woman is fickle see La donna e mobile
Woman, lovely woman (from The Serenade) G3
Woman washing by the river see A bhean ud thios
The women are worse than the men: I2
The wonder of you: E5
The wonderful crocodile: L7
Wonderings: S6
Wonders still the world shall witness: S6
Wondrous love: B D I L P2 Z
Won't it be wonderful after the war: S12
O won't you sit down: L4
Won't you sit with me awhile: C6
Woodman, spare that tree: E4 F4 F5 F7 W7
The woodsman's alphabet: C6 F3
O word of God incarnate: L3
Work and play: W7
Work for the night is coming: A3 L3 W3 W7
The work of the weavers: C8
Workers' carol (Coldly the night winds winging) R
Workers together (Finnish song) T6
Working on the railroad see I've been working on the
    railroad
The world has come awake: S6
The world has gone to rest see Souvenir
The world itself is blithe and gay: L3
The world itself rejoices now: S6
The world turned upside down: I
Worldes blis ne last: G2
Worried blues: S13
Worried man blues: B6 H5 S13
O worship the king: A3 L3 P2 W4
Would God I were the tender apple-blossom see
    Londonderry air
Would I were that pigeon see Ach, keby som bola
Would you know (the baby's skies) W5
The wraggle taggle gipsies see The raggle taggle gypsies

Wrap me up in my tarpaulin jacket: I3 L4 Tarpaulin
  jacket: G3
Wreath of carnations (Lei poni moi) G3
The wreck of the John B see The John B sails
The wreck on the C&O: L7
The wreck on the Somerset Road: L8
Wszystkich to ciekawosc bodzi: P(e.p.)
The Wyandotte's farewell song: C

X

Xango: L2

Y

Y deryn pur see The dove
Y gwcw vach see Cuckoo dear
Yafim haleylot bichna-an: R5(e.h.)
Yah-nah-nee (American Indian song) S12
Yangtze boatmen's chantey: T6
Yankee Doodle: B D E2 E4 F F4 F5 I L7 P2 S11
  W3 W5 W7 W9
The Yankee Doodle boy (by Cohan) B2
Yankee Doodle dandy-o: L6
Yankee maid: J
The Yankee man-of-war: H I I3
Yankee manufactures: J
A Yankee ship and a Yankee crew: G3
Yankee tars: H
Yankele: B7(e.y.) R5(e.y.)
Yanko grazed his oxen see Pasol Janko dva voly
The yard of pudding: C7
Yasashii okasan: W2(e.ja.)
ye see next word of title
Year of jubilo see Kingdom coming
Years ago beggars see Dawniej dziadowie
The yellow and blue (University of Michigan song) G3

The yellow bittern see An bunnan bui
The yellow pony see An poni beag bui
The yellow rose of Texas: G3 L4 S5
Yemen National Anthem: S4(e. ar.)
Yeo, heave ho: B4
Yerakina: B7(e. gk.)
Yes, I love you (from Eugene Onegin) W3
Yes, my darling daughter: C4
Yes, yes, no, no: T
Yesterday at the spring see Ayer vite en la fonte
Yeu ei chi sou: K(e. f.)
Yield not to temptation: L3
Yis'm'chu adirim: R5(e. h.)
Y'mey hanoar: R5(e. h.)
Yo dee oh dee oh: B6
Yo soy de la tierra: L8(s.)
Yo soy farolero: L9(e. s.)
The yodel song (When the college bell is ringing) G3
Yom l'yabasha: R5(e. h.)
Yonder comes Sister Mary: S
Yonder flew a nightingale see Przelecial-ci slowiczek
Yonder in Krakow in a mill see A tam w Krakowie
Yonders tree: B9
York: B Z
The Yorkshire bite: F3
You(Asi eres tu) see Asi eres tu
You (Tu) see Tu(En Cuba)
You and I (We sat by the river) F5 F6 We sat by the
    river: W3
You and the night and the music: H2
You are free: T8
You are making fun of me, girl see Ty ze mnie
    szydzisz, dziewucho
You are the only girl I'll ever care about: G3
You are too beautiful: S9
O you beautiful doll: T8
You can dig my grave: B6
You can't lose-a me, Cholly: L6
You dear little night see Akh ty, nochenka

You do something to me: S10
You do the darndest things, baby: E5
You don't know my mind: S13
You gave me your love: G3
You go to my head: C5
You gotta go down see You've got to go down
You have taken my heart: J2
You kicked and stomped and beat me: L8
You must have been a beautiful baby: C5
You never miss the water till the well runs dry: E3 F6
    G3
O you New York girls: I3
You old fool see Our goodman
You remember that night, love see An cuimhin leat an
    oiche ud
You scoundrels, you Mazovians see A wy juchy
You tell me your dream: A F4 F6 G3 M
You turn for sugar and tea: L8
You turned the tables on me: E5
You wander far and wide, dear see An Irish folk song
You were meant for me: T5
You were only fooling: T3
You who don't believe it: I
O you wretches see Bodaj by vas
You, you, in my heart living see Du, du liegst mir im
    herzen
You'll never miss your mother till she's gone: A
Young Beichan: N
Young Charlotte: F3 L6
Young Collins: N
Young hunting: N
Young lad see 'Oganaigh oig
The young man who wouldn't hoe corn: I I3 L S11
The young men's song (New England) F3
The young recruit: W6
The young shepherd (Tsobanakos imoona) B3(e.gk.)
Young Strongbow: F3
The young volunteer: S5
The young voyageur: B4

Your eyes have told me so: T8
Your morning tribute bring: Z
You're a heavenly thing: T4
You're dangerous: J2
You're in the army now: F4 F5 L5
You're my everything: H2
You're my poem of love: F7
You're not in my arms tonight: J2
You're the flower of my heart, sweet Adeline see
    Sweet Adeline
You're the one I care for: J2
You're the only star (in my blue heaven) T4
Yours see Quiereme mucho
Youth (We have tomorrow bright before us) T6
Youth of the ringlets see Buachaill an chuil dualaigh
Youth's stick dance: L2
You've got to go down (and join the union) F8 H5
Yr hen wr mwyn see The kind old man
Yuazuray: B6
Yugnt-hymn: R5(e. y.)
Yugoslav National Anthem see Hej slaveni
La yunsita: C12(s.)
Yuyake, koyake: W2(e. ja.)

                         Z

Z brezoveho dreva: D2(e. sl.)
Z tamtej strony jeziora: P(e. p.)
Za gorami: P(e. p.)
Zakochalem-ci sie: P(e. p.)
Zalongo dance see Khoros tou Zalongou
Ay, zamba: L9(e. s.)
La zamba de Vargas: C12(s.)
Zamboanga: L5
Zamiloval som si dievca: D2(e. sl.)
Zamri-li: R5(e. h.)
Zasadil som fialenku: D2(e. sl.)
Zasnal Jasio na murawie: P(e. p.)

Zayt gezunterheyt: R5(e.y.)
Zebra dun: F2 L5
Zebym ja tak miala: P(e.p.)
O Zeke (put that banjo down) G3
Zemer lach: R5(e.h.)
Zeszla gwiazdka nad koscolkiem: P(e.p.)
Zhamele: R5(e.y.)
Zhankoye: H5(e.y.)
Zhdi menia: R4(e.r.)
Zhdi soldata: R4(e.r.)
Zielona ruta jalowiec: P(e.p.)
Zigeuner: H2
Zing! went the strings of my heart: H2
Zinga-za: L2
La zingarella (from Il Trovatore) E(e.i.)
O Zion, haste, thy mission high fulfilling: L3
Zip-a-dee doo-dah: J2
Zip Coon see Old Zip Coon
Zirmu galim: R5(e.h.)
Zits ich mir oyfn benkele: R5(e.y.)
Zog nit keynmol: R5(e.y.)
Zorty: K(e.Lusatian)
Zu Bethlehem geboren see O Christmas babe
Zui, zui zukorobashi: W2(e.ja.)
Zuleika: B8
A Zulu king: B6
Zum gali gali: F8(h.) H5(h.)
Zum leiden bin ich auserkoren: G4(g.)
Di zun vet arunter geyn: B7(e.y.)
Zuntig - bulbe: R5(e.y.)
Zvenit gitara nad rekoiu: R4(e.r.)
Zwei konigskinder: K(e.g.)